AF679617

Global Perspectives on Social Empowerment Using Current Technology

Miftachul Huda
https://orcid.org/0000-0001-6712-0056
Sultan Idris Education University, Malaysia

IGI Global
Scientific Publishing
Publishing Tomorrow's Research Today

Vice President of Editorial Melissa Wagner
Director of Acquisitions Mikaela Felty
Director of Book Development Jocelynn Hessler
Production Manager Mike Brehm
Cover Design Jose Rosado

Published in the United States of America by
IGI Global Scientific Publishing
701 East Chocolate Avenue
Hershey, PA, 17033, USA
Tel: 717-533-8845 | Fax: 717-533-7115
Website: https://www.igi-global.com E-mail: cust@igi-global.com

Copyright © 2026 by IGI Global Scientific Publishing. All rights reserved. No part of this publication may be reproduced, stored or distributed in any form or by any means, electronic or mechanical, including photocopying, without written permission from the publisher. Use of this publication to train generative artificial intelligence (AI) technologies is expressly prohibited. The publisher reserves all rights to license its use for generative AI training and machine learning model development.

Product or company names used in this set are for identification purposes only. Inclusion of the names of the products or companies does not indicate a claim of ownership by IGI Global Scientific Publishing of the trademark or registered trademark.

Library of Congress Cataloging-in-Publication Data

Names: Huda, Miftachul, 1990- editor.
Title: Global perspectives on social empowerment using current technology / edited by: Miftachul Huda.
Description: Hershey, PA : IGI Global Scientific Publishing, [2026] | Includes bibliographical references and index. | Summary: "The objective of this book is to exchange expert theories, methodologies, and applications in all areas related to the social empowerment using current technology"-- Provided by publisher.
Identifiers: LCCN 2024059930 (print) | LCCN 2024059931 (ebook) | ISBN 9798337306292 (hardcover) | ISBN 9798337306308 (paperback) | ISBN 9798337306315 (ebook)
Subjects: LCSH: Power (Social sciences) | Social change--Technological innovations.
Classification: LCC HN49.P6 (print) | LCC HN49.P6 (ebook) | DDC 303.48/3--dc23/eng/20250327
LC record available at https://lccn.loc.gov/2024059930
LC ebook record available at https://lccn.loc.gov/2024059931

British Cataloguing in Publication Data
A Cataloguing in Publication record for this book is available from the British Library.

All work contributed to this book is new, previously-unpublished material.
The views expressed in this book are those of the authors, but not necessarily of the publisher.
This book contains information sourced from authentic and highly regarded references, with reasonable efforts made to ensure the reliability of the data and information presented. The authors, editors, and publisher believe the information in this book to be accurate and true as of the date of publication. Every effort has been made to trace and credit the copyright holders of all materials included. However, the authors, editors, and publisher cannot assume responsibility for the validity of all materials or the consequences of their use. Should any copyright material be found unacknowledged, please inform the publisher so that corrections may be made in future reprints.

Table of Contents

Detailed Table of Contents

The rapid expansion of technology has fundamentally reshaped human society, driving transformative changes across education, healthcare, economics, culture, and governance. This chapter explores the dual role of technological innovation as both a catalyst for opportunity and a source of complex challenges. It highlights the immense potential of technologies such as artificial intelligence, blockchain, and virtual reality to bridge societal gaps, empower marginalized communities, and foster sustainability. Case studies illustrate how digital tools have revolutionized access to essential services like education and healthcare, while e-commerce and digital payments have democratized economic participation. At the same time, the chapter critically examines the challenges posed by the digital divide, algorithmic biases, misinformation, and privacy concerns, emphasizing the need for inclusive policies and ethical frameworks.

In the 21st century, the intersection of technology and society has become an undeniable force shaping people's lives, work, and their global interconnectivity. Beyond its initial use as a straightforward tool, technology has evolved into a dynamic, all-pervasive force influencing practically every aspect of human life. Every element of society is already heavily reliant on technology. The introduction of cutting-edge technologies like Artificial Intelligence and Internet of Things, the proliferation of social media platforms, and the use of smartphones are all indicators of a rapidly evolving technological landscape, which redefine the meaning and implications of human existence. Despite its ability to empower the society, it poses some challenges such as threat to privacy, misinformation, polarization, and several

This chapter discusses how technology integration in education becomes a crucial tool for promoting social empowerment and enhancing learning. It highlights how innovations, such as online learning management systems, interactive multimedia, and collaborative digital spaces, can transform traditional pedagogy and create inclusive environments. In a discussion, challenges like access, equity, and the digital divide have to be overcome to ensure technology is enhancing rather than merely being an ornament in the educational practices of institutions. Using case studies and empirical evidence, we have demonstrated how effective technological integration indeed empowers students and teachers through promoting critical thinking, creativity, and collaboration. In conclusion, we recommend an integrative approach to educational technology that takes into consideration global perspectives on social empowerment and equity in education.

This chapter explores the transformative role of Artificial Intelligence (AI) in addressing the escalating issue of plastic waste accumulation, a critical environmental challenge. It delves into AI-driven strategies that enhance the efficiency of plastic sorting by accurately identifying types and recyclability, thereby minimizing contamination in recycling streams. The chapter also investigates AI models designed to predict the degradation rates of various plastics in diverse environmental conditions, offering valuable insights for long-term planning in waste management. Highlighting potential cost savings, financial benefits, and operational efficiencies, the discussion is enriched with case studies showcasing real-world applications and challenges in implementing AI for recycling. Ethical considerations and the environmental implications of adopting AI in this sector are analyzed to provide a balanced perspective.

Ensuring safe travel on roads with automobiles or cabs is crucial for creating secure urban environments. Women traveling face significant risks, including harassment, unwanted physical touch, kidnapping, and assault. With rising urban crime rates, addressing safety and security for women has become a pressing concern. To tackle this challenge, this project introduces an innovative Travelers Safety Solution, utilizing advanced technologies to enhance the safety and experience of women commuters. By integrating Google Maps API, Yolov8 for object detection, The system actively monitors route deviations using map-matching algorithms, triggering immediate emergency alerts if deviations occur, notifying both the user and their emergency contacts. Additionally, users can review and provide feedback on driver performance post-journey. This solution not only addresses the safety concerns of women travelers but also empowers them with real-time information and communication, fostering a safer and more secure commuting experience.

This work's main objective is to explore interpersonal communication. The focus is directed to verbal communication, however, the same is also shared with non-verbal communication. In this context, the importance that internal communication has in an organization/company is analyzed. It is well known that the professional success of companies is slightly dependent on internal communication. Barriers and their

Preface

INTRODUCTION

It is with great pleasure that I present this edited volume, *Global Perspectives on Social Empowerment Using Current Technology*. This book emerges at a critical juncture in human history, where rapid technological advancement—particularly in Artificial Intelligence (AI)—is reshaping the very foundations of how societies function, interact, and evolve.

The latest advancements and improvements in existing technologies have significantly impacted societal frameworks by introducing advanced systems and platforms that enhance methods of communication, learning, production, governance, and social interaction. Amid these developments, Artificial Intelligence is at the leading edge. Digital applications powered by AI have been tailored for various sectors, providing transformative support systems that empower both individuals and communities. From AI-driven instructional design in education to smart systems in business, administration, social engagement, and entertainment, technology now offers both impactful and efficient avenues for sustainable human growth when implemented mindfully and ethically.

In my role as the Editor of this volume, I acknowledge that although AI and similar technological advancements hold great potential, they also bring intricate challenges. These encompass issues of ethical leadership, fair access, digital know-how, and the incorporation of new technologies into daily human experiences. Thus, the primary aim of this book is to investigate thoroughly how AI and modern technological advancements can be intentionally crafted and executed to promote authentic social empowerment. The chapters compiled in this volume analyze existing trends, beliefs, and practices in various human sectors, enhancing a holistic understanding of how technological systems can harmonize with human values and societal requirements.

This volume unites a global community of researchers, scientists, engineers, professionals, business leaders, scholars, and academic researchers. Their contributions illustrate a variety of theoretical viewpoints, methodological strategies, empirical research, and practical implementations. Together, these creations offer a space for significant discussions and knowledge sharing to promote social empowerment via technology.

This book seeks to deepen professional comprehension of the strategic importance of modern technology in reinforcing social structures by showcasing pertinent theoretical frameworks together with recent empirical evidence. It is designed not just as an academic resource, but as a driver for innovation, teamwork, and ethical execution.

The intended audience consists of experts and scholars across different fields, especially in information and communication technology, education, business, administrative sciences, and management. Additionally, this volume provides essential perspectives for leaders and decision-makers focused on knowledge management, organizational growth, and fostering expertise within various work communities. Viewed through these lenses, the book highlights the ability of modern technology to enhance the social aspects of human existence.

I genuinely hope this collection will encourage thoughtful reflection, cross-disciplinary cooperation, and progressive approaches that utilize technology not just as a means of efficiency, but as a powerful catalyst for inclusive and sustainable social advancement.

ORGANIZATION OF THE BOOK

As Editor, I am pleased to introduce the rich and multidimensional contributions that compose this volume, each chapter offering a distinctive yet interconnected perspective on social empowerment through current technology.

In **Chapter 1**, the author presents a comprehensive examination of how rapid technological expansion has fundamentally reshaped human society across education, healthcare, economics, governance, and culture. The discussion situates innovations such as artificial intelligence, blockchain, and virtual reality as powerful instruments for bridging social divides and expanding access to essential services. Through carefully selected case studies, the chapter illustrates how digital platforms democratize participation while simultaneously confronting pressing concerns such as algorithmic bias, misinformation, privacy, and the persistent digital divide. The chapter sets a critical foundation for the volume by balancing technological optimism with ethical vigilance.

Chapter 2 advances this conversation by positioning technology as a transformative and all-pervasive force in the 21st century. Here, the contributors reflect on the evolution of technology from a functional tool to an ecosystem shaping identity, work, and global interconnectivity. Drawing conceptual alignment with the aspirations of the United Nations 2030 Agenda, the chapter frames social empowerment within broader sustainable development goals. While celebrating the empowering potential of artificial intelligence, the Internet of Things, and social media platforms, it also addresses the societal risks of polarization, privacy erosion, and misinformation, urging a balanced and forward-looking approach to technological integration.

In **Chapter 3**, the focus turns to gendered dimensions of digital empowerment, particularly within women's entrepreneurship. This chapter introduces the "Online Patriarchy Model," a compelling analytical framework that interrogates how digital platforms both enable and constrain women's economic agency. By examining how algorithmic systems and platform structures may replicate existing hierarchies, the author illuminates the concept of "online patriarchal bargains"—strategic negotiations women undertake to gain visibility and legitimacy in digital markets. This chapter contributes a critical gender lens to the broader discourse on empowerment, revealing both expanded opportunity and persistent structural inequality in digital environments.

Chapter 4 addresses the strategic importance of current technology instruction within the business sector. Emphasizing the growing demand for competencies in artificial intelligence, blockchain, data analytics, and cybersecurity, the chapter underscores the necessity of continuous and diversified learning ecosystems. Through global case illustrations, it demonstrates how corporate training, certifications, and online learning platforms not only strengthen competitiveness but also promote economic inclusion by equipping underserved populations with market-relevant skills. The discussion of micro-credentials and personalized learning further highlights the evolving nature of professional education in the digital economy.

Chapter 5 deepens the educational perspective by exploring technological integration within teaching and learning processes. The contributors argue that digital learning management systems, multimedia tools, and collaborative platforms can transform pedagogy and create inclusive learning environments. Yet, they caution that technology must be meaningfully integrated rather than superficially adopted. Drawing on empirical evidence and case studies, the chapter illustrates how thoughtful integration cultivates critical thinking, creativity, and collaboration while addressing persistent challenges such as access inequities and the digital divide. The integrative framework proposed here reinforces the book's global vision of equity-centered empowerment.

In **Chapter 6**, attention shifts to environmental sustainability through the lens of AI-powered plastic waste management. This chapter demonstrates how artificial intelligence can optimize sorting processes, predict degradation rates, and enhance recycling efficiency. By integrating technical analysis with real-world case studies, the authors reveal the economic and operational benefits of AI-driven systems while also examining ethical and ecological implications. The chapter exemplifies how technological innovation, when responsibly applied, can align environmental stewardship with social and economic value creation.

Chapter 7 presents a socially urgent and technologically innovative contribution addressing women's travel safety. The proposed Travelers Safety Solution integrates advanced tools such as Google Maps API and YOLOv8 object detection to monitor route deviations and trigger emergency alerts in real time. By combining geospatial intelligence, algorithmic monitoring, and user feedback systems, the chapter demonstrates how digital infrastructure can directly enhance personal security in urban mobility contexts. Beyond technological design, the chapter emphasizes empowerment through information, responsiveness, and autonomy in public spaces.

Chapter 8 redirects the discussion toward organizational dynamics, examining internal communication and its influence on institutional performance. Through a case study conducted at Portway Handling in Portugal, the authors investigate verbal communication barriers and mitigation strategies within corporate environments. Utilizing quantitative survey methods, the chapter evaluates how communication obstacles affect operational efficiency and professional success. By linking interpersonal communication practices to organizational outcomes, it broadens the concept of empowerment to include workplace culture and managerial responsibility.

Finally, **Chapter 9** explores the relationship between communication styles and gender within the organizational setting of Nespresso in Portugal. Through a quantitative case study approach, the chapter analyzes how gender dynamics influence verbal and non-verbal communication patterns, knowledge transmission, and goal attainment. By interrogating perceptions of gender equality and communicative effectiveness, the authors shed light on subtle yet impactful differences in professional interaction. This chapter complements earlier gender-focused discussions by situating empowerment within corporate communication structures.

Collectively, these nine chapters embody the intellectual ambition of this volume: to interrogate, contextualize, and advance the role of current technology as a driver of inclusive social empowerment. Each contribution, while grounded in a specific domain, speaks to the broader imperative of aligning technological innovation with ethical responsibility, equity, and human-centered development.

CONCLUSION

As I conclude this volume's final thoughts, I recall that technology, with all its intricacies and changes, is neither purely liberating nor purely obstructive—it is ultimately influenced by human intent, regulation, and shared accountability. The sections compiled in Global Perspectives on Social Empowerment Using Current Technology illustrate that true empowerment stems not just from innovation but from the intentional incorporation of technology with moral values, inclusive approaches, and designs that respond to social needs.

In various fields—education, business, environmental sustainability, gender equity, entrepreneurship, mobility safety, and organizational communication—our contributors have demonstrated how modern technologies, especially Artificial Intelligence and digital platforms, are reshaping the structure of opportunity. They have warned against being complacent, highlighting the ongoing digital divide, bias in algorithms, privacy issues, and systemic inequalities that could worsen if technological advancements unfold without thorough scrutiny.

What becomes clear throughout this volume is that social empowerment in the digital age necessitates a multifaceted strategy. It requires collaboration across disciplines among researchers, practitioners, policymakers, and industry experts. It necessitates investment in digital skills and ongoing education. It demands frameworks that emphasize equity, sustainability, and human dignity in addition to efficiency and growth. Crucially, it encourages us to reconceptualize technology not just as a tool for productivity, but as a transformative influence that can promote justice, participation, and collective prosperity.

As Editor, I see this collection not as a definitive conclusion, but as a continuing conversation—one that promotes additional exploration, creativity, and critical involvement. I aspire for this book to act as a scholarly reference and a practical resource, encouraging meaningful action in institutions, organizations, and communities around the globe.

The potential for social empowerment via today's technology is still to be determined. However, through knowledgeable leadership, ethical dedication, and a shared vision, we have the resources to responsibly and inclusively shape that future. May this book make a significant contribution to that collective effort.

Chapter 1

Human Society Empowerment Through Technology Expansion: An Empirical Research Review

S. Ida Evangeline
http://orcid.org/0000-0003-2997-7897
Government College of Engineering, Tirunelveli, India

Miftachul Huda
http://orcid.org/0000-0001-6712-0056
Sultan Idris Education University, Malaysia

ABSTRACT

The rapid expansion of technology has fundamentally reshaped human society, driving transformative changes across education, healthcare, economics, culture, and governance. This chapter explores the dual role of technological innovation as both a catalyst for opportunity and a source of complex challenges. It highlights the immense potential of technologies such as artificial intelligence, blockchain, and virtual reality to bridge societal gaps, empower marginalized communities, and foster sustainability. Case studies illustrate how digital tools have revolutionized access to essential services like education and healthcare, while e-commerce and digital payments have democratized economic participation. At the same time, the chapter critically examines the challenges posed by the digital divide, algorithmic biases, misinformation, and privacy concerns, emphasizing the need for inclusive policies and ethical frameworks.

DOI: 10.4018/979-8-3373-0629-2.ch001

ght © 2026, IGI Global Scientific Publishing. Copying or distributing in print or electronic forms without written permission of IGI Global Scientific Publishing is prohibited. Use of this chapter to generative artificial intelligence (AI) technologies is expressly prohibited. The publisher reserves all rights to license its use for generative AI training and machine learning model development.

1. INTRODUCTION

1.1 Context of Technological Expansion in Human Society

The evolution of technology has been a defining feature of human progress, shaping societies through successive waves of innovation. From the agricultural revolution to the industrial age and now the digital era, technology has consistently transformed the way humans live, work, and interact (Marquardt & Kearsley, 2024). Today, we are witnessing an unprecedented acceleration in technological advancement, driven by innovations in artificial intelligence, blockchain, quantum computing, biotechnology, and other cutting-edge fields (Neethirajan, 2024). These technologies permeate every facet of human life, influencing communication, education, healthcare, governance, and economic activities. This rapid expansion underscores technology's dual role as both a driver of opportunity and a source of complex challenges.

As humanity navigates the digital age, the integration of technology into everyday life has revealed its immense potential to address pressing societal issues (Okoro et al. 2024). From enabling remote education and healthcare access in underserved regions to fostering global collaboration and innovation, technology acts as a catalyst for empowerment (Prestoza, 2024). However, alongside these opportunities lie significant challenges, including widening digital divides, ethical dilemmas, and concerns over equity, privacy, and social cohesion. The transformative power of technology thus demands a careful examination of its broader implications for society.

1.2 Overview of Opportunities and Challenges

The opportunities presented by technological expansion are vast and multifaceted. Technology has democratized access to knowledge, resources, and markets, enabling individuals and communities to overcome traditional barriers of geography and socio-economic status. For instance, digital platforms facilitate remote learning, telemedicine, and global entrepreneurship, empowering individuals with tools to achieve personal and collective aspirations (Alnasser et al. 2024). In governance, technological innovations enhance transparency, efficiency, and citizen participation, while in culture, digital tools preserve and celebrate heritage in innovative ways.

Conversely, these advancements are accompanied by significant challenges. The digital divide—the gap between those who can access and benefit from technology and those who cannot—remains a critical barrier to inclusive progress (Peruzzo & Allan, 2024). Ethical concerns such as data privacy, surveillance, algorithmic bias, and job displacement due to automation pose threats to individual autonomy and social equity. Furthermore, the misuse of digital tools has led to societal issues like misinformation, polarization, and a decline in trust in institutions (Afrouz & Vassos, 2024). Addressing these challenges requires deliberate action to ensure that technological progress aligns with the principles of equity, sustainability, and human dignity.

1.3 Central Notion of Responsible and Inclusive Empowerment

This chapter argues that the transformative potential of technology must be harnessed responsibly to empower human society inclusively. Responsible technological development and deployment involve embedding ethical considerations, fostering collaboration across disciplines, and ensuring equitable access to technology's benefits (Sarker, 2024). By addressing systemic barriers and creating safeguards against misuse, society can leverage technology to foster empowerment in education, healthcare, economic participation, civic engagement, cultural preservation, and environmental sustainability.

The central notion of this chapter underscores the importance of a balanced approach to technology expansion—one that maximizes its potential to uplift individuals and communities while mitigating its risks. By critically examining the interplay between technological innovation and societal development, this chapter aims to contribute to the discourse on shaping a future where technology serves as a force for good, bridging divides and enabling a more inclusive, equitable, and empowered global society.

2. BRIDGING GAPS IN ESSENTIAL SERVICES

2.1 Education: Digital Tools and Remote Learning

Education is a cornerstone of societal development, yet access to quality education remains unequal across the globe. Technological advancements have emerged as a transformative force in bridging these gaps, offering innovative tools and platforms that democratize learning opportunities (Kizilcec, 2024). Digital tools such as online learning platforms, virtual classrooms, and interactive educational apps have significantly expanded access to knowledge, enabling learners in remote or underserved areas to overcome barriers of geography and infrastructure (Rafiq et al. 2024).

Remote learning, particularly during the COVID-19 pandemic, has demonstrated the potential of technology to maintain educational continuity in the face of disruption (Rahiem, 2024). Platforms such as Khan Academy, Coursera, and regional digital initiatives have connected millions of students to free or affordable courses, empowering them to pursue education independently of physical classrooms. Similarly, gamified learning applications like Duolingo and coding platforms like Code.org have made skill acquisition engaging and accessible, fostering lifelong learning.

The benefits of digital tools extend beyond access. They offer personalized learning experiences through artificial intelligence (AI)-powered algorithms that adapt content to individual needs, pacing, and preferences (Ayeni et al. 2024). Tools like adaptive testing and real-time feedback enhance the quality of learning, helping educators identify and address student weaknesses effectively. Moreover, collaborative tools such as Google Classroom and Microsoft Teams have fostered interaction and community among students and teachers, even across great distances.

However, despite these advances, challenges remain. The digital divide limits access to these technologies for students in low-income or rural areas, where internet connectivity and digital devices are scarce (Raihan et al. 2024). Addressing this gap requires investments in infrastructure, such as expanding broadband access and providing affordable devices. Equally important are initiatives to enhance digital literacy among both students and educators, ensuring that technology serves as a bridge rather than a barrier to education. Through targeted policies and collaborative efforts, technology can transform education into a more inclusive and equitable domain.

2.2 Healthcare: Telemedicine and AI Diagnostics

Healthcare is another critical sector where technology has bridged gaps, bringing essential services to underserved populations and improving the quality of care. Telemedicine, which allows patients to consult healthcare professionals remotely, has emerged as a game-changer in extending medical services to rural and isolated regions (Su et al. 2024). Platforms such as Teladoc and Doctor on Demand have enabled patients to access timely consultations, prescriptions, and follow-ups, significantly reducing travel burdens and wait times.

AI-driven diagnostic tools further amplify healthcare's reach and efficiency. Algorithms capable of analyzing medical images, such as X-rays and MRIs, have demonstrated remarkable accuracy in detecting conditions ranging from cancers to retinal diseases (Kasula, 2024). Tools like Google's DeepMind and IBM Watson Health are transforming diagnostic processes by providing clinicians with data-driven insights, aiding early detection and improving patient outcomes. Wearable devices like Fitbit and Apple Watch offer continuous health monitoring, enabling individuals to track vital signs, detect anomalies, and manage chronic conditions more effectively (Gupta & Pandey, 2024).

In addition to diagnostics, AI-powered systems are improving treatment planning and resource allocation (Arefin, 2024). Predictive analytics help healthcare providers anticipate disease outbreaks and optimize supply chains, ensuring timely responses to public health crises. Telehealth platforms integrated with electronic health records (EHRs) are streamlining patient care, allowing healthcare professionals to access and share information seamlessly (Bouabida et al. 2024).

Nevertheless, these advancements are not without challenges. The unequal distribution of technology often excludes marginalized populations, exacerbating health inequities (Hajat et al. 2024). Ensuring access to telemedicine and AI diagnostics requires addressing systemic barriers such as affordability, infrastructure deficits, and digital literacy. Privacy concerns related to patient data also necessitate robust regulatory frameworks to protect sensitive information and build trust in digital healthcare systems.

By addressing these challenges through inclusive policies, public-private partnerships, and community engagement, technology can revolutionize healthcare delivery. Its transformative potential lies in making quality healthcare accessible to all, transcending barriers of geography and socio-economic status, and fostering healthier, more resilient communities.

3. ECONOMIC EMPOWERMENT

3.1 E-Commerce, Digital Payments, and Entrepreneurship

The digital revolution has significantly reshaped economic participation, creating opportunities for individuals and communities to engage in markets that were previously inaccessible. E-commerce platforms, digital payment systems, and entrepreneurship tools have democratized access to economic resources, enabling individuals to start businesses, reach global audiences, and generate income with minimal capital investment (Bhuiyan et al. 2024).

E-commerce platforms such as Amazon, Alibaba, and Shopify have lowered the barriers to entry for small businesses and independent entrepreneurs (Costa & Rodrigues, 2024). These platforms provide the infrastructure needed to market, sell, and distribute goods globally, empowering sellers from diverse backgrounds to compete on an international scale. Small artisans, for example, can now showcase their products to a worldwide audience, bypassing traditional intermediaries and achieving economic independence.

Digital payment systems, including PayPal, Stripe, and mobile payment solutions like M-Pesa and Alipay, have further facilitated this economic empowerment (Rohatgi et al. 2024). By enabling secure and convenient transactions, these systems have expanded financial inclusion, particularly in regions where access to traditional banking services is limited. Mobile wallets and peer-to-peer payment apps have empowered individuals to participate in the digital economy, fostering entrepreneurship in underserved communities.

Crowdfunding platforms such as Kickstarter and GoFundMe have revolutionized how entrepreneurs and creators secure funding for their projects (Yáñez-Valdés & Guerrero, 2024). By connecting innovators with potential investors and supporters, these platforms have enabled individuals to realize their visions without relying on traditional financial institutions. This democratization of access to capital has opened new pathways for innovation, job creation, and economic growth.

However, the benefits of digital commerce and entrepreneurship are not evenly distributed. Limited digital literacy, inadequate infrastructure, and regulatory challenges often prevent marginalized populations from fully participating in the digital economy. To address these disparities, targeted interventions such as digital literacy training, investments in infrastructure, and supportive policy frameworks are essential. By fostering an inclusive digital ecosystem, technology can enable broader economic empowerment and reduce inequality.

3.2 Challenges in the Gig Economy

The rise of the gig economy, driven by digital platforms like Uber, Fiverr, and TaskRabbit, has redefined the nature of work, offering flexibility and autonomy to millions of workers worldwide. These platforms connect workers with short-term contracts or freelance opportunities, enabling individuals to earn income on their own terms. For many, the gig economy provides a pathway to economic participation, particularly in regions with limited formal employment opportunities (Salmah et al. 2024).

Despite its potential, the gig economy presents significant challenges that undermine its promise of empowerment. One of the primary concerns is job insecurity, as gig workers typically lack stable income, benefits, and legal protections (Lo & Kun-Lin, 2024). Unlike traditional employees, they are often considered independent contractors, which excludes them from labor protections such as minimum wage laws, health insurance, and retirement benefits. This precariousness leaves many gig workers vulnerable to economic shocks and exploitation.

Another challenge lies in the algorithms that govern gig platforms. These algorithms determine job allocation, pricing, and worker ratings, often in opaque and unregulated ways (Zhu et al. 2024). Workers may experience unfair treatment, such as deactivation or pay reductions, without clear recourse or transparency. The lack of bargaining power and collective representation further exacerbates the imbalance between workers and platform operators.

Additionally, the gig economy has been criticized for perpetuating income disparities and regional inequalities (Dong et al. 2024). While some workers benefit from high-paying opportunities in affluent markets, others struggle with low wages in less lucrative regions. This uneven distribution of opportunities highlights the need for equitable policies that address these disparities and ensure fair treatment for all gig workers.

To mitigate these challenges, stakeholders must prioritize the regulation and formalization of the gig economy. Policies that establish minimum standards for worker protections, promote transparency in platform governance, and enable collective bargaining are crucial. Public-private partnerships can also play a role in developing social safety nets tailored to gig workers, such as portable benefits and accessible upskilling programs (Martindale et al. 2024).

By addressing these challenges, the gig economy can evolve into a more inclusive and sustainable model of economic empowerment. Combined with the opportunities created by e-commerce and digital payment systems, technology has the potential to transform livelihoods, foster innovation, and create a more equitable global economy.

4. CIVIC ENGAGEMENT AND SOCIAL PARTICIPATION

4.1 Amplifying Voices Through Social Media and Digital Tools

The advent of social media and digital platforms has profoundly transformed the ways individuals and communities engage in civic and social activities. These technologies have democratized access to information, amplified marginalized voices, and enabled unprecedented levels of participation in public discourse and advocacy (Yap et al. 2024). Platforms such as Twitter, Facebook, and Instagram, along with specialized tools like Change.org and GoFundMe, empower individuals to mobilize for causes, influence policy decisions, and foster community action (Fazil et al. 2024).

Social media has become a powerful tool for civic engagement, providing a platform for real-time communication and collaboration. Activists and organizations have leveraged these platforms to organize grassroots movements, raise awareness about critical issues, and drive social change (Fornander et al. 2024). Movements like #MeToo, Black Lives Matter, and Fridays for Future have gained global traction through social media, demonstrating the potential of these tools to unite individuals across geographic and cultural boundaries (Herrada-Lores et al. 2024). The ease of sharing multimedia content, creating petitions, and crowdfunding initiatives has further enabled individuals to contribute to causes they care about, fostering a sense of empowerment and collective purpose.

Digital tools also enhance participation in governance and policymaking (Esposito et al. 2024). Online platforms for e-governance, such as MyGov in India or petitions.whitehouse.gov in the United States, allow citizens to engage directly with policymakers, submit grievances, and propose solutions (Malhotra, 2024). Virtual town halls and community forums facilitate dialogue between governments and constituents, increasing transparency and accountability. Additionally, tools for citizen science and crowdsourcing, such as Zooniverse and Ushahidi, encourage public involvement in research and data collection, enabling collaborative problem-solving on societal issues (Cui & Yasseri, 2024).

4.2 Risks of Misinformation and Polarization

While digital platforms have empowered civic engagement, they have also introduced significant risks, particularly concerning misinformation and societal polarization (Altay et al. 2024). The speed and scale at which information spreads on social media make these platforms vulnerable to the dissemination of false or misleading content. Misinformation campaigns, often driven by malicious actors, exploit these dynamics to manipulate public opinion, disrupt democratic processes, and undermine trust in institutions.

One of the most concerning aspects of misinformation is its impact on critical societal issues (Shahbazi & Bunker, 2024). False narratives about public health, for example, have fueled vaccine hesitancy and resistance to COVID-19 measures, endangering public safety. Similarly, the spread of fake news during elections has sown confusion, eroded trust in electoral systems, and exacerbated political divisions (Iida et al. 2024). The use of sophisticated techniques, such as deepfakes and algorithmic amplification, further complicates efforts to combat misinformation, making it increasingly difficult for users to distinguish credible information from falsehoods.

In addition to misinformation, digital platforms have contributed to societal polarization (Kreiss & McGregor, 2024). Echo chambers and filter bubbles—created by algorithms that prioritize content aligned with users' existing beliefs—reinforce biases and limit exposure to diverse perspectives. This phenomenon amplifies divisions within society, fostering hostility and reducing opportunities for constructive dialogue. Polarization is particularly evident in politically charged discussions, where opposing groups become entrenched in their viewpoints, making consensus and cooperation increasingly challenging.

To address these risks, a multifaceted approach is needed. Digital literacy programs can equip users with critical thinking skills to evaluate information and identify misinformation (Buchan et al. 2024). Social media platforms must take greater responsibility by implementing robust content moderation policies, enhancing algorithmic transparency, and collaborating with fact-checking organizations. Governments and civil society can play a role by promoting media literacy education, supporting independent journalism, and establishing regulatory frameworks that balance freedom of expression with the need to prevent harm.

By addressing the risks of misinformation and polarization, society can harness the transformative potential of digital tools while safeguarding the integrity of civic and social participation. Through deliberate efforts to promote inclusivity, accountability, and trust, technology can continue to empower individuals and communities to shape a more informed and cohesive world.

5. ETHICAL AND STRUCTURAL CONCERNS

5.1 Privacy, Surveillance, and Ethical AI

As technology becomes increasingly integrated into daily life, concerns about privacy, surveillance, and the ethical use of artificial intelligence (AI) have emerged as critical issues (Santos & Radanliev, 2024). These challenges stem from the vast amounts of data generated by individuals' interactions with digital systems, coupled with the rapid development of AI-driven tools that analyze, predict, and influence human behavior.

Privacy concerns revolve around the collection, storage, and use of personal data (Wu et al. 2024). From social media platforms to smart devices, digital technologies continuously gather detailed information about individuals, often without their explicit consent or understanding. This data is frequently monetized or used for targeted advertising, raising questions about ownership, transparency, and accountability. The pervasive nature of data collection has led to growing fears of misuse, such as identity theft, unauthorized surveillance, or the creation of detailed behavioral profiles for manipulative purposes.

Surveillance technologies have added another layer of complexity to privacy concerns. While tools such as facial recognition and smart city infrastructure can enhance public safety and operational efficiency, they also enable unprecedented levels of monitoring and control (Wang et al. 2024). The use of such technologies by governments and corporations raises ethical questions about individual autonomy, consent, and the potential for misuse in authoritarian contexts. For instance, widespread surveillance may erode trust in institutions, suppress dissent, and disproportionately target marginalized communities.

Ethical concerns extend to the development and deployment of AI. Algorithms often reflect the biases present in the data they are trained on, leading to discriminatory outcomes in critical areas such as hiring, lending, and law enforcement (Tortora, 2024). Moreover, the lack of transparency in AI decision-making processes—often described as the "black box" problem—makes it difficult to hold systems accountable for their actions. The unchecked application of AI in sensitive domains, such as predictive policing or healthcare, underscores the urgent need for ethical oversight and regulation.

5.2 Strategies for Embedding Ethical Principles

Addressing the ethical and structural concerns associated with technology requires a proactive and collaborative approach to embedding ethical principles into its design, development, and use. The following strategies can guide efforts to ensure that technology aligns with societal values and priorities:

1. **Privacy-by-Design:**

Privacy considerations should be integrated into the development process of technologies from the outset. This includes adopting practices such as data minimization, anonymization, and encryption to protect user information (Shehzadi, 2024). Clear and accessible privacy policies, along with mechanisms for user consent and control, can enhance transparency and trust.

2. **Transparent and Accountable AI:**

AI systems should be designed to be explainable and auditable, allowing users to understand how decisions are made and enabling stakeholders to identify and address biases or errors. Open-source AI models and independent audits can contribute to greater accountability (Akinrinola et al. 2024). Developers should prioritize fairness, equity, and inclusivity in their algorithms, using diverse and representative datasets to minimize bias.

3. **Ethical Governance Frameworks:**

Governments, industry leaders, and civil society must collaborate to establish regulatory frameworks that promote ethical technology use (Camilleri, 2024). These frameworks should define standards for data protection, AI accountability, and responsible innovation. International cooperation is essential to address cross-border challenges and ensure consistency in ethical practices.

4. **Ethics Committees and Review Boards:**

Organizations developing and deploying technology should establish internal ethics committees to evaluate potential societal impacts and guide decision-making

(Schuett et al. 2024). These committees can provide multidisciplinary perspectives, including those of ethicists, sociologists, and affected communities, to address ethical dilemmas comprehensively.

5. **Public Engagement and Education:**

Engaging the public in discussions about the ethical implications of technology can foster awareness and participation in shaping its use (Nguyen et al. 2024). Digital literacy programs that emphasize ethical considerations can empower individuals to make informed decisions about their data and technology use.

6. **Responsible Innovation Incentives:**

Policymakers can encourage ethical technology development through incentives such as grants, tax breaks, or certifications for companies that prioritize responsible innovation (Blank et al. 2024). Industry standards and best practices can also promote a culture of accountability.

7. **Global Ethical Standards:**

Given the global nature of technology, international organizations can play a crucial role in establishing ethical standards and promoting their adoption across countries (Stahl & Eke, 2024). Initiatives such as the UNESCO Recommendation on the Ethics of AI exemplify efforts to create globally recognized principles.

By embedding ethical principles into technological innovation, society can mitigate the risks associated with privacy violations, surveillance, and biased AI. These strategies ensure that technology serves as a tool for empowerment rather than exploitation, aligning its growth with the values of equity, inclusivity, and respect for human rights.

6. ADDRESSING THE DIGITAL DIVIDE

6.1 Factors Contributing to Unequal Access

The digital divide refers to the gap between individuals, communities, and countries that have access to information and communication technologies (ICTs) and those that do not. This divide has significant implications for social equity, economic opportunity, and overall human development, as technology increasingly serves as a gateway to essential services, education, and civic participation.

Several factors contribute to this unequal access to technology:

1. **Economic Barriers:**

The cost of devices, internet connectivity, and digital services remains prohibitive for many individuals, particularly in low-income households and developing countries (Samuel-Okon & Abejide, 2024). Even in regions with widespread connectivity, affordability often dictates the quality and frequency of access.

2. **Geographic Disparities:**

Rural and remote areas frequently lag behind urban centers in terms of technological infrastructure (Chee, 2024). The lack of broadband coverage, cellular networks, and reliable electricity in these regions limits access to digital tools and services.

3. **Educational Inequalities:**

Digital literacy is a crucial determinant of individuals' ability to engage with technology effectively (Val & López-Bueno, 2024). Those with limited educational opportunities are less likely to possess the skills needed to navigate digital platforms, exacerbating disparities in access and utilization.

4. **Gender and Social Norms:**

In some societies, cultural and social norms restrict access to technology for certain groups, particularly women and girls. Gender disparities in education and economic participation further compound this issue.

5. **Disabilities and Accessibility Challenges:**

Individuals with disabilities often face barriers in accessing technology that is not designed to accommodate diverse needs. The lack of accessible software, hardware, and user interfaces excludes many from benefiting fully from digital advancements.

6. **Policy and Regulatory Gaps:**

Inadequate policies and weak regulatory frameworks can hinder efforts to expand technology access. Factors such as monopolistic pricing, lack of competition among providers, and insufficient public investment exacerbate the digital divide.

6.2 Policies and Initiatives for Equitable Technology Access

Closing the digital divide requires comprehensive policies and initiatives that address its root causes while fostering inclusive and equitable access to technology. The following approaches have proven effective in promoting digital inclusion:

1. **Investing in Digital Infrastructure:**

Expanding broadband networks, especially in rural and underserved areas, is a fundamental step toward bridging the digital divide. Public-private partnerships can mobilize resources for infrastructure development, while government subsidies and incentives can encourage investment in high-cost regions (Guo et al. 2024).

2. **Promoting Affordable Access:**

Policies aimed at reducing the cost of devices, connectivity, and digital services can make technology more accessible to low-income populations. Initiatives like zero-rating services, subsidized internet packages, and community Wi-Fi programs have been successful in providing affordable access (Stjernborg & Svensson, 2024).

3. **Enhancing Digital Literacy:**

Education and training programs that focus on digital skills are essential for empowering individuals to use technology effectively. Schools, community centers, and non-governmental organizations can play a pivotal role in delivering these programs, particularly in marginalized communities (Chan, 2024).

4. **Addressing Gender Inequities:**

Targeted interventions are needed to address the gender gap in technology access. Initiatives that provide women and girls with devices, training, and support can empower them to participate fully in the digital economy (Kuteesa et al. 2024). Programs like UN Women's "Global Innovation Coalition for Change" exemplify such efforts.

5. **Designing for Accessibility:**

Technology must be inclusive of individuals with disabilities. Developers should adhere to accessibility standards and incorporate features like screen readers, voice commands, and customizable interfaces. Policies that mandate compliance with accessibility guidelines can drive systemic change (Chemnad & Othman, 2024).

6. **Fostering Community-Based Solutions:**

Localized initiatives, such as community technology hubs and telecenters, provide shared access to digital resources. These centers can serve as points of connection, training, and support, particularly in regions where individual access is limited.

7. **Policy and Regulatory Reform:**

Governments can enact policies that promote competition among internet service providers, regulate fair pricing, and protect consumer rights. National digital strategies that align with international frameworks, such as the Sustainable Development Goals (SDGs), can guide coordinated efforts (Komolafe et al. 2024).

8. **Leveraging Global Partnerships:**

International organizations and coalitions play a vital role in addressing the digital divide. Initiatives such as the World Bank's Digital Development Partnership and the ITU's "Connect 2030 Agenda" focus on mobilizing resources, sharing knowledge, and scaling successful models across regions.

9. **Incentivizing Innovation:**

Supporting research and development in low-cost technologies, such as affordable smartphones and solar-powered internet solutions, can accelerate progress in bridging the digital divide. Governments and private sector actors can collaborate to develop innovative solutions tailored to underserved populations.

By implementing these policies and initiatives, governments, organizations, and communities can work together to close the digital divide. Ensuring equitable access to technology is not only a matter of fairness but also a prerequisite for achieving broader social, economic, and cultural empowerment in an increasingly digital world.

7. CULTURAL EMPOWERMENT AND PRESERVATION

7.1 Role of VR and AR in Cultural Heritage

Virtual Reality (VR) and Augmented Reality (AR) technologies are revolutionizing the way cultural heritage is experienced, preserved, and shared (Ramtohul & Khedo, 2024). These immersive tools allow communities to document, recreate, and celebrate their cultural traditions in ways that were previously unimaginable, empowering individuals and groups to maintain and transmit their cultural identities in a rapidly globalizing world.

VR offers the ability to create fully immersive experiences that transport users to historical sites, events, or cultural spaces. For example, VR applications allow users to virtually explore ancient ruins, museums, or historically significant landmarks without leaving their homes. Projects like Google Arts & Culture and UNESCO's VR initiatives provide virtual access to cultural treasures that may otherwise be inaccessible due to geographical or financial barriers (Stachel & Cantoni, 2024). Such experiences foster global appreciation of cultural diversity while enabling local communities to take pride in their heritage.

AR complements VR by overlaying digital content onto the physical world, enhancing how people interact with cultural artifacts and traditions. Museums and cultural institutions are increasingly leveraging AR to provide enriched experiences for visitors (Khalil et al. 2024). For instance, AR-enabled apps can animate historical objects, provide detailed context, or allow users to visualize how ancient sites once appeared. These technologies not only make learning about cultural heritage more engaging but also ensure that the stories and significance behind artifacts are preserved for future generations.

Both VR and AR play a crucial role in safeguarding endangered cultural practices. Communities can use these tools to document oral histories, traditional dances, and crafts, creating digital archives that preserve cultural knowledge for posterity. Additionally, VR and AR are being used to revive lost or destroyed heritage, such as reconstructing historical sites damaged by conflict or natural disasters. This aspect of cultural empowerment emphasizes the resilience of human heritage in the face of adversity.

7.2 Balancing Cultural Diversity and Digital Homogenization

While digital tools like VR and AR provide powerful means of cultural preservation, they also introduce the risk of cultural homogenization (Oladokun et al. 2024). As technology connects cultures and facilitates the exchange of ideas, there is a growing concern that dominant cultural narratives may overshadow or dilute local and minority traditions. This homogenization could lead to the loss of unique cultural identities and practices, undermining the diversity that enriches human society (Sa'idah & Juhana, 2024).

One challenge lies in the unequal representation of cultures in digital spaces. Wealthier and more technologically advanced nations often have greater access to the resources needed to digitize their cultural heritage, while underrepresented communities struggle to have their stories told (Liu & Darvin, 2024). This imbalance risks perpetuating cultural hegemony, where certain traditions and narratives dominate global discourse.

Another concern is the commercialization of cultural heritage. As digital platforms increasingly monetize cultural experiences, there is a risk that heritage will be commodified, losing its intrinsic value and authenticity (Zhu & bin Azahari, 2024). For example, the reproduction of sacred rituals or artifacts in virtual environments could be misrepresented or appropriated, leading to cultural insensitivity and exploitation.

To balance cultural diversity with the risks of digital homogenization, several strategies are essential:

1. **Empowering Local Communities:**

Communities must have control over how their cultural heritage is digitized, represented, and shared. Initiatives should prioritize local voices and perspectives, ensuring that the technology serves the needs and aspirations of the communities it represents (Porter, 2024).

2. **Inclusive Digitization Efforts:**

Governments, NGOs, and international organizations should invest in digitization projects for underrepresented cultures, providing the necessary funding and technical support to document and preserve their heritage (Giacobone et al. 2024).

3. **Ethical Guidelines for Cultural Representation:**

Developers and organizations must adhere to ethical guidelines when creating digital representations of cultural heritage. These guidelines should emphasize respect for cultural ownership, authenticity, and sensitivity to the significance of traditions and artifacts (Quinlan, 2024).

4. **Promoting Cultural Exchange and Collaboration:**

Digital tools should be used to foster mutual understanding and appreciation between cultures. Virtual and augmented experiences can serve as platforms for intercultural dialogue, highlighting the shared values and unique contributions of diverse communities (Eden et al. 2024).

5. **Leveraging Open Access:**

Making digital cultural heritage resources openly accessible can promote global inclusivity and ensure that no single entity monopolizes cultural narratives. Open-source platforms and collaborations can democratize access to cultural knowledge, encouraging broader participation (Sabarirajan et al. 2024).

By embracing these strategies, societies can leverage VR and AR to empower cultural preservation and celebrate diversity while guarding against the risks of homogenization. In doing so, digital technologies can serve as a bridge between tradition and innovation, ensuring that cultural heritage continues to thrive in the digital age.

8. SUSTAINABILITY AND ENVIRONMENTAL IMPACT

8.1 Technological Solutions for Climate Change and Resource Efficiency

Technology is playing a pivotal role in addressing the urgent challenges of climate change and resource efficiency. Innovative solutions are transforming the way societies produce, consume, and manage resources, helping mitigate environmental degradation while promoting sustainable practices.

One of the most impactful technological advancements is the development of renewable energy systems. Solar panels, wind turbines, and hydroelectric systems are enabling the transition from fossil fuels to cleaner energy sources (Moosavian et al. 2024). Advances in battery storage technologies, such as lithium-ion and emerging solid-state batteries, are making renewable energy more reliable and accessible by addressing intermittency issues (Njema et al. 2024). Smart grid systems further enhance energy efficiency by optimizing power distribution and integrating decentralized energy production into national grids.

Artificial intelligence (AI) and big data analytics are also revolutionizing climate change mitigation efforts. AI-powered systems can monitor and predict climate patterns, optimize energy usage in buildings and industrial processes, and enhance agricultural productivity while reducing waste (Shaamala et al. 2024). For example, precision agriculture technologies use AI, IoT (Internet of Things) sensors, and drones to monitor soil health, water usage, and crop conditions, enabling farmers to minimize inputs like water and fertilizer while maximizing yields.

In urban planning, technologies such as digital twins and smart city solutions are improving resource efficiency. Digital twins create virtual replicas of physical environments, allowing planners to simulate and optimize resource use in real time. Smart city initiatives deploy IoT sensors to monitor air quality, manage traffic flow, and optimize waste management systems, reducing environmental footprints and improving urban livability (El-Hajj, 2024).

Carbon capture, utilization, and storage (CCUS) technologies represent another critical frontier in combating climate change. These systems capture carbon dioxide emissions from industrial processes and power plants, preventing them from entering the atmosphere. Captured carbon can then be stored underground or repurposed into valuable products, such as construction materials or synthetic fuels (Saxena et al. 2024).

Despite these advancements, challenges remain in scaling and deploying technological solutions equitably. Developing countries often lack the infrastructure and resources needed to adopt sustainable technologies, exacerbating global inequalities. Addressing these barriers requires coordinated global efforts, including funding, technology transfer, and capacity building.

8.2 Promoting Sustainable Development Practices

While technological innovation provides tools for sustainability, fostering a culture of sustainable development requires comprehensive strategies that integrate technological solutions into broader societal frameworks. Promoting sustainable practices involves aligning economic growth, environmental stewardship, and social equity.

1. **Encouraging Circular Economies:**

Technology can drive the transition from linear economic models, which rely on resource extraction and waste, to circular economies that emphasize reuse, recycling, and regeneration. Innovations such as blockchain can improve transparency in supply chains, ensuring that materials are sourced, used, and recycled responsibly (Vann Yaroson et al. 2024).

2. **Enhancing Public Awareness and Engagement:**

Digital tools can educate individuals and communities about sustainable practices. Apps and platforms that track carbon footprints, provide energy-saving tips, or encourage recycling can empower people to make environmentally conscious choices. Gamification and rewards systems can further motivate sustainable behaviors (Odoom et al. 2024).

3. **Integrating Sustainability into Policy and Regulation:**

Governments play a crucial role in promoting sustainability by implementing policies that incentivize the adoption of green technologies. Tax credits for renewable energy projects, subsidies for energy-efficient appliances, and penalties for excessive emissions are examples of regulatory measures that drive sustainable development (Adanma & Ogunbiyi, 2024).

4. **Fostering Public-Private Partnerships:**

Collaboration between governments, businesses, and non-governmental organizations can accelerate the development and deployment of sustainable technologies. Public-private partnerships can fund research and innovation, scale pilot projects, and create market conditions that favor sustainability (Ramolobe & Khandanisa, 2024).

5. **Leveraging Green Finance and Investment:**

Green financing mechanisms, such as climate bonds and sustainable investment funds, are critical to mobilizing resources for environmental projects. Financial technologies (fintech) enable individuals and institutions to invest in sustainable initiatives, expanding the reach of green funding (Hussain et al. 2024).

6. **Ensuring Equity in Access to Green Technologies:**

The benefits of sustainable development must be distributed equitably. International cooperation is essential to provide developing nations with access to sustainable technologies, financial support, and expertise. Programs like the Green Climate Fund aim to bridge this gap, ensuring that vulnerable populations can participate in and benefit from global sustainability efforts (Meka & Venkateswarlu, 2024).

7. **Innovating for Future Resilience:**

Emerging technologies, such as biodegradable materials, water purification systems, and bioenergy, hold promise for addressing long-term sustainability challenges. Investment in research and development can unlock new solutions to environmental problems while fostering economic growth (Xue & Wang, 2024).

By integrating technological solutions with sustainable development practices, societies can address the dual imperatives of mitigating climate change and achieving global sustainability. These efforts require collaboration across sectors and borders, ensuring that technology serves as a catalyst for a more resilient, equitable, and environmentally conscious world.

9. FUTURE PERSPECTIVES

9.1 Emerging Technologies and Their Potential

As society progresses deeper into the digital age, emerging technologies are poised to redefine the boundaries of what is possible, offering transformative solutions to complex societal challenges. These technologies hold immense potential to empower individuals, enhance quality of life, and address pressing global issues.

1. **Artificial Intelligence and Machine Learning:**

AI is at the forefront of innovation, with applications spanning diverse domains such as healthcare, education, transportation, and environmental conservation. Machine learning models can analyze vast datasets to uncover insights, optimize decision-making, and predict outcomes with unprecedented accuracy. For example, AI-driven drug discovery is accelerating the development of treatments for diseases, while autonomous vehicles promise to revolutionize transportation safety and efficiency (Hirsch-Kreinsen, 2024).

2. **Blockchain Technology:**

Blockchain offers a decentralized and secure method for recording transactions and managing data. Its applications go beyond cryptocurrency to include supply chain transparency, secure voting systems, and the protection of intellectual property. In emerging economies, blockchain can enable financial inclusion by providing unbanked populations with access to digital financial services (Zhuk, 2024).

3. **Quantum Computing:**

Quantum computing has the potential to solve problems that are currently intractable for classical computers, such as optimizing supply chains, modeling complex chemical reactions, and enhancing cryptographic security. This technology promises to unlock new possibilities in fields ranging from climate modeling to artificial intelligence (Troyer et al. 2024).

4. **Biotechnology and Genetic Engineering:**

Advances in biotechnology, such as CRISPR-Cas9 gene editing, are opening doors to breakthroughs in medicine, agriculture, and environmental sustainability. Genetic engineering can address global food security challenges by developing climate-resilient crops and reducing agricultural waste (Sharma et al. 2024).

5. **Extended Reality (XR):**

Extended reality technologies, including virtual reality (VR), augmented reality (AR), and mixed reality (MR), are expanding the possibilities for immersive experiences in education, training, and entertainment. In industries like healthcare, XR is being used for surgical training and patient therapy, while in cultural preservation, it allows for interactive exploration of heritage sites (Bekaroo, 2024).

6. **Green Technologies:**

Innovations in renewable energy, carbon capture, and sustainable materials are critical to combating climate change. Technologies such as perovskite solar cells, energy-efficient building materials, and bio-based plastics are making sustainability more achievable and scalable (Ahmed & Elfaki, 2024).

7. **Space Technologies:**

Space exploration and satellite technologies are enabling advances in global connectivity, disaster response, and environmental monitoring. Projects like SpaceX's Starlink aim to provide internet access to remote areas, while satellite imaging supports precision agriculture and wildlife conservation (Salykov et al. 2024).

These emerging technologies have transformative potential, but their integration into society requires thoughtful planning, regulation, and oversight to ensure they serve as tools for empowerment rather than sources of harm.

9.2 Governance Frameworks for Responsible Innovation

The rapid pace of technological advancement necessitates governance frameworks that balance innovation with ethical considerations, societal well-being, and environmental sustainability. Responsible innovation requires collaboration among governments, private sectors, academia, and civil society to establish shared principles and practices.

1. **Ethical Guidelines and Standards:**

Ethical frameworks should guide the development and use of emerging technologies, ensuring alignment with societal values such as equity, transparency, and accountability. For example, guidelines for AI development should emphasize fairness, privacy, and the prevention of bias in algorithms (Olorunfemi et al. 2024).

2. **Regulatory Oversight:**

Governments must implement policies and regulations that ensure technology is developed and deployed responsibly. This includes addressing potential risks such as data misuse, job displacement, and environmental harm. Regulations should strike a balance between fostering innovation and protecting public interests (Gilbert & Gilbert, 2024).

3. **Inclusive Stakeholder Engagement:**

Governance frameworks should involve diverse stakeholders, including marginalized communities, to ensure that technological benefits are distributed equitably. Public consultations, citizen panels, and multi-sector partnerships can provide valuable perspectives and foster inclusivity (Olorunsogo et al. 2024).

4. **Global Collaboration:**

Given the transnational nature of many emerging technologies, international cooperation is critical for addressing global challenges. Initiatives like the UN's Global Digital Compact and UNESCO's AI Ethics Recommendations provide platforms for collaborative governance and standard-setting (AllahRakha, 2024).

5. **Transparency and Accountability Mechanisms:**

Developers and organizations should be held accountable for the societal impacts of their technologies. Transparency in decision-making processes, regular impact assessments, and mechanisms for redress can build public trust and encourage ethical practices (Adeusi et al. 2024).

6. **Fostering Innovation for Public Good:**

Governments and institutions can incentivize responsible innovation by funding research in socially beneficial areas, such as sustainable development, public health, and education. Public-private partnerships can further drive innovation that aligns with societal priorities (Molloy et al. 2024).

7. **Education and Capacity Building:**

Building a tech-savvy workforce and informed citizenry is essential for navigating the opportunities and challenges of emerging technologies. Investments in education and digital literacy programs can empower individuals to participate in and shape the future of innovation (van Grunsven et al. 2024).

8. **Adaptive and Agile Policies:**

Governance frameworks must remain flexible to keep pace with rapid technological advancements. Regular updates to regulations and policies, informed by ongoing research and stakeholder feedback, can ensure relevance and effectiveness (Andriyani et al. 2024).

By adopting these governance strategies, society can harness the transformative potential of emerging technologies while safeguarding against their risks. Responsible innovation ensures that technological progress serves as a catalyst for a more equitable, sustainable, and empowered global future.

10. CONCLUSION

10.1 Recap of Key Insights

The rapid expansion of technology is reshaping every facet of human society, from education and healthcare to economic participation, cultural preservation, and environmental sustainability. This transformative wave of innovation has created unprecedented opportunities for empowerment, enabling individuals and communities to overcome traditional barriers and access critical resources, knowledge, and markets. Technologies like AI, blockchain, VR/AR, and renewable energy systems are driving progress across sectors, fostering inclusivity and efficiency.

At the same time, the integration of technology into daily life poses significant challenges. Issues such as the digital divide, ethical dilemmas in AI, data privacy concerns, and the risks of misinformation and polarization underscore the need for a balanced approach to technological development. Without thoughtful governance, these challenges can exacerbate existing inequalities and create new societal risks.

This chapter has explored how technology can serve as a powerful tool for societal empowerment, offering insights into its role in bridging gaps in essential services, fostering economic and civic participation, preserving cultural diversity, and addressing environmental challenges. By critically analyzing these opportunities and challenges, the chapter highlights the importance of aligning technological innovation with principles of equity, sustainability, and ethical responsibility.

10.2 Recommendations for Inclusive and Sustainable Technological Empowerment

To ensure that technology serves as a force for good, stakeholders across sectors must adopt strategies that promote inclusive and sustainable development. The following recommendations outline key steps for achieving this goal:

1. **Invest in Digital Infrastructure and Literacy:**

Expanding access to technology in underserved regions through investments in broadband networks, affordable devices, and digital literacy programs is critical to bridging the digital divide. Governments, private companies, and international organizations should collaborate to provide equitable access to digital tools and skills.

2. **Embed Ethics in Technology Development:**

Ethical considerations must be integral to the design and deployment of emerging technologies. Developers should prioritize transparency, accountability, and fairness, ensuring that technologies align with societal values and address potential biases or harms.

3. **Promote Inclusive Policies and Frameworks:**

Policymakers should establish regulations that protect vulnerable populations, promote equitable access, and encourage responsible innovation. Policies should address issues such as data privacy, algorithmic accountability, and the equitable distribution of technological benefits.

4. **Foster Public-Private Partnerships:**

Collaboration between governments, businesses, and civil society can accelerate the development and adoption of technologies that address societal challenges.

Joint initiatives can fund research, scale successful models, and create inclusive ecosystems for innovation.

5. **Support Global Cooperation:**

International collaboration is essential for tackling transnational challenges like climate change and cybersecurity. Organizations such as the United Nations and the International Telecommunication Union can facilitate dialogue, set global standards, and mobilize resources for inclusive technology development.

6. **Encourage Sustainable Practices:**

Technological advancements should prioritize environmental sustainability. Initiatives that promote renewable energy, circular economies, and resource efficiency should be incentivized and scaled globally to mitigate climate change and ensure long-term resilience.

7. **Empower Marginalized Communities:**

Special attention must be given to empowering women, minorities, and marginalized groups through targeted initiatives that address systemic barriers. Programs that enhance digital skills, provide access to financial resources, and amplify underrepresented voices can foster greater inclusion.

8. **Cultivate a Culture of Digital Responsibility:**

Public awareness campaigns and education programs can promote responsible technology use and critical thinking. Encouraging ethical behavior in digital spaces, combating misinformation, and fostering digital literacy are key to creating a safe and inclusive online environment.

9. **Adopt Adaptive Governance Models:**

Governance frameworks should remain agile to keep pace with rapid technological advancements. Regular assessments, stakeholder feedback, and iterative policy-making can ensure that regulations are effective and future-proof.

By adopting these strategies, society can leverage the transformative power of technology to build a more equitable, sustainable, and empowered future. The path forward requires collaboration, innovation, and a steadfast commitment to aligning technological progress with the broader goals of human development. In doing so, we can harness the full potential of technology to uplift individuals and communities worldwide, fostering a world where no one is left behind.

REFERENCES

Adanma, U. M., & Ogunbiyi, E. O. (2024). A comparative review of global environmental policies for promoting sustainable development and economic growth. *International Journal of Applied Research in Social Sciences*, *6*(5), 954–977. DOI: 10.51594/ijarss.v6i5.1147

Adeusi, K. B., Jejeniwa, T. O., & Jejeniwa, T. O. (2024). Advancing financial transparency and ethical governance: Innovative cost management and accountability in higher education and industry. *International Journal of Management & Entrepreneurship Research*, *6*(5), 1533–1546. DOI: 10.51594/ijmer.v6i5.1099

Afrouz, R., & Vassos, S. (2024). Adolescents' experiences of cyber-dating abuse and the pattern of abuse through technology, a scoping review. *Trauma, Violence & Abuse*, *25*(4), 15248380241227457. DOI: 10.1177/15248380241227457 PMID: 38323421

Ahmed, E. M., & Elfaki, K. E. (2024). Green technological progress implications on long-run sustainable economic growth. *Journal of the Knowledge Economy*, *15*(2), 6860–6877. DOI: 10.1007/s13132-023-01268-y PMID: 40479028

Akinrinola, O., Okoye, C. C., Ofodile, O. C., & Ugochukwu, C. E. (2024). Navigating and reviewing ethical dilemmas in AI development: Strategies for transparency, fairness, and accountability. *GSC Advanced Research and Reviews*, *18*(3), 050-058.

AllahRakha, N. (2024). Rethinking digital borders to address jurisdiction and governance in the global digital economy. *International Journal of Law and Policy*, *2*(1).

Alnasser, Y., Proaño, A., Loock, C., Chuo, J., & Gilman, R. H. (2024). Telemedicine and Pediatric Care in Rural and Remote Areas of Middle-and-Low-Income Countries: Narrative Review. *Journal of Epidemiology and Global Health*, *14*(3), 1–8. DOI: 10.1007/s44197-024-00214-8 PMID: 38478166

Altay, S., Nielsen, R. K., & Fletcher, R. (2024). News can help! The impact of news media and digital platforms on awareness of and belief in misinformation. *The International Journal of Press/Politics*, *29*(2), 459–484. DOI: 10.1177/19401612221148981

Andriyani, Y., Yohanitas, W. A., & Kartika, R. S. (2024). Adaptive innovation model design: Integrating agile and open innovation in regional areas innovation. *Journal of Open Innovation*, *10*(1), 100197. DOI: 10.1016/j.joitmc.2023.100197

Arefin, S. (2024). Chronic disease management through an ai-powered application. *Journal of Service Science and Management*, *17*(4), 305–320. DOI: 10.4236/jssm.2024.174015

Ayeni, O. O., Al Hamad, N. M., Chisom, O. N., Osawaru, B., & Adewusi, O. E. (2024). AI in education: A review of personalized learning and educational technology. *GSC Advanced Research and Reviews, 18*(2), 261–271. DOI: 10.30574/gscarr.2024.18.2.0062

Bekaroo, G. (2024). Extended Reality and the Implementation of the UN Sustainable Development Goals: Opportunities, Challenges and Future Directions. *Digital Technologies to Implement the UN Sustainable Development Goals*, 215-233.

Bhuiyan, M. R. I., Akter, M. S., & Islam, S. (2024). How does digital payment transform society as a cashless society? An empirical study in the developing economy. *Journal of Science and Technology Policy Management.*

Blank, S., Mason, C., Steinicke, F., & Herzog, C. (2024). Tailoring responsible research and innovation to the translational context: The case of AI-supported exergaming. *Ethics and Information Technology, 26*(2), 22. DOI: 10.1007/s10676-024-09753-x

Bouabida, K., Lebouché, B., & Pomey, M. P. (2024). The paradoxes of telehealth platforms: What did we learn from the use of telehealth platforms? *Frontiers in Digital Health, 6*, 1346039. DOI: 10.3389/fdgth.2024.1346039 PMID: 38414713

Buchan, M. C., Bhawra, J., & Katapally, T. R. (2024). Navigating the digital world: Development of an evidence-based digital literacy program and assessment tool for youth. *Smart Learning Environments, 11*(1), 8. DOI: 10.1186/s40561-024-00293-x

Camilleri, M. A. (2024). Artificial intelligence governance: Ethical considerations and implications for social responsibility. *Expert Systems: International Journal of Knowledge Engineering and Neural Networks, 41*(7), e13406. DOI: 10.1111/exsy.13406

Chan, G. H. (2024). Enhancing digital literacy in education: Educational directions. *Education + Training, 66*(1), 127–142. DOI: 10.1108/ET-09-2022-0390

Chee, S. Y. (2024). Age-related digital disparities, functional limitations, and social isolation: Unraveling the grey digital divide between baby boomers and the silent generation in senior living facilities. *Aging & Mental Health, 28*(4), 621–632. DOI: 10.1080/13607863.2023.2233454 PMID: 37424361

Chemnad, K., & Othman, A. (2024). Digital accessibility in the era of artificial intelligence—Bibliometric analysis and systematic review. *Frontiers in Artificial Intelligence, 7*, 1349668. DOI: 10.3389/frai.2024.1349668 PMID: 38435800

Costa, P., & Rodrigues, H. (2024). The ever-changing business of e-commerce-net benefits while designing a new platform for small companies. *Review of Managerial Science, 18*(9), 2507–2545. DOI: 10.1007/s11846-023-00681-6

Cui, H., & Yasseri, T. (2024). AI-enhanced Collective Intelligence: The State of the Art and Prospects. *arXiv preprint arXiv:2403.10433*.

Dong, Z., Peng, J., & Liu, S. (2024). Gender Pay Gap in the Gig Economy. *China Finance and Economic Review, 13*(1), 3–22. DOI: 10.1515/cfer-2024-0001

Eden, C. A., Chisom, O. N., & Adeniyi, I. S. (2024). Cultural competence in education: Strategies for fostering inclusivity and diversity awareness. *International Journal of Applied Research in Social Sciences, 6*(3), 383–392. DOI: 10.51594/ijarss.v6i3.895

El-Hajj, M. (2024). Leveraging digital twins and intrusion detection systems for enhanced security in IoT-based smart city infrastructures. *Electronics (Basel), 13*(19), 3941. DOI: 10.3390/electronics13193941

Esposito, G., Terlizzi, A., Guarino, M., & Crutzen, N. (2024). Interpreting digital governance at the municipal level: Evidence from smart city projects in Belgium. *International Review of Administrative Sciences, 90*(2), 301–317. DOI: 10.1177/00208523231167538

Fazil, A. W., Hakimi, M., Akrami, K., Akrami, M., & Akrami, F. (2024). Exploring the Role of Social Media in Bridging Gaps and Facilitating Global Communication. *Studies in Media. Journal of Communication, 2*(1), 13–21.

Fornander, L., Laukkanen, K., Molin, I., Nilsson, L., & Berggren, P. (2024). Team communication patterns during real and simulated trauma resuscitation—A social network analysis. *Ergonomics, 67*(2), 225–239. DOI: 10.1080/00140139.2023.2221000 PMID: 37273191

Giacobone, G. A., Mincolelli, G., & Imbesi, S. (2024). Inclusive cultural heritage in Europe: Co-designing an accessible user experience for digital architectural conservation. *Journal of Architectural Conservation, 30*(1), 19–34. DOI: 10.1080/13556207.2023.2296216

Gilbert, C., & Gilbert, M. A. (2024). The Convergence of Artificial Intelligence and Privacy: Navigating Innovation with Ethical Considerations. *International Journal (Toronto, Ont.), 3*(9).

Guo, B., Hu, P., & Lin, J. (2024). The effect of digital infrastructure development on enterprise green transformation. *International Review of Financial Analysis, 92*, 103085. DOI: 10.1016/j.irfa.2024.103085

Gupta, P., & Pandey, M. K. (2024). Role of AI for Smart Health Diagnosis and Treatment. In *Smart Medical Imaging for Diagnosis and Treatment Planning* (pp. 23–45). Chapman and Hall/CRC. DOI: 10.1201/9781003464884-4

Hajat, A., Andrea, S. B., Oddo, V. M., Winkler, M. R., & Ahonen, E. Q. (2024). Ramifications of precarious employment for health and health inequity: Emerging trends from the Americas. *Annual Review of Public Health*, *45*(1), 45. DOI: 10.1146/annurev-publhealth-071321-042437 PMID: 38012123

Herrada-Lores, S., Estrella-Ramón, A., Gálvez-Rodríguez, M. M., & Iniesta-Bonillo, M. A. (2024). The role of hashtags for non-profit causes: The# fridaysforfuture movement. *International Review on Public and Nonprofit Marketing*, •••, 1–22. DOI: 10.1007/s12208-024-00401-0

Hirsch-Kreinsen, H. (2024). Artificial intelligence: A "promising technology". *AI & Society*, *39*(4), 1641–1652. DOI: 10.1007/s00146-023-01629-w

Hussain, S., Rasheed, A., & Rehman, S. U. (2024). Driving sustainable growth: exploring the link between financial innovation, green finance and sustainability performance: banking evidence. *Kybernetes*, *53*(11), 4678–4696. DOI: 10.1108/K-05-2023-0918

Iida, T., Song, J., Estrada, J. L., & Takahashi, Y. (2024). Fake news and its electoral consequences: A survey experiment on Mexico. *AI & Society*, *39*(3), 1065–1078. DOI: 10.1007/s00146-022-01541-9

Kasula, B. Y. (2024). Advancements in AI-driven Healthcare: A Comprehensive Review of Diagnostics, Treatment, and Patient Care Integration. *International Journal of Machine Learning for Sustainable Development*, *6*(1), 1–5.

Khalil, S., Kallmuenzer, A., & Kraus, S. (2024). Visiting museums via augmented reality: An experience fast-tracking the digital transformation of the tourism industry. *European Journal of Innovation Management*, *27*(6), 2084–2100. DOI: 10.1108/EJIM-09-2022-0479

Kizilcec, R. F. (2024). To advance AI use in education, focus on understanding educators. *International Journal of Artificial Intelligence in Education*, *34*(1), 12–19. DOI: 10.1007/s40593-023-00351-4 PMID: 37359103

Komolafe, M. O., Agu, E. E., Ejike, O. G., Ewim, C. P. M., & Okeke, I. C. (2024). A digital service standardization model for Nigeria: The role of NITDA in regulatory compliance. *International Journal of Frontier Research in Science, 2*(2), 069-079.

Kreiss, D., & McGregor, S. C. (2024). A review and provocation: On polarization and platforms. *New Media & Society*, *26*(1), 556–579. DOI: 10.1177/14614448231161880

Kuteesa, K. N., Akpuokwe, C. U., & Udeh, C. A. (2024). Gender equity in education: Addressing challenges and promoting opportunities for social empowerment. *International Journal of Applied Research in Social Sciences*, *6*(4), 631–641. DOI: 10.51594/ijarss.v6i4.1034

Liu, G., & Darvin, R. (2024). From Rural China to the Digital Wilds: Negotiating digital repertoires to claim the right to speak. *TESOL Quarterly*, *58*(1), 334–362. DOI: 10.1002/tesq.3233

Lo, Y. F., & Kun-Lin, H. (2024). The study of working patterns in the Gig Economy. *Management Analytics and Social Insights*, *1*(1), 70–87.

Malhotra, C. (2024). Digital India: Past, Present and Future. In *Indien im 21. Jahrhundert– Auf dem Weg zur postindustriellen Ökonomie: India in the 21st Century–On its way to a post-industrial economy* (pp. 325–345). Springer Fachmedien Wiesbaden.

Marquardt, M. J., & Kearsley, G. (2024). *Technology-based learning: Maximizing human performance and corporate success*. CRC Press. DOI: 10.4324/9781003579175

Martindale, N., Wood, A. J., & Burchell, B. J. (2024). What do platform workers in the UK gig economy want? *British Journal of Industrial Relations*, *62*(3), 542–567. DOI: 10.1111/bjir.12797

Meka, J. S., & Venkateswarlu, P. (2024). Progress, Challenges, and Strategies towards attaining Sustainable Development Goals. *Educational Administration: Theory and Practice*, *30*(4), 2145–2161.

Molloy, C., Bankins, S., Kriz, A., & Barnes, L. (2024). Innovating for the greater good: Examining innovation champions and what motivates them. *Australian Journal of Public Administration*, *83*(1), 24–49. DOI: 10.1111/1467-8500.12577

Moosavian, S. F., Noorollahi, Y., & Shoaei, M. (2024). Renewable energy resources utilization planning for sustainable energy system development on a stand-alone island. *Journal of Cleaner Production*, *439*, 140892. DOI: 10.1016/j.jclepro.2024.140892

Neethirajan, S. (2024). Artificial intelligence and sensor innovations: Enhancing livestock welfare with a human-centric approach. *Human-Centric Intelligent Systems*, *4*(1), 77–92. DOI: 10.1007/s44230-023-00050-2

Nguyen, A., Kremantzis, M., Essien, A., Petrounias, I., & Hosseini, S. (2024). Enhancing student engagement through artificial intelligence (AI): Understanding the basics, opportunities, and challenges. *Journal of University Teaching & Learning Practice*, *21*(06). Advance online publication. DOI: 10.53761/caraaq92

Njema, G. G., Ouma, R. B. O., & Kibet, J. K. (2024). A review on the recent advances in battery development and energy storage technologies. *Journal of Renewable Energy*, *2024*(1), 2329261. DOI: 10.1155/2024/2329261

Odoom, D., Mensah, E. O., Dick-Sagoe, C., Lee, K. Y., Opoku, E., & Obeng-Baah, J. (2024). Examining the level of public awareness on the Sustainable Development Goals in Africa: An empirical evidence from Ghana. *Environment, Development and Sustainability*, *26*(3), 6221–6238. DOI: 10.1007/s10668-023-02959-x PMID: 36721466

Okoro, Y. O., Ayo-Farai, O., Maduka, C. P., Okongwu, C. C., & Sodamade, O. T. (2024). The Role of technology in enhancing mental health advocacy: A systematic review. *International Journal of Applied Research in Social Sciences*, *6*(1), 37–50. DOI: 10.51594/ijarss.v6i1.690

Oladokun, B. D., Ajani, Y. A., Ukaegbu, B. C., & Oloniruha, E. A. (2024). Cultural Preservation Through Immersive Technology: The Metaverse as a Pathway to the Past. *Preservation. Digital Technology & Culture*, *53*(3), 157–164. DOI: 10.1515/pdtc-2024-0015

Olorunfemi, O. L., Amoo, O. O., Atadoga, A., Fayayola, O. A., Abrahams, T. O., & Shoetan, P. O. (2024). Towards a conceptual framework for ethical AI development in IT systems. *Computer Science & IT Research Journal*, *5*(3), 616–627. DOI: 10.51594/csitrj.v5i3.910

Olorunsogo, T., Jacks, B. S., & Ajala, O. A. (2024). Leveraging quantum computing for inclusive and responsible AI development: A conceptual and review framework. *Computer Science & IT Research Journal*, *5*(3), 671–680. DOI: 10.51594/csitrj.v5i3.927

Peruzzo, F., & Allan, J. (2024). Rethinking inclusive (digital) education: Lessons from the pandemic to reconceptualise inclusion through convivial technologies. *Learning, Media and Technology*, *49*(2), 244–258. DOI: 10.1080/17439884.2022.2131817

Porter, S. M. (2024). Making big bets and leaning into operational excellence: Building the future of cultural heritage institutions. *Journal of Library Administration*, *64*(2), 168–193. DOI: 10.1080/01930826.2024.2305071

Prestoza, M. J. (2024). Assessing remote learning's feasibility: A comprehensive analysis of Philippine public-school teachers' use of learning management systems and blended learning approaches. *Journal of Research. Policy & Practice of Teachers and Teacher Education*, *14*(1), 21–27. DOI: 10.37134/jrpptte.vol14.1.3.2024

Quinlan, C. L. (2024). Framing and determining science content and standards for cultural representation of African American heritage in science content knowledge. *Cultural Studies of Science Education, 19*(1), 47–75. DOI: 10.1007/s11422-023-10195-y

Rafiq, S., Iqbal, S., & Afzal, A. (2024). The Impact of Digital Tools and Online Learning Platforms on Higher Education Learning Outcomes. [MRJ]. *Al-Mahdi Research Journal, 5*(4), 359–369.

Rahiem, M. D. (2024). Early childhood education contingencies for sustaining learning during school closures: Lessons from preschool remote education home visits in Indonesia during the COVID-19 pandemic. *Children and Youth Services Review, 166*, 107955. DOI: 10.1016/j.childyouth.2024.107955

Raihan, M. M., Subroto, S., Chowdhury, N., Koch, K., Ruttan, E., & Turin, T. C. (2024). *Dimensions and barriers for digital (in) equity and digital divide: A systematic integrative review*. Digital Transformation and Society.

Ramolobe, K. S., & Khandanisa, U. (2024). The role of public–private partnership in achieving local government sustainable development. *Africa's Public Service Delivery & Performance Review, 12*(1), 6. DOI: 10.4102/apsdpr.v12i1.816

Ramtohul, A., & Khedo, K. K. (2024). Augmented reality systems in the cultural heritage domains: A systematic review. *Digital Applications in Archaeology and Cultural Heritage, 32*, 00317. DOI: 10.1016/j.daach.2024.e00317

Rohatgi, S., Gera, N., & Nayak, K. (2024). Has digital banking usage reshaped economic empowerment of urban women? *The Journal of Management and Governance, 28*(2), 543–563. DOI: 10.1007/s10997-023-09676-7

Sa'idah, S., & Juhana, A. (2024). The Effectiveness of Virtual Reality in Increasing Visitor Satisfaction of Cultural Heritage Sites: A Systematic Literature Review:-. [JOINT]. *Journal of Information System and Technology, 5*(3), 7–14. DOI: 10.37253/joint.v5i3.9981

Sabarirajan, A., Reddi, L. T., Rangineni, S., Regin, R., Rajest, S. S., & Paramasivan, P. (2024). Leveraging MIS Technologies for Preserving India's Cultural Heritage on Digitization, Accessibility, and Sustainability. In *Data-Driven Intelligent Business Sustainability* (pp. 122–135). IGI Global.

Salmah, E., Astuti, E., & Harsono, I. (2024). Employee Engagement in the Gig Economy. [PRODUCTIVITY]. *Management Studies and Business Journal, 1*(1), 116–122.

Salykov, A., Aimbetov, A., Yesmagulova, N., & Jussibaliyeva, A. (2024). Factors and trends in the development of the space industry in the context of the digitalization of the economy of the Republic of Kazakhstan. *Environment, Development and Sustainability*, *26*(3), 6703–6718. DOI: 10.1007/s10668-023-02983-x PMID: 36747988

Samuel-Okon, A. D., & Abejide, O. O. (2024). Bridging the digital divide: Exploring the role of artificial intelligence and automation in enhancing connectivity in developing nations. *Journal of Engineering Research and Reports*, *26*(6), 165–177. DOI: 10.9734/jerr/2024/v26i61170

Santos, O., & Radanliev, P. (2024). *Beyond the Algorithm: AI, Security, Privacy, and Ethics*. Addison-Wesley Professional.

Sarker, I. H. (2024). LLM potentiality and awareness: A position paper from the perspective of trustworthy and responsible AI modeling. *Discover Artificial Intelligence*, *4*(1), 40. DOI: 10.1007/s44163-024-00129-0

Saxena, A., Prakash Gupta, J., Tiwary, J. K., Kumar, A., Sharma, S., Pandey, G., Biswas, S., & Raghav Chaturvedi, K. (2024). Innovative Pathways in Carbon Capture: Advancements and Strategic Approaches for Effective Carbon Capture, Utilization, and Storage. *Sustainability (Basel)*, *16*(22), 10132. DOI: 10.3390/su162210132

Schuett, J., Reuel, A. K., & Carlier, A. (2024). How to design an AI ethics board. *AI and Ethics*, •••, 1–19.

Shaamala, A., Yigitcanlar, T., Nili, A., & Nyandega, D. (2024). Algorithmic green infrastructure optimisation: Review of artificial intelligence driven approaches for tackling climate change. *Sustainable Cities and Society*, *101*, 105182. DOI: 10.1016/j.scs.2024.105182

Shahbazi, M., & Bunker, D. (2024). Social media trust: Fighting misinformation in the time of crisis. *International Journal of Information Management*, *77*, 102780. DOI: 10.1016/j.ijinfomgt.2024.102780

Sharma, A., Arya, S. K., Singh, J., Kapoor, B., Bhatti, J. S., Suttee, A., & Singh, G. (2024). Prospects of chitinase in sustainable farming and modern biotechnology: An update on recent progress and challenges. *Biotechnology & Genetic Engineering Reviews*, *40*(1), 310–340. PMID: 36856523

Shehzadi, S. (2024). Privacy by Design: Integrating Information Theoretical Privacy in AI Development. *Integrated Journal of Science and Technology*, *1*(2).

Stachel, C., & Cantoni, L. (2024, June). Creating an Online Exhibition About Shoe Heritage: A Story on Swiss Footwear on Google Arts & Culture. In *International Conference on Human-Computer Interaction* (pp. 369-385). Cham: Springer Nature Switzerland. DOI: 10.1007/978-3-031-61353-1_25

Stahl, B. C., & Eke, D. (2024). The ethics of ChatGPT–Exploring the ethical issues of an emerging technology. *International Journal of Information Management*, *74*, 102700. DOI: 10.1016/j.ijinfomgt.2023.102700

Stjernborg, V., & Svensson, G. L. (2024). Rural mobility in later life; counteracting accessibility poverty with digital service solutions. *Transportation Research Part D, Transport and Environment*, *126*, 104030. DOI: 10.1016/j.trd.2023.104030

Su, Z., Li, C., Fu, H., Wang, L., Wu, M., & Feng, X. (2024). Development and prospect of telemedicine. *Intelligent Medicine*, *4*(1), 1–9. DOI: 10.1016/j.imed.2022.10.004

Tortora, L. (2024). Beyond Discrimination: Generative AI Applications and Ethical Challenges in Forensic Psychiatry. *Frontiers in Psychiatry*, *15*, 1346059. DOI: 10.3389/fpsyt.2024.1346059 PMID: 38525252

Troyer, M., Benjamin, E. V., & Gevorkian, A. (2024). Quantum for good and the societal impact of quantum computing. *arXiv preprint arXiv:2403.02921.*

Val, S., & López-Bueno, H. (2024). Analysis of Digital Teacher Education: Key Aspects for Bridging the Digital Divide and Improving the Teaching–Learning Process. *Education Sciences*, *14*(3), 321. DOI: 10.3390/educsci14030321

van Grunsven, J., Stone, T., & Marin, L. (2024). Fostering responsible anticipation in engineering ethics education: How a multi-disciplinary enrichment of the responsible innovation framework can help. *European Journal of Engineering Education*, *49*(2), 283–298. DOI: 10.1080/03043797.2023.2218275

Vann Yaroson, E., Chowdhury, S., Mangla, S. K., Dey, P., Chan, F. T., & Roux, M. (2024). A systematic literature review exploring and linking circular economy and sustainable development goals in the past three decades (1991–2022). *International Journal of Production Research*, *62*(4), 1399–1433. DOI: 10.1080/00207543.2023.2270586

Wang, X., Wu, Y. C., Zhou, M., & Fu, H. (2024). Beyond surveillance: Privacy, ethics, and regulations in face recognition technology. *Frontiers in Big Data*, *7*, 1337465. DOI: 10.3389/fdata.2024.1337465 PMID: 39027377

Wu, X., Duan, R., & Ni, J. (2024). Unveiling security, privacy, and ethical concerns of ChatGPT. *Journal of Information and Intelligence*, *2*(2), 102–115. DOI: 10.1016/j.jiixd.2023.10.007

Xue, C., & Wang, J. (2024). Proactive boundary-spanning search, organizational resilience, and radical green innovation. *Business Strategy and the Environment, 33*(3), 1834–1852. DOI: 10.1002/bse.3576

Yáñez-Valdés, C., & Guerrero, M. (2024). Equity crowdfunding platforms and sustainable impacts: Encountering investors and technological initiatives for tackling social and environmental challenges. *European Journal of Innovation Management, 27*(7), 2326–2350. DOI: 10.1108/EJIM-03-2022-0127

Yap, J. M., Barat, A. H., & Kiszl, P. (2024). Civic roles of libraries in combating information disorders in social media: A scoping review. *Education for Information*, (Preprint), 1-24.

Zhu, G., Huang, J., Lu, J., Luo, Y., & Zhu, T. (2024). Gig to the left, algorithms to the right: A case study of the dark sides in the gig economy. *Technological Forecasting and Social Change, 199*, 123018. DOI: 10.1016/j.techfore.2023.123018

Zhu, Y. (2024). Research on the Branding of Intangible Cultural Heritage Enabled by Digital Technology. *International Journal of Education and Humanities, 13*(2), 104–107. DOI: 10.54097/ks839493

Zhuk, A. (2024). Crypto-anarchy: a paradigm shift for society and the legal system. *Journal of Computer Virology and Hacking Techniques*, 1-27.

Chapter 2

Technology as a Catalyst for Social Empowerment: Shaping the Future of Human Society

Ananya Pandey
http://orcid.org/0000-0002-2419-6314
Christ University, Bangalore, India

Jipson Joseph
http://orcid.org/0009-0005-1795-5051
Christ University, Bangalore, India

ABSTRACT

In the 21st century, the intersection of technology and society has become an undeniable force shaping people's lives, work, and their global interconnectivity. Beyond its initial use as a straightforward tool, technology has evolved into a dynamic, all-pervasive force influencing practically every aspect of human life. Every element of society is already heavily reliant on technology. The introduction of cutting-edge technologies like Artificial Intelligence and Internet of Things, the proliferation of social media platforms, and the use of smartphones are all indicators of a rapidly evolving technological landscape, which redefine the meaning and implications of human existence. Despite its ability to empower the society, it poses some challenges such as threat to privacy, misinformation, polarization, and several unintended repercussions. In light of the above perspective, this chapter explores the role of technology in social empowerment and enhancing the future of society as envisioned by the United Nations' 2030 agenda.

DOI: 10.4018/979-8-3373-0629-2.ch002

ht © 2026, IGI Global Scientific Publishing. Copying or distributing in print or electronic forms without written permission of IGI Global Scientific Publishing is prohibited. Use of this chapter to generative artificial intelligence (AI) technologies is expressly prohibited. The publisher reserves all rights to license its use for generative AI training and machine learning model development.

INTRODUCTION: THE POWER OF TECHNOLOGY IN SOCIAL CHANGE

Historical advancements like the printing press, telephone, computer, and internet have reduced physical barriers to communication and enabled people to freely and actively engage on a global scale. The emergence of a leisure class and the development of advanced economies like the contemporary global economy, are both results of technological growth. Together with the unparalleled technological advancements, there also takes place social transformation. However, technology alone cannot make decisive changes in the society. It is thus crucial to take into account all the other factors at play, including the current and past status of society, its cultural norms, infrastructure, and much more (Lee, 2002). It is quite interesting that different people perceive societal change differently. Recency bias, for example, may influence how one views social change and contributes to the development of the society. While analyzing the social changes in the last century, one can easily determine the positive changes resulting from the interaction between technological innovation and social development, but this was not always the case (Floridi, 2007).

Social empowerment entails equal chances, control over one's life, and the ability to make significant life decisions for all segments of the society. A country can never have a healthy growth trajectory if all facets of society are not given equal importance. All segments of the society need to be empowered. This progressive vision of empowerment improves their capacity to make decisions and turn them into required actions and results. However, it specifically aims at elevating the underprivileged and oppressed communities (Mayo, 2004). It guarantees that everyone in the community can participate in and gain from the developmental processes. In order to establish a fair and just society where each person has the chance to realize their full potential, social empowerment is essential. By addressing systemic injustices, it provides the marginalized groups with the resources that are required to go beyond the obstacles and participate on an equitable basis. It shows the reciprocal interaction of technology and society. That is, technological change is driven by society, and society is shaped by evolving technologies (Du et al., 2020). However, while making technological decisions, effective consideration should be given to the calculation of costs and benefits. Computing and communications have undergone a revolution in recent decades, and all signs point to continued rapid advancements in technology and the application of information technology. As a result of both greater competition and technological advancements, the cost of communication has been falling in tandem with and supporting the sharp rises in the capability and application of new information technologies. Electronic commerce via the internet, a new method of conducting business, is arguably one of the most important results of information technology advancements. Despite being relatively new, it has the potential to drastically change social and economic dynamics. It already has an impact on major industries like retail, finance, and communications, and it may soon spread to industries like healthcare and education (Sarkar, 2012). It denotes the smooth integration of information and communication technology throughout the electronic business's whole value chain.

Keeping in view the above-mentioned perspective, this chapter aims to describe the role of technology in empowering the society towards a better future. Further this chapter also explains the technological advancements and its enhancement in shaping human society besides examining various social and ethical challenges.

EVOLUTION OF TECHNOLOGY AND SOCIAL STRUCTURE

Since the pre-historians and anthropologists differ greatly with regard to the estimates of the emergence of the human species, comparing the history of technology to the history of human-like species does not help pinpoint its exact genesis (Finley, 1965). Occasionally, animals would utilize natural tools like twigs or stones, and before the first great step of creating their own tools, the creatures that eventually became humans probably used them for hundreds of thousands of years. Even so, it took a very long time before they began regularly producing such tools, and more eons went by before they finally reached the later stages of standardizing their basic stone pounders and choppers and producing them, which involved setting up locations and designating experts for the task (Hodges, 1992). Humans have lived almost exclusively in small nomadic societies for all but the last 10,000 years, relying on their abilities to hunt, fish, gather food, and evade predators to survive (Romano et al., 2020). A few communities that were most favored by geographic location and climate started to shift from the lengthy Paleolithic or Old Stone Age lifestyles to a more settled way of life reliant on agriculture and animal husbandry towards the end of the last ice age, some 15,000 to 20,000 years ago. The Neolithic Period, also known as the New Stone Age, was a time of transition that ultimately resulted in a notable increase in population, expansion of settlements, and the emergence of town life. From this point, the transition following the development from stones to manufacturing units (Stones → Power → Tools and weapons → Building techniques → Manufacturing unit) gradually escalated.

In response to only the most fundamental social demands—the need for food and shelter—and with few social resources available for any other activity rather than meeting these wants, the technological progress so far detailed occurred extremely slow over a lengthy period of time (Clark & Wu, 2016). However, a significant cultural shift started to occur in a few fortunate geographic locations around 5,000 years ago. It led to a considerable rise in technological innovation as well as the creation of new demands and resources. It marked the start of the innovation of city (Jemala, 2021).

The below described points explain the evolution of technology in socially empowering several domains such as agricultural, industrial, and digital fields.

Agriculture

Agriculture made extensive use of Information Age technologies in the early decades of the twenty-first century. In order to increase farm performance, digital agriculture and agricultural accuracy required a lot of data collecting and computing, while agricultural robots, agricultural drones, and non-motorized tractors were frequently utilized on farms (Hemathilake et al., 2022). Around 10,000 years ago, agricultural technology first appeared. The mechanical repair tools that farmers now frequently use were progressively developed from simple hand tools that made the starting easier. The commercial solutions that are accessible to practically every agricultural enterprise that can be readily mechanized are revealed by a closer examination of the body of current technology (Chase et al., 2018). Significant changes throughout the history of agricultural technology have revolutionized the farming practices. "Agriculture 4.0," often known as the "fourth agricultural revolution," has already started. At the time of each preceding agricultural revolution, it was radical. The shift from hunting and gathering to settled agriculture was the first revolution (Kaledio et al., 2023). The second has to do with the shift to commercial farming that occurred during the 18th-century agricultural revolution. The Green Revolution in the developing world and the post-war productivity gains linked to automation were the subjects of the third revolution. Significant technological advancements were made during each age advancing significant changes. Increased productivity and scalability were made possible by the shift from conventional to contemporary methodologies (Phuyal et al., 2020). By creating drip irrigation, Israel transformed agriculture in the contemporary era. The AgTech industry was only getting started. More modern technologies are embedded into the fabric of agriculture today. Farmers have a wide range of technologies at their disposal, from biotechnology to data-driven decision-making. Increased yields, resource efficiency, and the ability to address issues like pests and diseases are just a few of the many advantages (Jafarpanah & Karshenas, 2023).

Industrial

The transition from an agrarian and handicraft economy to one centered on industry and machine production is known as the "Industrial Revolution" in modern history. New patterns of living and methods of working were brought about by these technological advancements, which also profoundly altered the society. In the 18th century, this approach started in Britain and then rapidly extended to other countries (Rafferty, 2017). The proto-industrialization era was followed by the first industrial revolution. It took place from the end of the 18th century until the start of the 19th. The mechanization of industries brought about the most significant developments (Mager, 1993). Agriculture began to give way to industry as the foundation of the society's economy due to mechanization. The world experienced the second Industrial Revolution nearly a century after the first. The advent of a new energy source—oil, gas, and electricity—was aided by significant technological developments in industries toward the end of the 19th century (Sharma & Singh, 2020). Electronics, telecommunications, and, of course, computers all emerged during the third revolution. The third Industrial Revolution made biotechnology, research, and space travel possible. At the beginning of the third millennium, Industry 4.0 began with the Internet, which is something that everyone utilizes on a daily basis (Troxler, 2013). The shift from the first Industrial Revolution, which was based on technological phenomena, to Industry 4.0, which creates virtual reality environments and permits humans to defy the laws of physics, is evident. The world is extensively shaped by the four industrial revolutions. They are the foundation of global economies. Around the world, initiatives and programs are being put into place with the goal of assisting people in utilizing the wonders of the fourth revolution in their daily lives. The future is bright, from augmented reality gaming to digital flipbooks (Yin et al., 2018) affirming the importance of technology in human life and societal growth.

Digital

In reaction to shifts in the market, consumer insights, and business requirements, digital transformation is the process of using digital technology to alter or develop new organizational culture, customer experiences, and business processes (Kraus et al., 2022). The fundamental building blocks of the digital revolution and digital transformation were developed during the pre-internet era, which spanned from 1950 to 1989. The conversion of manual operations into digital technologies was made possible by the development of microchips and semiconductors. The period after the origin of internet, or 1990–2006, new digital technology and significant change were brought about by the next digital era (Hilbert, 2020). The transition from a fragmented to a globalized world was initiated by the internet revolution. The launch of the iPhone and the move to mobile devices occurred during the Mobile Era, which spanned from 2007 to 2019, just as businesses were starting to feel at ease with the modern internet and how it affected their operations (Xinzhou, 2015). Another significant era in the interaction of technology and society is the post-Pandemic Era, or 2020–2022. As businesses were compelled to reconsider how they catered to their clients in a remote and non-contact environment, the epidemic spurred digital advancements (Ben & Luftman, 2022). This led to the Generative AI Era (2022–Present). Generative artificial intelligence or Gen AI is the era, the world is living in at the moment. As businesses were compelled to reconsider how they catered to their clients in a remote and non-contact environment, the epidemic spurred digital advancements (Hutson et al., 2023).

RESHAPING SOCIETAL NORMS AND HIERARCHY WITH TECHNOLOGY

Technology has an impact on the thinking, learning, and communication patterns of people. It benefits society and influences how individuals engage with one another on a regular basis. Today's society depends heavily on technology and its impacts. It affects people's daily lives and has both positive and harmful consequences on the planet (Vannoy & Palvia, 2010). These days, technical advancements are commonplace. Examples include cell phones and the internet. But there is a drawback to all technological advancements. The way that technology impacts education is one area that has significantly impacted society. People are better able to interact with the information they are learning and struggle with because it has made learning more collaborative and engaging (Raja & Nagasubramani, 2018). It also improves the access to resources. Since the invention of the internet, one has had constant access to information, and they can find nearly anything on the internet. Additionally, it makes it easy for the students to complete their assignments. Exams and quizzes are easier for students to complete, and online learning can be highly beneficial for professors. Also, it promotes self-paced learning by extending the confines of the classroom (Haleem et al., 2022). Social media and YouTube also provide access to education. Compared to listening to lectures and reading textbooks, this aids students' learning. Learning is now more convenient and enjoyable due to these technological developments. The way one converse and interact with one another globally is another way that technology has changed the society. Numerous new electronic communication techniques were made possible by technology. People can facetime someone who lives on the other side of the world, use social networking, send emails, and have conferences virtually with video conferencing (Geladi, 2018). Finally, the health sector's technology innovations have contributed to people's safety and well-being. Numerous cutting-edge smartphone apps allow users to monitor their weight, caloric consumption, heart rate, and other health metrics at any time of the day. The availability of treatment has expanded, healthcare has changed to benefit the aged, and hospitals are utilizing cutting-edge technology in their operating rooms (Kang & Exworthy, 2022).

Today's human behavior is shaped by technological factors. However, research indicates that mobile communication has a negative impact on people's ability to interact socially and in person. People's relationships and communication might be negatively impacted by mobile technology. Because people are constantly interacting with someone, they find that they do not have enough time for themselves (Saptasagar, 2022). It may also divert one's attention from their academic tasks. Because anyone can locate anyone anywhere, at any time of the day, also one loses their privacy. In summary, each of these factors influences how people behave in the modern world. One would not have such a sophisticated way of living without technical improvements (Koessmeier & Büttner, 2021).

BRIDGING INEQUALITIES WITH TECHNOLOGY

Equitable resource distribution, education and skill development investments, social protection measures, anti-discrimination efforts, assistance for marginalized groups, and international collaboration for fair trade and financial systems are all necessary to reduce inequality within and between nations.

Education

Education is supposed to be a powerful equalizer, giving everyone access to possibilities regardless of their location, upbringing, or financial situation. However, many children are frequently unable to get high-quality instruction due to a lack of resources and access. Democratizing access to top-notch teaching resources, platforms, and tools is one way that educational technology advancements are assisting the attempts to eliminate these disparities (Barcellos et al., 2020). Quality education is becoming more accessible and inclusive because of advancements in fields like artificial intelligence (AI), cloud computing, adaptive learning, and rich digital content. Teachers, all throughout the world, are using technology to scale expertly created content, reach distant populations, tailor education, and analyze data to improve learning (Kellner, 2004; Ng, 2023)). Technology has enormous potential to empower people worldwide and provide access to high-quality education. Geographically unrestricted access is provided by cloud platforms. Each student receives training that is tailored to them through adaptive learning. Through simulations and interaction, digital content immerses the users. By offering accessible platforms, accommodations for people with impairments, and connectivity to remote locations, technology is eliminating long-standing barriers to education. It increases access to high-quality education (Grover & Nandal, 2024).

Healthcare

Leading the charge to democratize healthcare and transform the sector as a whole are health tech startups. Offering services that empower patients with ease, accessibility, and a satisfying experience is the key to success. The consumerization of the healthcare sector will eventually improve health outcomes and steer the sector in the right direction, despite the fact that conventional voices in the field initially viewed it with mistrust (Thomason, 2021). It may seem paradoxical, but providing end-to-end care allows people to focus more on their lives and less on their health. Now that they are not alone on their path to wellness, they can concentrate on what makes them happy while feeling secure in the knowledge that they are being looked after. Because this treatment modality is so much more democratic and efficient, there are a lot of benefits for everyone, including insurers (Rubeis et al., 2022). If one cannot afford the best doctor, they will not have as much access to care if they do not reside in a big city. Technology with AI capabilities can lessen the effects of these deserts. AI-powered diagnostic technologies have the potential to level the playing field and increase access to healthcare by giving people trustworthy health insights regardless of their location or the availability of medical personnel (Topol, 2019). For instance, if a mother or baby does not have instant access to a clinician, software that employs AI to identify problems during labor could help protect them throughout childbirth. Depending on the medical condition, sometimes the patient merely has to have access to a smartphone in order to collect the data needed for a diagnosis. AI integration in healthcare typically creates a lot of buzz, reviving interest in and excitement for the potential applications of AI (Bajwa et al., 2021). AI's extraordinary ability to collect and evaluate vast amounts of patient data for improving diagnostic precision is at the core of its promise. AI systems are able to analyze a wide range of data, including imaging data, test findings, and medical histories, and derive conclusions that may be invisible to the human eye (Yelne et al., 2023).

Financial Services

The worldwide financial services sector is still driven by financial technology, or fintech. Fintech use has exploded worldwide since the COVID-19 outbreak began. The widespread use of digital wallets and mobile banking is one-way fintech is democratizing access to financial services. Mobile banking apps remove the requirement for physical bank offices by enabling users to conveniently conduct a variety of financial operations from their cellphones (World Bank, 2022). According to the FinTech companies, the need for a more democratic financial system appears to be the driving force behind the financial technology sector. The real legacy of finance sector will come from the long-term effects of those businesses (Feyen et al., 2021). Democratizing of the financial system implies that an industry gives access to fundamental and equitable financial services to those who are underbanked or unbanked, such as minorities, people with disabilities, or marginalized groups. Due to lack of physical infrastructure, internet, smartphones, and computer access, low-income and rural populations are unable to access many financial services that one takes for granted (McKendrick, 2023). Furthermore, financial goods lack openness and simple language, and they are frequently excessively costly for those with less money. This makes it challenging to comprehend the true price and risks of those items. In order to overcome or mitigate those flaws, the financial industry can undergo a more rapid, differentiated, and democratizing transformation with the aid of technology like AI. It can therefore lessen the gap between the rich and poor people's access to financial services (Azeema et al., 2023).

Humanitarian Response

A key factor in improving disaster risk reduction (DRR) is the emerging technologies. To improve their response, humanitarian relief agencies are increasingly using digital techniques like machine learning (ML) and AI. Using digital tools gives decision-makers a much-needed advantage in tackling the most urgent humanitarian issues by facilitating quicker decision-making, better resource allocation, and more focused actions (Baraldo & di Franco, 2024). AI and ML-powered predictive analytics are essential for disaster response. Machine Learning for Anticipatory Actions (ML4AA) forecasts drought hazards by utilizing cutting-edge technology and climate data to provide prompt warnings and aid. With the use of tools like these, humanitarian efforts may become more proactive rather than reactive in the future, saving lives through preventative, economic measures (Venkadesh et al., 2024). Blockchain provides a vital basis for improving the effectiveness, accountability, and transparency of humanitarian aid. Blockchain's tamper-proof, decentralized ledger system is its power, and it has the potential to completely transform financial inclusion and aid distribution. Additionally, blockchain creates new opportunities for microfinance and asset tokenization, enabling underserved groups to engage in decentralized financial systems (Adideran et al., 2024). Smartphones and mobile networks are now commonplace, even in remote locations, due to considerable advancements in mobile technology. By lowering the danger of fraud and guaranteeing prompt help, mobile payment solutions for cash-based transfers enable safe, direct transfers of money to people in need (Upreti, 1994). Humanitarian help today relies heavily on data, and advanced analytics is enabling faster, impactful, and well-informed decisions. Real-time analysis of large datasets is revolutionizing everything from the distribution of food and medical supplies to the management of refugee camps (Kondraganti, 2021).

Environment Sustainability

One of the most important areas of concern in the continuous pursuit of world development is the nexus between environmental sustainability and technology. The need to address environmental issues including pollution, resource depletion, and climate change has grown more urgent in recent years (Beder, 1994). Technology has become a ray of hope as humanity struggles with the effects of unsustainable activities, providing creative ways to slow down environmental damage and foster long-term resilience. Fundamentally, sustainable development aims to satisfy current demands without endangering the capacity of future generations to satisfy their own. It stands for intergenerational and intragenerational positivity. Technology has a dual function in this setting, acting as a force for advancement and a catalyst for change (Lambertini, 2018). The use of technology, from cutting-edge waste management systems to renewable energy technologies, has the potential to completely transform how humans interact with the environment and influence the course of our planet. To fully realize this promise, though, a determined effort must be made to combine technology advancements with social programs, policy frameworks, and cross-sector partnerships (Khawaja et al., 2024). Recognizing the transformative power of technology in promoting sustainable development and protecting the valuable natural resources is crucial as one stands at the intersection of environmental stewardship and technological growth. Since they offer answers to environmental problems, technological advancements are essential to the advancement of sustainable development (Jianing et al., 2024). The extensive use of renewable energy technologies like solar, wind, and hydro power is one significant example. By providing clean and renewable substitutes for fossil fuels, these technologies lessen reliance on limited resources and greenhouse gases (GHGs) emissions. By reducing energy use and carbon emissions, energy-efficient construction and transportation systems also support sustainable development (Osman et al., 2023). Furthermore, waste management technologies, such as recycling and waste-to-energy procedures, aid in resource efficiency and landfill trash reduction. Farmers may maximize resource utilization, reduce their impact on the environment, and sustainably boost crop yields through precision agriculture, which is made possible by technologies like sensors, drones, and data analytics (Sinha et al., 2021). Additionally, developments in carbon capture and storage technology present viable ways to reduce emissions from power plants and industry. Beyond the energy sector, technology makes it easier to implement sustainable practices in waste management, urban planning, and agriculture, which lowers emissions and increases resilience to the effects of climate change (Bose et al., 2024).

EMPOWERING COMMUNITIES THROUGH CONNECTIVITY

People's interactions with politics have changed as a result of social media, which has made it simpler than ever to raise awareness and spur change. Through social media sites like Facebook, Instagram, and Twitter, people and groups can mobilize support, advocate for causes, and reach a global audience. Since information spreads swiftly in today's society, political activism has become more accessible to anybody with an internet connection. Social media is a potent instrument for underrepresented groups to raise awareness of problems that traditional media frequently ignores. Advocates and activists utilize social media sites like Twitter to interact with like-minded others, exchange personal narratives, and voice their concerns about injustice (Olaniran & Williams, 2020). Social media provides a platform for people who might not otherwise be heard to question the status quo and call for structural change. The use of digital technology to unite communities and residents in order to address local issues is growing. Although many strategies have been devised to help towns and residents make their communities better, these strategies are frequently not financially viable (Yang & Su, 2020). Some social media strategies to address the problem of financial unsustainability include crowdsourcing and crowdfunding. Crowdsourcing is the process of using the combined abilities and contributions of a wide range of people to complete a task, obtain data, or resolve an issue. Crowdsourcing involves asking a huge number of people on social media sites like Facebook, Instagram, or Twitter for ideas, information, or contributions, or on specialized crowdsourcing websites like Kickstarter (Cai et al., 2021). Through crowdfunding, a new company initiative can be financed by a large number of people contributing modest sums of money. By connecting investors and entrepreneurs through the extensive reach of social media and crowdfunding platforms, it has the potential to boost entrepreneurship by broadening the pool of investors beyond the conventional circle of owners, family members, and venture capitalists. Crowdfunding gained popularity as a result of the 2008 financial crisis (Macht & Weatherston, 2014). Small firms found it difficult to obtain credit after the crisis as banks imposed more stringent lending guidelines, which caused many of them to look for alternate sources of finance. The expected size of the global crowdfunding market in 2023 was $1.17 billion, indicating a modest growth over prior years. According to Statista, the global crowdfunding market is predicted to reach a market volume of $1.27 billion by 2028, with an annual growth rate of 1.48% (Statista, n.d.).

Furthermore, the open-source movement has transformed software development in recent years, encouraging a collaborative and innovative culture that has radically altered the way software is developed, shared, and enhanced. This strategy has supplanted the conventional notion of competition with a new paradigm in which technological achievements are driven by the combined efforts of global community (Spinellis & Szyperski, 2004). The open-source movement exemplifies the notion that the secret to maximizing software development's potential is cooperation rather than rivalry. Open source's capacity to spur innovation is among its most important effects on software development. Developers from all over the world can contribute their ideas, knowledge, and experience to open-source projects (Brains, 2024). Faster problem-solving and innovative solutions that might not surface in a closed, proprietary setting are the results of this collaborative approach. Without having to wait for formal updates from a single vendor, developers can experiment, alter, and enhance software by making the source code publicly available (O'Reilly, 1999). As a result, new features and capabilities are introduced much more quickly and the development cycle is accelerated. Open source has been adopted by various major tech firms like Google, Facebook, and Microsoft, who both contribute to and profit from this cooperative ecosystem.

ETHICAL AND SOCIAL CHALLENGES

In the connected digital age, technology greatly influences our perceptions of politics, society, and the economy. The well-being of society and human lives could be greatly improved by information and communication technologies. However, hate speech and fake news operations have also flourished in digital arenas, escalating division among people and endangering social harmony. Even while the literature acknowledges this negative aspect, the socio-technical nature of fake news and the intricacy of polarization as a phenomenon call for a fresh strategy to fully understand its complexities (Vasist et al., 2024). Social media platforms are used by fake news to propagate quickly, creating echo chambers and polarizing society. Preconceptions are strengthened when people are exposed to biased information that supports their preexisting opinions. This effect erodes the shared identity of the humans by causing societal opinions to fracture and undermining faith in traditional media sources. Additionally, the presence of fake news fuels conspiracy theories, widening societal divides and impeding productive communication and collaboration (Mwangi, 2023). Technology creation and use can have both positive and harmful effects on people, society, and the environment. These possible repercussions and conundrums are known as the ethical implications of technical breakthroughs. A number of ethical issues are frequently linked to technological developments, such as privacy, security, employment displacement, environmental effect, and the possibility of technology abuse (Khogali & Mekid, 2023). There are now serious privacy and security problems due to the quick growth of digital technology and the growing interconnectedness of gadgets. The risk of identity theft, data breaches, and illegal spying increases with the amount of personal information that is gathered, saved, and shared online. Furthermore, there are ethical questions around possible biases, discrimination, and invasions of privacy when using AI and machine learning for data analysis and facial recognition (Alawida et al., 2022). Concerns regarding the possible abuse of emerging technology by people, businesses, or governments are also raised by their development. Examples include the development of deadly autonomous weapons systems, the use of biotechnology to create biological weapons, and the application of AI and machine learning in surveillance. When creating and regulating these technologies, ethical issues must be taken into account to guarantee that they are applied sensibly and for the good of society (Kavanagh, 2022). A digital divide can result from technological improvements, whereby people or communities with less access to technology are left behind and suffer in areas like social inclusion, employment, and education. This presents moral questions regarding the duty of governments, tech firms, and society at large to guarantee that everyone may profit from technology, irrespective of socioeconomic background, geographic location, or other considerations (Hanna, 2022).

Technology's unintended repercussions are not a new phenomenon in the twenty-first century. A paradigm for comprehending various kinds of unintended consequences—unexpected advantages, perverse outcomes, and unanticipated drawbacks—was put forth by Robert Merton in the 1930s (Healy, 2012). Indeed, the globe has seen throughout history how important innovations, like the Industrial Revolution or high fructose corn syrup, may have long-lasting negative repercussions on society, like diabetes and air pollution. However, because of the exponential growth in compounding rate, the effects of modern technologies are more sinister. Moore's and Metcalfe's laws have accelerated scaling, which has both helped and hurt the technology sector by escalating its unforeseen consequences (Nohria & Taneja, 2021).

CONCLUSION: TECHNOLOGY FOR THE GREATER GOOD

In an age when technology permeates every part of human life, its capacity to influence society is greater than ever. Technology is a potent instrument that can aid in closing socioeconomic inequalities, whether it be by expanding access to education, improving healthcare delivery, or empowering underserved populations. Digital literacy is one of the best methods to make a difference in society. Numerous chances for education, entrepreneurship, and employment are made possible by having access to the internet and digital tools. Underprivileged populations can be given the opportunity to engage in the digital economy through initiatives that teach digital skills, including the establishment of Digital Literacy Centers (DLCs) (Lowenthal et al., 2022). Economic growth, sustainable development, and national security are all fueled by technology and applied sciences. The national security, including economic security, food security, water security, health security, environmental security, and our capacity to adapt to climate change, may be impacted by an over-reliance on foreign suppliers for essential technologies in today's technologically advanced world. In all major socioeconomic and strategic sectors, such as capital goods, electronics components and products, computers, telecom equipment, biomedical equipment, aircraft, and contemporary transportation systems, this calls for a swift transition from a state of "technology-dependence" to "technology-adequacy" (Mirzabaev et al., 2023). A national initiative to raise the technological intensity of our manufactured products exports should be started, in addition to a renewed focus on materials, engineering, and manufacturing technology. The world must focus on being leaders in a few specific areas of technology. The rapid advancement of technology is expected to influence governance methods in the future. "Disruption" has replaced the phrase "transformation"! If the events of the past five years are any indication, the future holds an accelerated speed that the globe has never seen or anticipated. Clearly, disruptive technologies are changing how people live, communicate, travel, shop, sleep, and enjoy entertainment.

Technology has the power to significantly alter society when used wisely. In addition to promoting entrepreneurship and environmental sustainability, it offers scalable and affordable answers to some of the most important problems that the present globe is facing. But for technology to have a real social impact, it needs to be sustainable, inclusive, and adapted to the requirements of local communities. As governments and organizations keep coming up with new ideas, the future of social impact appears to be becoming more digital and more optimistic.

REFERENCES

Alawida, M., Omolara, A. E., Abiodun, O. I., & Al-Rajab, M. (2022). A deeper look into cybersecurity issues in the wake of Covid-19: A survey. *Journal of King Saud University. Computer and Information Sciences*, *34*(10), 8176–8206. DOI: 10.1016/j.jksuci.2022.08.003 PMID: 37521180

Azeema, N., Nawaz, H., Gill, M. A., Khan, M. A., Miraj, J., & Lodhi, K. (2023). Impact of Artificial Intelligence on Financial Markets: Possibilities & Challenges. *Journal of Computing & Biomedical Informatics*, *6*(01), 287–299.

Bajwa, J., Munir, U., Nori, A., & Williams, B. (2021). Artificial intelligence in healthcare: Transforming the practice of medicine. *Future Healthcare Journal*, *8*(2), e188–e194. DOI: 10.7861/fhj.2021-0095 PMID: 34286183

Baraldo, M., & di Franco, P. D. G. (2024). Place-centred emerging technologies for disaster management: A scoping review. *International Journal of Disaster Risk Reduction*, *112*, 104782. DOI: 10.1016/j.ijdrr.2024.104782

Barcellos, S. H., Carvalho, L. S., & Turley, P. (2020). Is education the great equalizer? *NBER Working Paper*.

Beder, S. (1994). The role of technology in sustainable development. *IEEE Technology and Society Magazine*, *13*(4), 14–19. DOI: 10.1109/44.334601

Ben-Zvi, T., & Luftman, J. (2022). Post-pandemic IT: Digital transformation and sustainability. *Sustainability (Basel)*, *14*(22), 15275. DOI: 10.3390/su142215275

Bose, D., Bhattacharya, R., Kaur, T., Pandya, R., Sarkar, A., Ray, A., Mondal, S., Mondal, A., Ghosh, P., & Chemudupati, R. I. (2024). Innovative approaches for carbon capture and storage as crucial measures for emission reduction within industrial sectors. *Carbon Capture Science & Technology*, *12*, 100238. DOI: 10.1016/j.ccst.2024.100238

Brains, E. (2024, September). The Impact of Open Source on Software Development: Collaboration Over Competition. Medium. https://medium.com/@emperorbrains/the-impact-of-open-source-on-software-development-collaboration-over-competition-4d8ce85c3bfa

Cai, W., Polzin, F., & Stam, E. (2021). Crowdfunding and social capital: A systematic review using a dynamic perspective. *Technological Forecasting and Social Change*, *162*, 120412. DOI: 10.1016/j.techfore.2020.120412

Chase, L. C., Stewart, M., Schilling, B., Smith, B., & Walk, M. (2018). Agritourism: Toward a conceptual framework for industry analysis. *Journal of Agriculture, Food Systems, and Community Development*, *8*(1), 13–19. DOI: 10.5304/jafscd.2018.081.016

Clark, H., & Wu, H. (2016). The sustainable development goals: 17 goals to transform our world. *Furthering the work of the United Nations*, 36-54.

Du, J. T., Xie, I., & Waycott, J. (2020). Marginalized communities, emerging technologies, and social innovation in the digital age: Introduction to the special issue. *Information Processing & Management*, *57*(3), 102235. DOI: 10.1016/j.ipm.2020.102235

Feyen, E., Frost, J., Gambacorta, L., Natarajan, H., & Saal, M. (2021). Fintech and the digital transformation of financial services: implications for market structure and public policy. *BIS papers*.

Finley, M. I. (1965). Technical innovation and economic progress in the ancient world. *The Economic History Review*, *18*(1), 29–45. DOI: 10.2307/2591872

Floridi, L. (2007). A look into the future impact of ICT on our lives. *The Information Society*, *23*(1), 59–64. DOI: 10.1080/01972240601059094

Geladi, N. (2018). Technology is affecting the quality of human face-to-face interaction. *Digital Society. Retrieved from:* https://medium. com/digital-society/technology-is-affecting-the-quality-of-human-face-to-face-interaction-146fe72a29c5

Grover, V., & Nandal, M. (2024). Education System Using Cloud Computing: A Proposed Model. In *Educational Perspectives on Digital Technologies in Modeling and Management* (pp. 178-194). IGI Global. DOI: 10.4018/979-8-3693-2314-4.ch009

Haleem, A., Javaid, M., Qadri, M. A., & Suman, R. (2022). Understanding the role of digital technologies in education: A review. *Sustainable operations and computers, 3*, 275-285.

Hanna, K. T. (2022). What Is The Digital Divide and How Is It Being Bridged. *TechTarget. Retrieved March, 15*, 2023.

Healy, T. (2012). The unanticipated consequences of technology. *Nanotechnology: ethical and social Implications*, 155-173.

Hemathilake, D. M. K. S., & Gunathilake, D. M. C. C. (2022). Agricultural productivity and food supply to meet increased demands. In *Future foods* (pp. 539–553). Academic Press. DOI: 10.1016/B978-0-323-91001-9.00016-5

Hilbert, M. (2020). Digital technology and social change: The digital transformation of society from a historical perspective. *Dialogues in Clinical Neuroscience*, *22*(2), 189–194. DOI: 10.31887/DCNS.2020.22.2/mhilbert PMID: 32699519

Hodges, H. (1992). *Technology in the ancient world*. Barnes & Noble Publishing.

Hutson, J., Lively, J., Robertson, B., Cotroneo, P., & Lang, M. (2023). Conclusion: Future Perspectives—Embracing the AI Renaissance. In *Creative Convergence: The AI Renaissance in Art and Design* (pp. 225–237). Springer Nature Switzerland.

Jafarpanah, I., & Karshenas, A. (2023). Technological Trends in Smart Agriculture. *Journal of Entrepreneurship and Agriculture*, *10*(2), 100–115.

Jemala, M. (2021). Long-term research on technology innovation in the form of new technology patents. *International Journal of Innovation Studies*, *5*(4), 148–160. DOI: 10.1016/j.ijis.2021.09.002

Jianing, P., Bai, K., Solangi, Y. A., Magazzino, C., & Ayaz, K. (2024). Examining the role of digitalization and technological innovation in promoting sustainable natural resource exploitation. *Resources Policy*, *92*, 105036. DOI: 10.1016/j.resourpol.2024.105036

Kaledio, E., Russell, E., Oloyede, J., & Olaoye, F. (2023). Cultivating Innovation: A Comprehensive Exploration of Agtech's Impact on Agriculture and Sustainable Food Systems.

Kang, H. S., & Exworthy, M. (2022). Wearing the future—wearables to empower users to take greater responsibility for their health and care: Scoping review. *JMIR mHealth and uHealth*, *10*(7), e35684. DOI: 10.2196/35684 PMID: 35830222

Kavanagh, C. (2022). *New tech, new threats, and new governance challenges: an opportunity to craft smarter responses?* Carnegie Endowment for International Peace.

Kellner, D. (2004). Technological transformation, multiple literacies, and the revisioning of education. *E-Learning and Digital Media*, *1*(1), 9–37. DOI: 10.2304/elea.2004.1.1.8

Khawaja, M. K., Alkayyali, K., Almanasreh, M., & Alkhalidi, A. (2024). Waste-to-energy barriers and solutions for developing countries with limited water and energy resources. *The Science of the Total Environment*, *926*, 172096. DOI: 10.1016/j.scitotenv.2024.172096 PMID: 38556009

Khogali, H. O., & Mekid, S. (2023). The blended future of automation and AI: Examining some long-term societal and ethical impact features. *Technology in Society*, *73*, 102232. DOI: 10.1016/j.techsoc.2023.102232

Koessmeier, C., & Büttner, O. B. (2021). Why are we distracted by social media? Distraction situations and strategies, reasons for distraction, and individual differences. *Frontiers in Psychology*, *12*, 711416. DOI: 10.3389/fpsyg.2021.711416 PMID: 34925123

Kondraganti, A. (2021). Big Data Analytics in Humanitarian and Disaster Operations: A Systematic Review. *arXiv preprint arXiv:2108.09800.*

Kraus, S., Durst, S., Ferreira, J. J., Veiga, P., Kailer, N., & Weinmann, A. (2022). Digital transformation in business and management research: An overview of the current status quo. *International Journal of Information Management*, *63*, 102466. DOI: 10.1016/j.ijinfomgt.2021.102466

Lambertini, M. (2018, August). Technology can help us save the planet. But more than anything, we must learn to value nature. In *World Economic Forum* (Vol. 23).

Lee, K. R. (2002). Impacts of Information Technology on Society in the New Century. *Business and management, 5*(6), 46-55.

Lowenthal, P. R., Persichini, G., Conley, Q., Humphrey, M., & Scheufler, J. (2022). Digital literacy in special education: Preparing students for college and the workplace. In *Research anthology on inclusive practices for educators and administrators in special education* (pp. 524–537). IGI Global. DOI: 10.4018/978-1-6684-3670-7.ch029

Macht, S. A., & Weatherston, J. (2014). The benefits of online crowdfunding for fund-seeking business ventures. *Strategic Change*, *23*(1-2), 1–14. DOI: 10.1002/jsc.1955

Mager, W. (1993). Proto-industrialization and proto-industry: The uses and drawbacks of two concepts. *Continuity and Change*, *8*(2), 181–215. DOI: 10.1017/S026841600000206X

Mayo, M. (2004). Exclusion, inclusion and empowerment: community empowerment? Reflecting on the lessons of strategies to promote empowerment. In *The politics of inclusion and empowerment: Gender, class and citizenship* (pp. 139–158). Palgrave Macmillan UK. DOI: 10.1057/9781403990013_9

McKendrick, J. (2023, January). The Coming Democratization Of Financial Services, Thanks To Artificial Intelligence. Forbes. https://www.forbes.com/sites/joemckendrick/2023/01/14/the-coming-democratization-of-financial-services-thanks-to-ai/

Mirzabaev, A., Kerr, R. B., Hasegawa, T., Pradhan, P., Wreford, A., von der Pahlen, M. C. T., & Gurney-Smith, H. (2023). Severe climate change risks to food security and nutrition. *Climate Risk Management*, *39*, 100473. DOI: 10.1016/j.crm.2022.100473

Mwangi, E. (2023). Technology and fake news: shaping social, political, and economic perspectives. *Authorea Preprints.*

Ng, D. (2023, September). How Technology is Democratizing Access to Quality Education in the Digital Era. Medium. https://medium.com/@nclairline/how-technology-is-democratizing-access-to-quality-education-in-the-digital-era-29f16d9897ea

Nohria, N., & Taneja, H. (2021). Managing the unintended consequences of your innovations. *Harvard Business Review*, •••, 19.

O'Reilly, T. (1999). Lessons from open-source software development. *Communications of the ACM, 42*(4), 32–37. DOI: 10.1145/299157.299164

Olaniran, B., & Williams, I. (2020). Social media effects: Hijacking democracy and civility in civic engagement. *Platforms, Protests, and the Challenge of Networked Democracy*, 77-94.

Osman, A. I., Chen, L., Yang, M., Msigwa, G., Farghali, M., Fawzy, S., Rooney, D. W., & Yap, P. S. (2023). Cost, environmental impact, and resilience of renewable energy under a changing climate: A review. *Environmental Chemistry Letters, 21*(2), 741–764. DOI: 10.1007/s10311-022-01532-8

Phuyal, S., Bista, D., & Bista, R. (2020). Challenges, opportunities and future directions of smart manufacturing: A state of art review. *Sustainable Futures : An Applied Journal of Technology, Environment and Society, 2*, 100023. DOI: 10.1016/j.sftr.2020.100023

Rafferty, J. P. (2017). The rise of the machines: Pros and cons of the industrial revolution.

Raja, R., & Nagasubramani, P. C. (2018). Impact of modern technology in education. *Journal of Applied and Advanced Research, 3*(1), 33–35. DOI: 10.21839/jaar.2018.v3iS1.165

Romano, V., Lozano, S., & Fernández-López de Pablo, J. (2020). A multilevel analytical framework for studying cultural evolution in prehistoric hunter–gatherer societies. *Biological Reviews of the Cambridge Philosophical Society, 95*(4), 1020–1035. DOI: 10.1111/brv.12599 PMID: 32237025

Rubeis, G., Dubbala, K., & Metzler, I. (2022). "Democratizing" artificial intelligence in medicine and healthcare: Mapping the uses of an elusive term. *Frontiers in Genetics, 13*, 902542. DOI: 10.3389/fgene.2022.902542 PMID: 36046243

Saptasagar, K. A. (2022). Effects of Digital Technology on Adolescents: Pros and Cons. In *Impact and Role of Digital Technologies in Adolescent Lives* (pp. 19–25). IGI Global. DOI: 10.4018/978-1-7998-8318-0.ch002

Sarkar, S. (2012). The role of information and communication technology (ICT) in higher education for the 21st century. *Science, 1*(1), 30–41.

Sharma, A., & Singh, B. J. (2020). Evolution of industrial revolutions: A review. *International Journal of Innovative Technology and Exploring Engineering, 9*(11), 66–73. DOI: 10.35940/ijitee.I7144.0991120

Sinha, A. K., Rakesh, S., Mitra, B., Roy, N., Sahoo, S., Saha, B. N., ... & Bhattacharya, P. M. (2021). Agricultural waste management policies and programme for environment and nutritional security. *Input use efficiency for food and environmental security*, 627-664.

Spinellis, D., & Szyperski, C. (2004). How is open source affecting software development? *IEEE Software, 21*(1), 28–33. DOI: 10.1109/MS.2004.1259204

Statista (n.d.). Estimated transaction value of crowdfunding worldwide from 2017 to 2023, with forecasts from 2024 to 2028. https://www.statista.com/statistics/1078273/global-crowdfunding-market-size/

Thomason, J. (2021). Big tech, big data and the new world of digital health. *Global Health Journal (Amsterdam, Netherlands), 5*(4), 165–168. DOI: 10.1016/j.glohj.2021.11.003

Topol, E. (2019). *Deep medicine: how artificial intelligence can make healthcare human again.*

Troxler, P. (2013). *Making the 3rd industrial revolution. Fab Labs: Of Machines, Makers and Inventors*. Transcript Publishers.

Upreti, G. (1994). Environmental conservation and sustainable development require a new development approach. *Environmental Conservation, 21*(1), 18–29. DOI: 10.1017/S0376892900024036

Vannoy, S. A., & Palvia, P. (2010). The social influence model of technology adoption. *Communications of the ACM, 53*(6), 149–153. DOI: 10.1145/1743546.1743585

Vasist, P. N., Chatterjee, D., & Krishnan, S. (2024). The polarizing impact of political disinformation and hate speech: A cross-country configural narrative. *Information Systems Frontiers, 26*(2), 663–688. DOI: 10.1007/s10796-023-10390-w PMID: 37361884

Venkadesh, P., Divya, S. V., Marymariyal, P., & Keerthana, S. (2024). Predicting Natural Disasters With AI and Machine Learning. In *Utilizing AI and Machine Learning for Natural Disaster Management* (pp. 39–64). IGI Global. DOI: 10.4018/979-8-3693-3362-4.ch003

World Bank. (2022). COVID-19 drives a global surge in use of digital payments. https://www.worldbank.org/en/news/press-release/2022/06/29/covid-19-drives-global-surge-in-use-of-digital-payments

Xinzhou, H. (2015, April). The development trend of mobile Internet and its impact on the global economy. In *2015 International Conference on Social Science and Technology Education* (pp. 598-600). Atlantis Press. DOI: 10.2991/icsste-15.2015.159

Yang, Y., & Su, Y. (2020). Public voice via social media: Role in cooperative governance during public health emergencies. *International Journal of Environmental Research and Public Health*, *17*(18), 6840. DOI: 10.3390/ijerph17186840 PMID: 32962172

Yelne, S., Chaudhary, M., Dod, K., Sayyad, A., & Sharma, R. (2023). Harnessing the power of AI: A comprehensive review of its impact and challenges in nursing science and healthcare. *Cureus*, *15*(11). Advance online publication. DOI: 10.7759/cureus.49252 PMID: 38143615

Yin, Y., Stecke, K. E., & Li, D. (2018). The evolution of production systems from Industry 2.0 through Industry 4.0. *International Journal of Production Research*, *56*(1-2), 848–861. DOI: 10.1080/00207543.2017.1403664

Chapter 3
From Social Capital to Economic Agency Through a Self-Efficacy Perspective on Women's Entrepreneurship

Benu Kesar
http://orcid.org/0000-0003-3207-5528
Symbiosis International University, Pune, India

Shaji Joseph
http://orcid.org/0000-0002-5268-1376
Symbiosis International University, Pune, India

Dev Kesar
http://orcid.org/0009-0004-0801-2257
Vellore Institute of Technology, Chennai, India

ABSTRACT

Social media platforms have transformed entrepreneurship for women by providing low-barrier access to markets. This study elucidates the mediating role of self-efficacy in translating social media participation into empowerment outcomes for women entrepreneurs, exemplified by platforms like Meesho. This study introduces the Self-Efficacy Enhancement Theory (SEET), which comprises psychological, social, and economic self-efficacy domains. Psychological self-efficacy is the belief in one's ability to control emotions and persist through challenges, built by reframing social media failures as useful learning opportunities to stay resilient. Social self-efficacy

DOI: 10.4018/979-8-3373-0629-2.ch003

ht © 2026, IGI Global Scientific Publishing. Copying or distributing in print or electronic forms without written permission of IGI Global Scientific Publishing is prohibited. Use of this chapter to generative artificial intelligence (AI) technologies is expressly prohibited. The publisher reserves all rights to license its use for generative AI training and machine learning model development.

is the confidence in building relationships that turn personal contacts into trusted business networks. Economic self-efficacy is the ability to manage money and grow sales, which transforms side hustles into steady income sources. Mastery experiences and vicarious learning are key factors in developing psychological self-efficacy.

1. INTRODUCTION

Entrepreneurship has long been a pathway to economic independence, innovation, and social mobility. However, women entrepreneurs have historically faced significant challenges, from cultural biases to limited access to financial resources and professional networks. Digital transformation and social media have reshaped the business landscape, providing women entrepreneurs with unprecedented opportunities to overcome these barriers (Agrawal, 2022).

The digital revolution has enabled women to build online enterprises, connect with global markets, and leverage digital marketing strategies to scale their businesses (Al-Dajani et al., 2014). Social media platforms such as Instagram, Facebook, LinkedIn, and TikTok have become crucial tools for women-led small businesses, offering direct customer engagement, brand visibility, and innovative marketing avenues (Akpuokwe et al., 2024).

In a patriarchy-driven society, which is driven by norms and values that prioritize male authority and control over economic matters, the empowerment of men and the subordination and bias against women can be seen as a crucial element for economic development (Amatucci & Swartz, 2011). For entrepreneurs to thrive in environments, they need to be resourceful in their approach to business by identifying new prospects. Different entrepreneurs have different needs, goals, and skills, it is important to recognize their differences to provide them with the best support and resources. Women are often stereotyped as having feminine characteristics such as empathy, sensitivity, and sensuality. Entrepreneurs must be innovative, recognize opportunities, manage risks, and take risks to succeed.

This study identifies self-efficacy as the crucial psychological factor that explains how social media participation results in empowerment outcomes. This overview emphasizes the psychological, social, and economic aspects of self-efficacy relevant to women entrepreneurs, stressing its significance for their personal and business success while recognising the barriers they face. Psychological self-efficacy is fundamental for women entrepreneurs, shaping their ability to manage stress and believe in their abilities. Research shows that higher self-efficacy is associated with optimistic attitudes toward challenges, resilience in overcoming setbacks, and adaptive coping strategies in business settings. Mastery experiences, vicarious learning, verbal persuasion, and emotional regulation are key factors in developing psychological self-efficacy, enabling women to navigate the complexities of entrepreneurship more effectively.

Patriarchy has a long and complex history that is deeply intertwined with social, economic, and technological developments. Most historians agree that patriarchal systems began to emerge centuries ago, coinciding with the transition from nomadic hunter-gatherer societies to more settled agricultural communities in regions such as Mesopotamia, Egypt, and Greece. This shift facilitated a division of labour in which men, often physically stronger, began to dominate the workforce, particularly in agriculture and warfare. As societies evolved, the consolidation of power among male elites became a hallmark of emerging states. Elites required a stable population to produce resources and defend their interests, leading to societal pressures that dictated women's roles primarily as mothers, tasked with bearing sons to ensure continuity and security for these patriarchal structures. This focus on producing male heirs reflected and reinforced the ideological underpinnings of patriarchy, which privileged men while subordinating women in both public and private spheres.

The impact of patriarchy is profound and can be observed in various facets of modern life, including gender roles, economic opportunities, and social justice. In traditionally patriarchal societies, such as India and China, this legacy has resulted in systemic preferences for sons, which has had dire consequences, including high rates of female foeticide and skewed sex ratios.

Despite progress in challenging these norms, the historical roots of patriarchy continue to shape contemporary societal dynamics, highlighting the need for ongoing efforts to address its lasting effects.

Empowerment in entrepreneurship is a multifaceted concept that involves both individual and community dimensions. Entrepreneurs must recognize their potential, plan effectively, and take decisive actions to achieve their goals. Psychological empowerment is a key factor in entrepreneurship, providing individuals with the mindset needed to pursue their goals and overcome challenges. It involves increasing self-efficacy and participation, which are essential for proactive entrepreneurial behaviour.

The concept of entrepreneurship dates back to the 18th century when economist Richard Cantillon first coined the term “entreprendre,” meaning “to undertake.” Historically, business ownership has been male dominated, particularly in industries that require significant capital investment. Women were largely relegated to informal trade, craft businesses, and small-scale service enterprises.

The rise of feminist economic thought in the 20th century challenged these norms, emphasizing the need for economic empowerment as a key driver of gender equality. Over the past few decades, governments and international organizations have launched policies to support women entrepreneurs through financial inclusion programs, business education, and mentorship initiatives.

Social media serves as a powerful platform for women entrepreneurs to reach their target audiences (Al-Dajani et al., 2014). Regularly posting engaging content and interacting with followers not only promotes products or services but also builds community and trust. Storytelling on social media allows women entrepreneurs to authentically showcase their brand's unique narrative. By expressing their values and experiences, they can engage their audience on a more personal level, which can enhance brand loyalty and emotional connection with customers. As competition intensifies, the importance of customer service and user experience grows. Women entrepreneurs must prioritize building strong relationships with their customers through personalized interactions on social media platforms. The ability to respond swiftly to customer inquiries and feedback helps foster loyalty and trust, which are crucial for long-term success.

We have introduced online patriarchy model which examines the pervasive influence of patriarchal structures within digital environments and their impact on women's experiences in online spaces. As the social media has evolved into a critical platform for social interaction, it has also become a battleground where traditional gender norms are both challenged and reinforced (Akpuokwe et al., 2024; Jiménez-Zarco et al., 2021). Notably, the rise of cyber harassment and misogynistic behaviour highlights the ongoing struggle for women to assert their agency amidst systemic victimization.

This model underscores the importance of understanding how both digital and societal dynamics contribute to the perpetuation of gender inequality. The analysis of the online patriarchy model reveals how race, class, and gender interweave to shape diverse online experiences. Critics argue that existing frameworks often overlook the nuanced challenges faced by marginalized women, thus calling for a more inclusive perspective that acknowledges the complexities of digital feminism. This discussion has led to significant debates about representation, digital safety, and the role of social media in both empowering and silencing women's voices. The model also highlights the dual role of social media platforms: while they can facilitate feminist activism and amplify marginalized voices, they simultaneously expose users to harassment and discriminatory practices.

We have introduced the Self-Efficacy Enhancement Theory (SEET) that combines sources of self-efficacy with platform affordances. SEET views empowerment as a three-part process involving psychological self-efficacy (confidence and resilience), social self-efficacy (network skills and influence), and economic self-efficacy (income growth and financial independence).

Psychological self-efficacy is reinforced through repeated mastery experiences such as successful product postings, positive customer feedback, and incremental sales growth. Social self-efficacy emerges through the affordances of digital networking. Women entrepreneurs convert bonding social capital (family and close networks) into bridging capital (extended digital communities), expanding access to information, mentorship, and customers. Economic self-efficacy manifests when women experience tangible financial returns from digital engagement.

1.1 Research Objectives

- To explore how social media affordances enhance self-efficacy for women entrepreneurs.
- To examine platform-specific empowerment strategies.
- To assess multidimensional impacts (psychological confidence, social networking, economic gains) via self-efficacy enhancement theory.

1.2 Research Questions

- How do social media platforms build psychological, social, and economic self-efficacy among women entrepreneurs?
- What role does Meesho's model play in democratizing entrepreneurship for homemakers and informal sellers?
- Which challenges hinder women's digital entrepreneurship, and what strategies mitigate them?

This study presents the Self-Efficacy Enhancement Theory (SEET), a flexible, intervention-focused framework that combines self-efficacy with platform affordances. SEET views empowerment as involving psychological self-efficacy (confidence and resilience), social self-efficacy (network skills and influence), and economic self-efficacy (financial independence).

A compelling illustration of platform-mediated empowerment is provided by Meesho, an Indian social commerce enterprise founded in 2015. Its zero-investment reselling model eliminates inventory requirements and logistical burdens, enabling women, particularly homemakers, to monetize social networks via WhatsApp and Facebook. By operationalizing "network entrepreneurship," the platform transforms relational trust into economic activity. Unlike conventional e-commerce giants that impose compliance and capital thresholds, Meesho's commission-free entry structure lowers structural barriers. Its vernacular language interface and mobile-first design further enhance inclusivity in Tier-2 and Tier-3 regions.Meesho's analytics dashboards offer feedback on mastery; community groups encourage vicarious learning; instant UPI-based payments boost economic confidence; and low-risk entry reduces fear of failure.

2. LITERATURE REVIEW

Social media has emerged as a transformative tool for women entrepreneurs, offering opportunities for business growth, empowerment, and overcoming traditional barriers (Wood & Khan, 2016). It facilitates brand building, customer engagement, and access to global markets, which are crucial for entrepreneurial success. However, women entrepreneurs face unique challenges in leveraging social media effectively, including algorithmic biases, digital literacy gaps, and societal barriers. These challenges necessitate strategic approaches and supportive measures to maximize the benefits of social media for women entrepreneurs.

The impact of entrepreneurship extends beyond individual success stories. These entrepreneurs serve as catalysts for localized socio-economic transformation through two primary mechanisms: the elevation of community living standards and the generation of increased household income. Their embedded position within local communities allows them to identify and address specific market needs while creating employment opportunities for fellow community members (Tang, 2022). Empowerment in entrepreneurship is a multifaceted concept that involves both individual and community dimensions (Connell, 2015; Behera et al., 2023). This empowerment manifests in various forms:

1. Economic empowerment, defined as increased income, financial independence, and access to markets, is greatly enhanced by social media's removal of middlemen from value chains, enabling direct-to-consumer transactions that bypass traditional gatekeepers.
2. Social empowerment manifests through network expansion, increased visibility, and the formation of solidarity, transforming peripheral actors into key influencers.
3. Psychological empowerment depends on self-efficacy beliefs about one's ability to perform goal-oriented actions (Bandura & Walters, 1977), which social media enhances through repeated feedback, public validation, and successful mastery. Women entrepreneurs creating Instagram Lives or Meesho listings internalise resilience from customer interactions and success metrics, fostering agentic mindsets that support persistence amid volatility. This aligns with SEET's core, psychological self-efficacy, leading to cognitive reframing and reduced self-doubt.

Online platforms are playing a transformative role in empowering women entrepreneurs by providing them with global market access, networking opportunities, financial resources, and educational tools (Yáñez-Valdés & Guerrero, 2024). E-commerce platforms and social media have eliminated geographical barriers, enabling women to sell products worldwide without requiring a physical storefront (Wood & Khan, 2016; Agrawal, 2022). Networking sites and digital communities foster collaboration, mentorship, and knowledge exchange, helping women expand their business networks (Iyer et al., 2021).

Digital entrepreneurship refers to the creation and management of business ventures using digital technologies. Social media enables individuals with minimal capital to enter the business world, making entrepreneurship more accessible than ever before. One of the biggest advantages of social media for entrepreneurs is its cost-effectiveness. Setting up a social media account is free, and entrepreneurs can begin promoting their products or services with minimal investment. Through organic posts, live sessions, influencer collaborations, and paid ads, entrepreneurs can reach wide and diverse audiences across the globe. Features like comments, likes, and direct messaging provide immediate feedback and foster stronger relationships with customers. Additionally, social media platforms offer built-in analytics tools that help entrepreneurs understand customer preferences and refine their business strategies in real time.

Each social media platform has unique strengths. For instance, Instagram and TikTok are ideal for visually appealing content, making them popular among fashion, beauty, and food entrepreneurs. Facebook provides access to a broader demographic and includes e-commerce tools like Facebook Shops. LinkedIn is more suited for B2B ventures, professional services, and thought leadership, while YouTube allows for long-form content such as tutorials and reviews, which are effective in building authority and trust in certain niches.

Despite the opportunities, digital entrepreneurship through social media comes with challenges. Platform algorithms can unpredictably reduce content visibility, making it hard for entrepreneurs to consistently reach their audience. The digital space is also highly competitive, requiring constant creativity and content production. Entrepreneurs, especially women, may also face issues such as online harassment or burnout due to the pressure of maintaining an active digital presence. Furthermore, relying too heavily on one platform can be risky if policies or user trends shift unexpectedly.

To succeed as a digital entrepreneur on social media, strategic planning is crucial. Entrepreneurs need to define a clear niche to stand out in a crowded market and post consistently high-quality content that resonates with their target audience. Engagement is key, responding to comments, hosting interactive sessions, and building community trust are just as important as selling products. Using platform analytics to guide decisions and maintaining a presence on multiple platforms can also help mitigate risks and sustain long-term growth.

Moreover, technological advancements in artificial intelligence (AI) and blockchain have further expanded entrepreneurial possibilities, offering tools for personalized marketing, financial inclusion, and operational transparency (Behera et al., 2023; Bose et al., 2024). Crowdfunding platforms and digital financial services are bridging the funding gap, offering alternative sources of capital for female entrepreneurs traditionally excluded from conventional funding avenues. Online education and training resources provide access to crucial business skills, ranging from digital marketing to financial management. Additionally, online platforms enhance brand visibility through influencer marketing, affiliate collaborations, and content-driven engagement. The ability to leverage data analytics and automation tools further empowers women by offering strategic insights into customer behaviour and market trends (Yusniza, 2011).

One of the key benefits of online spaces is social support and solidarity. Women in digital communities share experiences, exchange advice, and offer emotional support, creating virtual sisterhoods that counteract isolation. Additionally, online platforms provide discursive spaces where personal struggles can be transformed into public debates, following the feminist principle that "the personal is political" (Friedan, 1963). Women can use digital networks to challenge societal norms, question oppressive structures, and advocate for their rights (Reich, 2010). The ability to mobilize collective action through social media campaigns and online forums further amplifies women's agency in resisting patriarchal dominance.

2.1 The Online Patriarchy Model

The Online Patriarchal Model conceptualizes digital platforms as gendered sociotechnical systems where patriarchal values are embedded, operationalized, and reinforced through algorithmic governance, interface design, and capitalist logics. These platforms do not merely reflect existing social hierarchies; they institutionalize and scale them through automated decision-making, data-driven discrimination, and design cultures shaped predominantly by male technocratic elites.

The Online Patriarchy Model represents how structural patriarchy, which originates in offline, institutional domains, is extended and reconfigured within digital spaces. Structural Patriarchy is understood as the deep-rooted, institutionalized system of male dominance embedded in social, economic, and political institutions.

The Online Patriarchy Model is an extension of gendered power into digital life. This model outlines three interrelated mechanisms that operationalize patriarchal control within digital platforms.

1. Technological Gatekeeping: This refers to the structural exclusion that occurs at the design and governance levels of digital platforms. Platforms are often conceptualized and built by male-dominated teams, leading to the creation of systems that fail to account for diverse user needs. The lack of inclusive gover-

nance means that decision-making structures are not representative or responsive to gender-based concerns. As a result, women's voices and perspectives are frequently marginalized in platform policy and architecture.

2. Algorithmic Bias: Algorithms, trained on biased data, often replicate and reinforce historical gender disparities. In this context, women-led ventures suffer from reduced visibility, meaning their products, services, or content are less likely to be recommended, ranked, or promoted by the algorithm. Additionally, stereotyped content promotion means that women's work is often pigeonhole into narrowly defined, gender-conforming categories such as beauty, caregiving, or lifestyle regardless of its actual substance or innovation.
3. Digital Harassment and Emotional Labor: As women participate in digital economies, they are disproportionately subjected to gendered trolling, targeted abuse, and systemic neglect from platform moderation systems. This harassment results in a psychological burden, ranging from emotional exhaustion to anxiety and burnout. In many cases, the cumulative toll leads to forced silence, where women limit their online engagement or self-censor as a protective response. This silencing further entrenches the digital divide by curbing women's full participation in public digital life.

Together, these dimensions illustrate how patriarchal structures are not dismantled in digital spaces but rather reshaped and amplified through technological systems, algorithmic governance, and platform cultures. The model underscores the need to recognize digital space not as a neutral or emancipatory arena, but as a contested terrain shaped by offline hierarchies that require conscious, structural redress.

The Online Patriarchy Model (Figure 1) provides an essential theoretical tool for understanding contemporary digital gender dynamics.

Figure 1. Online patriarchy model

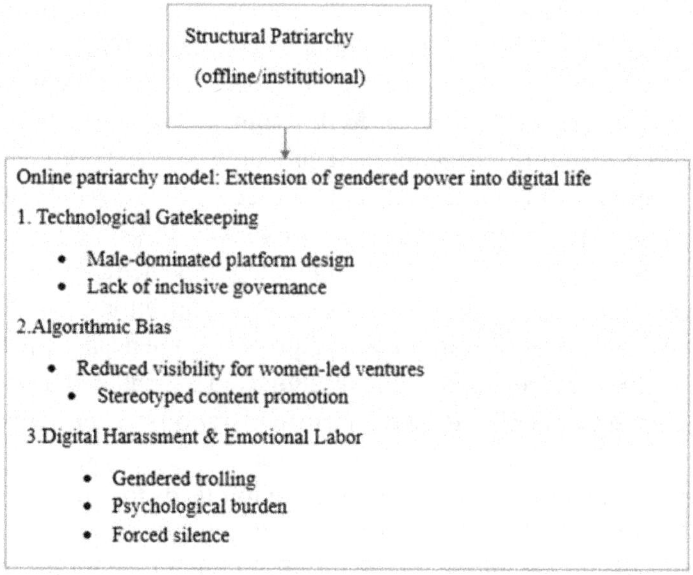

2.2 Theoretical Framework

We have introduced the Self-Efficacy Enhancement Theory (SEET), which focuses on strategies to strengthen individuals' beliefs in their capacity to execute actions to achieve desired outcomes. It shifts from static empowerment views to dynamic processes that foster personal agency through targeted interventions provides a lens to interpret social media's impact beyond adoption and network effects, focusing on agency, self-efficacy, and access to resources. Social media enhances women's autonomy by enabling independent income generation, expression of their voices, and public presence. The theory emphasises the mechanisms by which individuals gain control over their lives, make informed choices, and access resources that enable them to achieve both personal and collective goals. In the context of women entrepreneurs, empowerment is a dynamic, multidimensional process encompassing psychological confidence, social influence, and economic self-sufficiency.

a. Psychological Self-Efficacy

Psychological self-efficacy refers to an individual's belief in their capacity to think, decide, cope, and persist in the face of challenges. When users create content, articulate opinions, or manage online identities, they repeatedly test their competence.

Positive engagement (likes, comments, shares) reinforces confidence, while learning from failed posts fosters resilience and self-regulation. Over time, individuals develop a stronger sense of agency, self-expression, and control over outcomes. In short, the platform becomes a low-risk arena for psychological rehearsal where confidence is built one post at a time. Psychological self-efficacy encompasses dimensions of self-efficacy, confidence, motivation, and perceived control over one's business and environment. Social media engagement plays a vital role in this process by allowing women to visualize their professional identity and validate their entrepreneurial capabilities in a public domain.

b. Economic Self-Efficacy

Economic self-efficacy reflects beliefs about one's ability to generate income, manage resources, and achieve financial independence. Social media directly strengthens this dimension by lowering entry barriers to economic participation. Users can market products, offer services, build personal brands, or monetise content without formal institutional backing. Observing peers succeed economically through digital means further reinforces the belief that similar outcomes are attainable. Metrics such as reach, engagement, and sales provide concrete evidence of economic capability, transforming abstract confidence into measurable performance. The result is a shift from "I need permission to earn" to "I can create value myself," a psychologically radical but economically practical transition. Engaging in entrepreneurial activities enables women to attain financial independence and control over their futures, which is particularly important in socio-economic contexts.

c. Social Self-Efficacy

This refers to an individual's belief in their ability to interact and connect effectively with others, which can significantly influence various aspects of their life, particularly in the context of entrepreneurship. This facet of self-efficacy is crucial for women entrepreneurs, as it affects their ability to build networks, seek mentorship, and foster relationships essential to business success.Cultural factors also play a significant role in shaping social self-efficacy. In collectivist societies, individuals may exhibit greater persistence in the face of failure, reflecting a communal approach to support and encouragement. This contrasts with individualist cultures, where self-efficacy might be more closely tied to personal achievement. Understanding these cultural nuances can inform interventions to enhance social self-efficacy among women entrepreneurs, ultimately improving their quality of life and professional development.

Social Self-Efficacy Strategies

- **Daily Connection Challenges:** Start with messaging three prospects on WhatsApp; progress to group polls for feedback, building relational confidence through consistent interactions.
- **Story-Sharing Circles:** Host weekly Instagram Live sessions where participants share one "win" from stakeholder engagements, and peer inspiration.
- **Role-Play Rehearsals:** Practice objection-handling scripts (e.g., "price too high?") in small Facebook Groups, simulating live negotiations to sharpen interpersonal agility.

Psychological Self-Efficacy Strategies

- **Reframing Rituals:** End each posting day by listing three "lessons learned" from metrics, turning setbacks into stepping stones for mindset shifts.
- **Breathing Technique:** Before live streams, use 4-7-8 breathing technique (inhale 4s, hold 7s, exhale 8s) to calm nerves.
- **Gratitude Logging:** Maintain a simple journal of daily micro-achievements (one new follower), cultivating intrinsic resilience over time.

2.3 Methodology

This study uses a mixed-methods research design, integrating an extensive literature review with a case study of Meesho. To ensure academic rigor, peer-reviewed sources were drawn from the following databases: Scopus, Web of Science, Science Direct, and Google Scholar. A combination of primary and secondary keywords was used with Boolean operators to refine search results. Only articles published in English-language, peer-reviewed journals, books, and conference proceedings were included. The Meesho case study relied exclusively on secondary data. These included the Official Meesho website, blogs, and press releases.

Impact of Self-Efficacy on Business Performance

The connection between self-efficacy and business success is clear. Women with high self-efficacy are more likely to take on challenging tasks, recover quickly from setbacks, and see failures as due to factors they can control, like lack of effort or strategy.

Strategies to Enhance Self-Efficacy

a. Social Self-Efficacy Enhancement Strategies

- **Daily Connection Challenges:** Start with messaging 3 prospects on WhatsApp; progress to group polls for feedback, building confidence through consistent interactions.
- **Story-Sharing Circles:** Host weekly Instagram Live sessions where participants share one win from stakeholder engagements and peer inspiration.
- **Role-Play Rehearsals:** Practise objection-handling scripts (price too high) in small Facebook groups, simulating live negotiations to sharpen interpersonal agility.

b. Psychological Self-Efficacy Enhancement Strategies

- **Reframing Rituals:** End each posting day by listing 3 lessons learned from metrics, turning setbacks into stepping stones for mindset shifts.
- **Breathing Technique:** Before live streams, use the 4-7-8 breathing technique (inhale for 4s, hold for 7s, exhale for 8s) to calm nerves.
- **Gratitude Logging:** Maintain a simple journal of daily micro-achievements (one new follower) cultivating intrinsic resilience.

The Nature of Online Patriarchal Bargains

- **Strategic Adaptation, Not Submission:** Women's navigation of the digital realm is characterized by agency and calculated adaptation, not just acceptance of online patriarchy.
- **Structures of Power:** Algorithmic and technological systems frequently encode prevailing gender hierarchies, shaping what is seen, rewarded, and valued.
- **Contradictory Outcomes:** The same strategies that help secure safety, visibility, or income can also reinforce the structures they seek to circumvent.

Key Dimensions and Strategies

1. Negotiated Visibility
    - Women often tweak their online presentation (e.g., using gender-neutral usernames, professionalized images) to interact favourably with algorithms that privilege specific aesthetics or behaviours.
    - Highlighting values such as "authenticity," "community," or "care" becomes a tactical choice to resonate and gain recognition on content-

driven platforms.Such adjustments serve both to gain traction and to navigate the visibility–vulnerability trade-off online.

Case Study: Meesho's Positive Spillover Effects in India

Meesho is an Indian social commerce platform that has become a symbol of grassroots digital entrepreneurship. Founded in 2015 by IIT Delhi alumni Vidit Aatrey and Sanjeev Barnwal, Meesho initially launched as a hyperlocal fashion discovery app but later shifted to a social commerce marketplace. It enables everyday users, especially women, homemakers, and small business owners, to start online businesses with no upfront investment or inventory risk. Based in Bengaluru, this unicorn operates a three-sided marketplace connecting suppliers, resellers, and customers through WhatsApp, Facebook, and Instagram. Resellers earn commissions without needing inventory or capital, sharing catalogs from home.

Meesho's mission, encapsulated in its ethos "my shop," is democratizing e-commerce by transforming ordinary people into entrepreneurs through a digital platform that leverages social media networks and mobile technology.

Meesho began as Fashnear, an app intended for hyperlocal fashion discovery. But as the founders engaged with users and understood market needs, they discovered a distinct opportunity: many small merchants and homemakers wanted to sell online but lacked the capital, technical skills, and logistics support needed. This insight led to a pivot towards social commerce, where resellers could share products on social media and earn margins without owning stock.

Meesho's model relies on social features: zero-investment onboarding, social sharing tools, and analytics to improve. Co-founder Aatrey highlighted its women-centric approach: "We built it for homemakers needing flexible income without investments." Resellers promote through personal networks, earning profits per sale, making it an ideal model for multitasking moms. Meesho onboarded millions of women, boosting household incomes and fostering skills such as digital marketing.

Meesho App Features Driving Scale

1. **AI Product Recommendations:** Matches trending salwar suits to local tastes
2. **Sales Analytics Dashboard:** "Heat maps" show peak buying times by neighbourhood.
3. **Live Streaming:** 4x conversion via real-time styling demos
4. **UPI Instant Payments:** 100 commission hits the bank within 60 seconds
5. **Valmo Logistics:** Reaches 15K pincodes, including rural
6. **Cashback Gamification:** 50 incentives accelerate viral sharing

Meesho onboarded millions of women, boosting household incomes and fostering skills such as digital marketing. It bridges urban-rural divides by sourcing from manufacturers and reselling in underserved areas. Unlike Amazon and Flipkart's seller fees, Meesho's commission-only structure minimises barriers to entry, aligning with India's 100 million SMBs. Compared with peers, Meesho excels at transactions via WhatsApp, highlighting the influence of social trust. At the core of Meesho's success is its social reseller model.

Online patriarchal bargains reveal how women tactically negotiate visibility, safety, and success in algorithmically governed, gendered digital systems, often at the cost of reinforcing the very structures they must navigate. Understanding these bargains is crucial for building more equitable, inclusive, and critically aware digital futures.

The Challenges faced by Women Entrepreneurs in the digital entrepreneurship space, particularly in low-resource or unequal contexts, along with corresponding solutions or strategies, are mentioned below:

1. Digital Divide
   - Description: Unequal access to the internet, digital devices, and digital literacy, especially for women in rural or low-income areas.
   - Solutions: National and NGO-led programs for digital inclusion, Mobile-first digital literacy training, and Public Wi-Fi access and affordable data plans.
2. Online Gender-Based Violence (OGBV)
   - Description: Women face harassment, stalking, doxxing, and threats in digital spaces.
   - Solutions: Digital safety tools and platform moderation, Legal measures to criminalize online abuse, and Digital safety education.
3. Lack of Digital Skills & Tech Literacy
   - Description: Many women lack the technical skills required to benefit from digital tools like e-commerce or digital marketing.
   - Solutions: Upskilling programs (e.g., coding, SEO) and Peer mentoring and gender-sensitive digital content.
4. Cultural & Social Norms
   - Description: Societal expectations often discourage women from being public or entrepreneurial online.
   - Solutions:

Gender-awareness campaigns and community engagement. Highlighting successful female digital role models.

5. Time Poverty

- Description: Unpaid domestic responsibilities reduce the time women have to invest in entrepreneurship.
- Solutions: Family support policies and Flexible work/learning arrangements.

6. Limited Access to Finance
    - Description: Women often struggle to obtain loans or attract investors for digital ventures.
    - Solutions: Mobile-based microloans and fintech options. Gender-inclusive funding programs and women-focused crowdfunding.
7. Platform Bias & Algorithmic Disadvantage
    - Description: Algorithms often favor male-dominated content, reducing visibility for women entrepreneurs.
    - Solutions: Algorithm transparency and audits and policies that promote content diversity and visibility (e.g., niche platforms, hashtags).
8. Lack of Mentorship & Networking
    - Description: Limited access to experienced mentors or business networks hinders women's progress in digital fields.
    - Solutions: Digital mentorship platforms, entrepreneurial networks, and virtual incubators for women.
9. Regulatory & Policy Gaps
    - Description: Inadequate legal and policy frameworks to support digital entrepreneurship.
    - Solutions: Gender-inclusive policies and legal frameworks for digital businesses.

Table 1. Challenges faced by women entrepreneurs and suggested solutions

Challenges	Description	Solutions / Strategies
Digital Divide	Unequal access to the internet, devices, and digital literacy, especially in rural or low-income areas.	National & NGO-led digital inclusion programs; mobile-first training; public Wi-Fi & affordable data plans.
Online Gender-Based Violence (OGBV)	Harassment, stalking, doxxing, and threats that target women in digital spaces.	Platform moderation tools, digital safety training, and legal frameworks to criminalize OGBV.
Lack of Digital Skills & Tech Literacy	Limited technical skills prevent women from fully leveraging e-commerce, analytics, or social media marketing.	Digital upskilling programs (coding, e-commerce, SEO); peer mentoring; gender-sensitive training content.

continued on following page

Table 1. Continued

Challenges	Description	Solutions / Strategies
Cultural & Social Norms	Restrictive gender roles discourage women from being visible or leading businesses online.	Gender-awareness campaigns, community engagement, and showcasing successful female role models.
Time Poverty	Unpaid domestic labour limits women's availability to engage in digital ventures.	Flexible learning/work models; family support policies
Limited Access to Finance	Women face barriers in accessing loans or investors, especially for digital startups or scaling ventures.	Fintech solutions (e.g., mobile microloans), gender-inclusive funding programs; and women-focused crowdfunding platforms.
Platform Bias & Algorithmic Disadvantage	Algorithms often favor established, male-dominated networks or aesthetics, reducing women's online visibility.	Transparent algorithm audits, platform diversity policies, and alternative visibility strategies (hashtags, niche networks).
Lack of Mentorship & Networking	Women entrepreneurs lack access to high-value digital mentors and entrepreneurial networks.	Digital mentorship platforms, women's entrepreneur networks, virtual accelerators/ incubators.
Regulatory & Policy Gaps	Lack of supportive legal infrastructure for digital entrepreneurship (e.g., taxation, IP, online contracts).	Gender-inclusive digital policy frameworks, entrepreneur-friendly e-commerce regulation, and global policy harmonization.
Sustainability & Scaling Issues	Many women-led digital businesses struggle to grow due to limited capacity and market access.	E-commerce partnerships (Amazon, Etsy, Shopify for women); digital trade readiness programs; impact investment channels.

Source: Author's own work

3. PLATFORM-SPECIFIC EMPOWERMENT STRATEGIES

Instagram and Visual Commerce: Instagram has become the cornerstone platform for women entrepreneurs, particularly in fashion, beauty, lifestyle, and artisanal products. The platform's visual-first approach aligns with how many women naturally communicate about their products and services. Features like Instagram Shopping, Stories, Reels, provide multiple touchpoints for customer engagement and conversion.

Women entrepreneurs have mastered the art of storytelling through Instagram, sharing their journey from concept to creation, which builds authentic connections with their audience (Gleeson, 2012). The platform's algorithm rewards consistent, high-quality content, allowing skilled creators to reach substantial audiences organically without significant advertising spend (Reich, 2010).

Facebook and Community Building: Facebook's strength lies in its community-building capabilities through groups, pages, and marketplace functionality (Brahem & Boussema, 2022). Women entrepreneurs utilize Facebook Groups to create exclusive communities around their brands, fostering customer loyalty and generating valuable feedback. The platform's sophisticated advertising tools enable precise targeting, allowing businesses to reach specific demographics efficiently.

Facebook Marketplace has become particularly valuable for women selling handmade goods, vintage items, or local services, providing a trusted environment for peer-to-peer commerce. The integration of Facebook Shops has further streamlined the buying process, allowing customers to complete purchases without leaving the platform.

LinkedIn for Professional Services: Women entrepreneurs in consulting, coaching, and professional services have found LinkedIn invaluable for establishing thought leadership and generating B2B opportunities. The platform's professional focus helps women overcome gender biases that might exist in traditional networking environments, as expertise and content quality become the primary differentiators.

LinkedIn's publishing platform allows women to share insights, case studies, and industry expertise, building credibility and attracting potential clients. The networking capabilities enable strategic relationship building with other entrepreneurs, potential partners, and industry leaders.

TikTok and Viral Marketing: TikTok has emerged as a powerful platform for women entrepreneurs seeking to reach younger demographics and achieve rapid brand awareness. The platform's algorithm can propel content to millions of viewers regardless of follower count, creating opportunities for viral marketing that were previously accessible only to established brands with significant marketing budgets.

Women entrepreneurs have excelled at creating authentic, entertaining content that showcases their products in action, often leading to immediate sales spikes and brand recognition (Akpuokwe et al., 2024; Kelly & McAdam, 2023). The platform's short-form video format encourages creativity and allows for quick product demonstrations, tutorials, and behind-the-scenes content.

Social media platforms have enabled women entrepreneurs to generate substantial revenue streams through multiple channels. Direct sales through social commerce features, affiliate marketing partnerships, sponsored content, and digital product sales create diversified income sources that provide financial stability and growth potential.

Research indicates that women-owned businesses utilizing social media effectively report higher revenue growth compared to those relying solely on traditional marketing methods. The ability to track engagement metrics, conversion rates, and customer behavior through platform analytics enables data-driven decision-making that optimizes business performance.

Managing social media businesses requires women entrepreneurs to develop diverse technical skills, from content creation and basic graphic design to data analysis and digital marketing. This necessity has driven widespread upskilling among women entrepreneurs, making them more versatile and capable business leaders.

Online tutorials, platform-specific training programs, and community-shared knowledge have made technical skill acquisition more accessible than ever. Many women entrepreneurs report that managing their social media presence has given them confidence to tackle other technical aspects of business management.

The table 2 underscores the strategies and the inclusion of platform-specific examples such as Instagram, TikTok, LinkedIn, and Facebook which demonstrates how businesses can strategically select the right channels for their marketing efforts. By adopting these innovative approaches, women entrepreneurs can maximize their digital footprint, drive brand visibility, and create a sustainable online business model (Melissa et al., 2013; Jaman et al., 2020).

Table 2. Innovative marketing strategies using social media

Strategy	Description	Key Benefits	Example Platforms
AI-Powered Chatbots	Automates customer support with instant, personalized responses.	Enhances customer experience, improves response time.	Facebook Messenger, WhatsApp
Influencer Collaborations	Partners with niche influencers to increase brand credibility and reach new audiences.	Boosts brand trust and expands audience reach.	Instagram, TikTok, YouTube
Live Streaming & Q&A	Broadcasts live events, product launches, and Q&A sessions with audiences.	Increases real-time engagement and brand transparency.	Facebook Live, Instagram Live, LinkedIn Live
User-Generated Content (UGC)	Encouraging customers to share testimonials, reviews, and creative content featuring products.	Builds authenticity and community trust.	Instagram, Pinterest, Twitter
Short-Form Video Content	Creating engaging short videos showcasing product features, behind-the-scenes, or storytelling.	Increases content virality and engagement.	TikTok, Instagram Reels, YouTube Shorts
Augmented Reality (AR) Try-Ons	Implementing AR filters that allow customers to try on products virtually (e.g., makeup, fashion).	Enhances interactive shopping experiences.	Instagram, Snapchat, Facebook
Hashtag Challenges & Contests	Encouraging user participation in branded hashtag challenges and giveaways.	Drives brand visibility and audience engagement.	TikTok, Instagram, Twitter

continued on following page

Table 2. Continued

Strategy	Description	Key Benefits	Example Platforms
Social Commerce Integration	Selling products directly through social media storefronts and live shopping features.	Simplifies purchase process and boosts sales.	Facebook Shops, Instagram Shopping, Pinterest
AI-Driven Content Personalization	Using AI to analyze user behavior and deliver tailored content recommendations.	Improves content relevance and engagement.	LinkedIn, Facebook, Instagram
Cause-Driven Marketing	Aligning brand messaging with social causes and sustainability efforts.	Builds brand loyalty and emotional connection.	Instagram, Twitter, LinkedIn

Source: Author's own work

4. RESULTS AND DISCUSSION

This study provides an in-depth examination of the ways digital platforms simultaneously empower and constrain women entrepreneurs within patriarchal digital economies. The findings reveal a nuanced interplay between opportunity and structural inequality, shaped by platform design, algorithmic governance, and socio-cultural norms.

The research confirms that digital platforms have become indispensable tools for women entrepreneurs seeking economic independence and market expansion. Through social media, women utilize storytelling, influencer marketing, and e-commerce features to craft authentic brand narratives and drive engagement. These tools have enabled the rise of inclusive and community-centered business models, especially through platforms like Instagram, TikTok, Facebook, and LinkedIn, where visual communication, live interactions, and network building are central to business growth.

Moreover, digital entrepreneurship facilitates economic, social, and technical empowerment by expanding market access, providing financial tools, and supporting skill development. Women are increasingly leveraging AI-powered personalization, platform analytics, and crowdfunding technologies to overcome historical financial exclusions. However, these gains are mediated by complex structural and emotional costs.

The Online Patriarchy Model introduced in this study elucidates the embedded systems of male dominance that persist within digital spaces. Predominantly male platform developers shape environments that often fail to reflect the experiences and needs of women, resulting in exclusionary design and policy structures.

Participation on social media platforms enhances self-efficacy. SEET incorporates Bandura's sources of mastery, vicarious learning, and persuasion within digital environments across psychological, social, and economic areas. Meesho's zero-investment reselling model delivers maximum benefits through real-time analytics and accessible entry points, helping newcomers build step-by-step mastery and gain confidence as sellers. The mastery element of SEET is most apparent in the psychological boost women experience from repeated posting cycles, which surpasses that of traditional commerce, as they achieve practical success through metrics-based feedback loops.

Vicarious and persuasive factors operate in WhatsApp and Facebook groups, strengthening social self-efficacy via peer endorsements and friendly sessions that foster relational agility. Economically, integrated mechanisms improve retention and order volume, as UPI commissions turn hustles into sustainable ventures.

5. CONCLUSION

This study has examined the transformative potential of social media as a catalyst for entrepreneurial self-efficacy among women. We have introduced the Self-Efficacy Enhancement Theory (SEET) and its three domains: psychological, social, and economic self-efficacy.

At the psychological level, SEET illuminates how social media platforms contribute to the internal transformation of women entrepreneurs by strengthening their belief in their own capabilities. Meesho's progression from a hyperlocal fashion app to a publicly traded social commerce leader exemplifies the power of inclusive digital innovation. Its accessible business model, mobile-first strategy, and focus on empowering women have transformed millions into independent entrepreneurs. Its impact extends beyond trade, serving as a social and economic movement that shows how technology can foster inclusive growth in emerging markets.

REFERENCES

Agrawal, B. (2022). Use of Social media by small women entrepreneurs of India for growing their business. *SMS Journal of Enterpreneurship & Innovation*, *8*(01). Advance online publication. DOI: 10.21844/smsjei.v8i01.30007

Ahl, H. (2006). Why research on women entrepreneurs needs new directions. *Entrepreneurship Theory and Practice*, *30*(5), 595–621. DOI: 10.1111/j.1540-6520.2006.00138.x

Akpuokwe, C. U., Chikwe, C. F., & Eneh, N. E. (2024). Innovating business practices: The impact of social media on fostering gender equality and empowering women entrepreneurs. *Magna Scientia Advanced Research and Reviews, 10*(2), 032–043. https://doi.org/DOI: 10.30574/msarr.2024.10.2.0042

Al-Dajani, H., Bika, Z., Collins, L., & Swail, J. (2014). Gender and family business: New theoretical directions. *International Journal of Gender and Entrepreneurship*, *6*(3), 218–230. DOI: 10.1108/IJGE-11-2013-0069

Amatucci, F. M., & Swartz, E. (2011). Through a fractured lens: Women entrepreneurs and the private equity negotiation process. *Journal of Developmental Entrepreneurship: JDE, 16*(03), 333–F

Behera, R. K., Bala, P. K., & Rana, N. P. (2023). Creation of sustainable growth with explainable artificial intelligence: An empirical insight from consumer packaged goods retailers. *Journal of Cleaner Production*, *399*(136605), 136605. DOI: 10.1016/j.jclepro.2023.136605

Bose, T. K., Bonna, A. H., Bristy, J. F., & Moser, R. (2024). Evolving female entrepreneurship in emerging economies: Clarifying the linkages between institutional forces and online venture performance. *Journal of Small Business and Enterprise Development*, *31*(7), 1424–1454. Advance online publication. DOI: 10.1108/JSBED-01-2024-0026

Brahem, M., & Boussema, S. (2022). Social media entrepreneurship as an opportunity for women: The case of Facebook-commerce. *International Journal of Entrepreneurship and Innovation*, *146575032110660*. Advance online publication. DOI: 10.1177/14657503211066010

Connell, J. (2015, June 30). *3 Steps to Become the Empowered Entrepreneur You Want to Be*. Entrepreneur. https://www.entrepreneur.com/growing-a-business/3-steps-to-become-the-empowered-entrepreneur-you-want-to-be/246962

Gleeson, B. (2012). Critical commentary. The urban age: Paradox and prospect. *Urban Studies (Edinburgh, Scotland)*, *49*(5), 931–943. DOI: 10.1177/0042098011435846

Iyer, S., Kabanda, S., & Al-Haidari, N. N. (2021). The Use of Social Media by SMEs. In *AMCIS*.

Jaman, S. F. I. H., Damit, N. J. H., Ishak, N. A., Ason, M. L. A., Tamin, M. R., Tangphadungrutch, K., & Almunawar, M. N. (2020). The adoption of social media as marketing tools: Case small and medium enterprises in Brunei Darussalam. *International Journal of Asian Business and Information Management*, *11*(2), 28–50. DOI: 10.4018/IJABIM.2020040103

Jiménez-Zarco, A. I., Clemente-Almendros, J. A., González-González, I., & Aracil-Jordà, J. (2021). Female micro-entrepreneurs and social networks: Diagnostic analysis of the influence of social-media marketing strategies on brand financial performance. *Frontiers in Psychology*, *12*, 630058. DOI: 10.3389/fpsyg.2021.630058 PMID: 33912108

Kelly, G., & McAdam, M. (2023). Women entrepreneurs negotiating identities in liminal digital spaces. *Entrepreneurship Theory and Practice*, *47*(5), 1942–1970. DOI: 10.1177/10422587221115363

Melissa, E., Hamidati, A., Saraswati, M. S., & Flor, A. G. (2013). Investigating the potentials of social media to support women entrepreneurship in Indonesian urban areas. *Proceedings of the Sixth International Conference on Information and Communications Technologies and Development: Notes* - Volume 2. DOI: 10.1145/2517899.2517921

Reich, Y. (2010). My method is better! *Research in Engineering Design*, *21*(3), 137–142. DOI: 10.1007/s00163-010-0092-3

Tang, C. S. (2022). Innovative technology and operations for alleviating poverty through women's economic empowerment. *Production and Operations Management*, *31*(1), 32–45. DOI: 10.1111/poms.13349

Wood, J., & Khan, G. F. (2016). Social business adoption: An empirical analysis. *Business Information Review*, *33*(1), 28–39. DOI: 10.1177/0266382116631851

Yáñez-Valdés, C., & Guerrero, M. (2024). Determinants and impacts of digital entrepreneurship: A pre-and post-COVID-19 perspective. *Technovation*, 132, 102983.

Yusniza, K. (2011). E-Consumer Behaviour: Exploring the Drivers of E-Shopping. *European Journal of Social Sciences, 23*.

KEY TERMS AND DEFINITIONS

Algorithm Bias: The inherent preference of digital platforms that may favor male-led businesses in ad placements, search rankings, and visibility, leading to unequal opportunities for women entrepreneurs.

Artificial Intelligence (AI) in Entrepreneurship: The use of AI-driven tools such as customer analytics, automated marketing, chatbots, and predictive modelling to enhance business decision-making and efficiency.

Blockchain Technology: A decentralized and secure digital ledger that helps women entrepreneurs manage financial transactions, protect intellectual property, and improve financial inclusion without traditional banking constraints.

Cyber Harassment and Online Safety: The risks associated with gender-based abuse, trolling, and fraud that female entrepreneurs face while conducting business online.

Digital Empowerment: The process through which women entrepreneurs leverage digital tools, particularly social media, to overcome traditional barriers, access new markets, and grow their businesses.

Digital Financial Services: Online banking, mobile payments, and peer-to-peer lending platforms like M-Pesa and crowdfunding sites (GoFundMe, iFundWomen) that provide women with access to capital and financial management tools.

Digital Skill Gap: The disparity in technological knowledge and capabilities that can prevent women from fully utilizing digital platforms for business success.

E-Commerce Platforms: Online marketplaces such as Shopify, Etsy, and Amazon Handmade that enable women entrepreneurs to sell products and services without the need for a physical store.

Entrepreneurial Resilience Capital: A combination of psychological strength, strategic flexibility, and continuous learning that helps women entrepreneurs sustain and grow their businesses despite challenges.

Feminist Economic Thought: The economic perspective that emphasizes gender equality in entrepreneurship and the role of digital tools in reducing historical financial and social barriers for women.

Influencer Marketing: A digital marketing strategy where women entrepreneurs collaborate with social media influencers to boost brand credibility and reach a wider audience.

Social Capital in Entrepreneurship: The networks, relationships, and communities that women entrepreneurs build through digital platforms to access mentorship, collaboration, and business growth opportunities.

Social Commerce: The integration of e-commerce within social media platforms, allowing customers to make purchases directly through features like Instagram's "Shop Now" button.

Social Media Entrepreneurship: The practice of using social media platforms like Instagram, Facebook, and LinkedIn for business operations, marketing, customer engagement, and revenue generation.

Work-Life Balance in Digital Entrepreneurship: The challenge of managing business activities while maintaining personal and family responsibilities due to the 24/7 nature of online businesses.

Chapter 4
Empowering Business Through Contemporary Technology Instruction:
Global Perspectives, Practices, and Societal Impact

Satya Subrahmanyam
http://orcid.org/0000-0003-0441-2742
Holy Spirit University of Kaslik, Lebanon

ABSTRACT

This chapter, "Current Technology Instruction for the Business Sector," examines the pivotal role of technology education in shaping a skilled workforce for the digital economy. The rapid advancement of technologies like artificial intelligence, blockchain, data analytics, and cybersecurity has transformed business operations, creating a demand for digital competencies. Addressing this need, technology instruction is increasingly diverse, encompassing online platforms, corporate training, and certifications. Through global case studies, the chapter highlights how such education fosters economic growth, bridges skill gaps, and promotes inclusivity by empowering underserved communities. Challenges and future trends, including personalized learning and micro-credentials, underscore the essential nature of continuous learning for competitive and social advancement.

DOI: 10.4018/979-8-3373-0629-2.ch004

ht © 2026, IGI Global Scientific Publishing. Copying or distributing in print or electronic forms without written permission of IGI Global Scientific Publishing is prohibited. Use of this chapter to generative artificial intelligence (AI) technologies is expressly prohibited. The publisher reserves all rights to license its use for generative AI training and machine learning model development.

1. INTRODUCTION

1.1 Contextualizing Rapid Technological Transformation in the Global Business Environment

The global business landscape is experiencing an unprecedented pace of technological transformation driven by advances in artificial intelligence, big data analytics, cloud computing, and digital platforms. These technologies are fundamentally altering how organizations create value, coordinate work, and compete across markets. Recent scholarship emphasizes that digital transformation is not merely a technological upgrade but a systemic change affecting organizational structures, decision-making processes, and skill requirements (Brynjolfsson & McAfee, 2020). As firms increasingly rely on algorithmic systems and data-driven strategies, technological competence has become a central determinant of organizational performance and resilience. Consequently, the capacity of businesses to adapt depends heavily on the quality and relevance of technology instruction available to current and future workforces.

1.2 The Growing Importance of Technology Instruction for Workforce Readiness and Social Empowerment

In response to these shifts, technology instruction has emerged as a critical mechanism for workforce readiness. Contemporary research highlights that workers now require a hybrid skill set that combines digital, analytical, and socio-cognitive capabilities to effectively engage with advanced technologies (Autor et al., 2022). Technology instruction plays a pivotal role in equipping individuals with these competencies and enabling them to navigate increasingly complex and automated work environments. Beyond employability, such instruction contributes to broader social empowerment by expanding access to economic opportunities, supporting entrepreneurial activity, and enabling participation in digitally mediated markets. Scholars argue that when technology education is inclusive and context-sensitive, it can mitigate job polarization and reduce vulnerability to technological displacement (Acemoglu & Restrepo, 2020). On the contrary, inadequate access to high-quality instruction risks reinforcing existing inequalities, particularly for low-skilled workers and those in emerging economies.

1.3 Purpose, Scope, and Structure of the Chapter

The purpose of this chapter is to examine current technology instruction for the business sector through an integrated lens that connects skill development, organizational performance, and social empowerment. The chapter focuses on how instructional approaches - spanning higher education, vocational training, corporate learning, and micro-credentialing - can be designed to align with rapidly evolving business needs while fostering inclusive growth. Drawing on contemporary literature, the chapter explores key technologies shaping business instruction, pedagogical models that support applied learning, and institutional arrangements that enable scalable and sustainable skill development. Structurally, the chapter begins with conceptual foundations, followed by global perspectives, practical illustrations, and a discussion of challenges and future directions. This introductory section establishes the rationale for positioning technology instruction as both an economic and social imperative.

1.4 Relevance to Developed and Developing Economies

While the demand for technology instruction is global, its implications differ across economic contexts. In developed economies, the primary challenge lies in continuous upskilling and reskilling to prevent skill obsolescence as technologies evolve rapidly. Research suggests that lifelong learning systems and employer-led training initiatives are increasingly essential to maintain workforce adaptability and productivity (van Laar et al., 2019). In developing economies, however, the emphasis is often on foundational digital skills and applied business technologies that can enhance productivity, formalize enterprises, and support youth employment. Studies indicate that targeted technology instruction can generate significant social returns by enabling inclusion in global value chains and fostering local innovation ecosystems (Qureshi, 2023).

Across both contexts, the digital divide extends beyond access to infrastructure to include disparities in skills, instructional quality, and relevance to labor-market needs. Addressing these challenges requires coordinated efforts among educators, businesses, and policymakers to ensure that technology instruction supports equitable participation in the digital economy. As digital transformation continues to reshape business globally, understanding technology instruction as a socially embedded process is essential for achieving sustainable and inclusive development outcomes.

2. CONCEPTUAL FOUNDATIONS OF TECHNOLOGY INSTRUCTION IN BUSINESS

Technology instruction in business is grounded in theoretical perspectives that link learning, technology, and organizational practice. It draws on constructivist, experiential, and socio-technical frameworks to explain how digital tools shape knowledge creation, skill development, and decision-making. Understanding these conceptual foundations is essential for designing instructional models that align technological capabilities with managerial competence, ethical awareness, and evolving business realities.

2.1 Defining Current Technology Instruction in the Business Context

Current technology instruction in the business context refers to structured learning processes designed to develop competencies required to effectively deploy, manage, and critically engage with contemporary digital technologies. These technologies include artificial intelligence, data analytics, enterprise platforms, automation tools, and digital collaboration systems that increasingly underpin organizational operations. Unlike traditional IT training, contemporary technology instruction emphasizes applied digital fluency, data-informed decision-making, and the integration of technology with managerial and strategic functions (Vial, 2019). It is therefore interdisciplinary by nature, blending technical skills with business acumen, ethical awareness, and adaptive learning capabilities. In this sense, technology instruction is not limited to skill transmission but serves as a capability-building mechanism that enables organizations and individuals to respond to continuous technological change.

2.2 Evolution of Technology-Enabled Learning in Business Education and Training

Technology-enabled learning in business has evolved significantly over the past two decades. Early approaches focused primarily on computer literacy and enterprise software training. Since 2020, however, the emphasis has shifted toward digitally mediated, flexible, and personalized learning environments that support continuous upskilling. The proliferation of learning management systems, virtual simulations, AI-driven adaptive learning tools, and micro-credential platforms has transformed both academic and corporate training landscapes (Bond et al., 2021). Business education institutions increasingly integrate experiential learning through simulations and data labs, while organizations adopt blended and on-demand learning models aligned with rapidly changing skill needs. This evolution reflects a broader recognition that static curricula are insufficient in a context where technological competencies quickly become obsolete.

Table 1. Evolution of technology-enabled learning in business

Phase	Dominant Focus	Key Characteristics
Pre-2010	Computer literacy	Basic IT skills, software training
2010–2019	E-learning and LMS	Online courses, content digitization
2020–present	Intelligent and adaptive learning	AI-driven personalization, simulations, micro-credentials

2.3 Linking Technology Instruction to Social Empowerment, Employability, and Inclusion

Beyond organizational performance, technology instruction plays a crucial role in social empowerment. Research demonstrates that access to relevant digital and business-oriented instruction enhances employability by improving job readiness, career mobility, and entrepreneurial capacity (Acemoglu & Restrepo, 2020). For marginalized populations, including women, youth, and workers in informal sectors, targeted technology instruction can reduce entry barriers to the formal economy and support participation in digitally enabled value chains (Qureshi, 2023). Importantly, the social impact of instruction depends not only on access but also on relevance, quality, and contextual alignment with labor-market needs. Inclusive instructional design - such as flexible delivery modes, localized content, and competency-based assessment - has been shown to improve learning outcomes and promote equity in skill development (Van Laar et al., 2019).

2.4 Theoretical Lenses Informing Technology Instruction in Business

The conceptual grounding of technology instruction in business draws on multiple theoretical perspectives. **Human capital theory** frames technology instruction as an investment that enhances productivity and economic returns for both individuals and organizations. From this perspective, continuous upskilling is essential to maintaining competitiveness in technology-intensive environments (Autor et al., 2022). **Digital empowerment theory** extends this view by emphasizing agency, participation, and the capacity of individuals to leverage technology for social and economic advancement. This lens highlights the role of instruction in enabling informed and autonomous engagement with digital systems rather than passive usage.

A complementary perspective is offered by **socio-technical systems theory**, which stresses the interdependence between technological tools and social structures. According to this approach, effective technology instruction must address not only technical functionality but also organizational culture, work design, and human–technology interaction (Vial, 2019). Table 2 presents a comparative overview of these theoretical lenses and their implications for business-oriented technology instruction.

Table 2. Theoretical lenses underpinning technology instruction in business

Theory	Core Assumption	Implications for Instruction
Human capital theory	Skills increase economic productivity	Focus on measurable competencies and employability
Digital empowerment	Technology enables agency and inclusion	Emphasis on access, relevance, and learner autonomy
Socio-technical systems	Technology and social systems co-evolve	Integration of technical, organizational, and human factors

The conceptual foundations of technology instruction in business extend beyond technical training to encompass broader economic and social objectives. By grounding instructional strategies in robust theoretical frameworks and aligning them with evolving business realities, technology instruction can serve as a powerful lever for employability, inclusion, and sustainable development across diverse economic contexts.

3. CURRENT TECHNOLOGIES SHAPING BUSINESS INSTRUCTION

Business instruction is being reshaped by a range of digital technologies that influence both learning processes and educational outcomes. Advances in artificial intelligence, data analytics, digital platforms, automation, and immersive tools have transformed how knowledge is delivered, applied, and assessed. These technologies enable more personalized, interactive, and practice-oriented learning environments aligned with contemporary business needs.

3.1 Artificial Intelligence and Data Analytics in Business Learning

Artificial intelligence (AI) and data analytics have become foundational technologies shaping contemporary business instruction. AI-enabled learning systems are increasingly used to personalize educational pathways, recommend content, and provide real-time feedback based on learner behavior and performance. In business education, these systems support the development of analytical thinking, data literacy, and evidence-based decision-making - competencies that are now essential across managerial roles (Chui et al., 2018). Analytics-driven instructional tools allow learners to engage with real datasets, predictive models, and visualization platforms, thereby bridging the gap between theory and practice. Research indicates that exposure to AI-supported learning environments enhances problem-solving skills and improves learners' ability to interpret complex business information (Ransbotham et al., 2017). Scholars also caution that AI-driven instruction must be designed transparently to avoid reinforcing bias and over-reliance on automated judgment, particularly in management education contexts.

3.2 Digital Platforms, Learning Management Systems, and Virtual Collaboration Tools

Digital platforms and learning management systems (LMS) continue to play a central role in business instruction, particularly in blended and fully online formats. Since 2020, there has been a significant expansion in the use of cloud-based LMS, enterprise collaboration tools, and video-conferencing platforms to support synchronous and asynchronous learning. These technologies enable geographically dispersed learners to collaborate on projects, simulate organizational workflows, and engage in peer learning that mirrors contemporary workplace practices (Bond et al., 2021). Virtual collaboration tools such as shared workspaces, project management software, and communication platforms foster teamwork, leadership development, and cross-cultural competence. Empirical studies suggest that when effectively integrated into curricula, digital platforms enhance learner engagement and support the development of transferable business skills (Subrahmanyam, 20252). Nonetheless, their effectiveness depends on instructional design quality, faculty competence, and learners' digital readiness.

3.3 Automation, Robotics, and Process Technologies

Automation and robotics are increasingly embedded in business operations, particularly in manufacturing, logistics, retail, and service sectors. As a result, business instruction is adapting to include learning about robotic process automation (RPA), intelligent workflows, and technology-enabled process optimization. Instructional programs now incorporate process-mapping tools, automation software, and case-based simulations to help learners understand how routine tasks can be redesigned or augmented by machines (Acemoglu & Restrepo, 2020). Rather than focusing solely on technical operation, business-oriented instruction emphasizes strategic oversight, change management, and the human implications of automation. Research highlights that such instruction is critical for preparing managers to make informed decisions about technology adoption while mitigating workforce displacement and ethical risks (Autor et al., 2022). Consequently, automation-related learning increasingly blends technical awareness with organizational and social considerations.

3.4 Blockchain, Fintech, and Emerging Digital Infrastructures

Blockchain and financial technologies (fintech) represent another set of transformative tools influencing business instruction. Blockchain-based systems introduce new models of trust, transparency, and decentralized governance, with applications spanning supply chain management, digital identity, and smart contracts. Business education programs are incorporating blockchain concepts through experiential learning modules that simulate transactions, auditing processes, and decentralized decision-making environments (Treiblmaier, 2019). Likewise, fintech innovations - such as digital payments, peer-to-peer lending, and algorithmic credit scoring - are reshaping financial services and entrepreneurial ecosystems. Instruction in these areas equips learners with an understanding of digital infrastructures that underpin modern markets and supports financial inclusion initiatives, particularly in emerging economies (Gomber et al., 2017). The pedagogical challenge lies in balancing technical complexity with conceptual clarity, ensuring that learners grasp both operational mechanisms and regulatory, ethical, and social implications.

3.5 Immersive Technologies for Experiential Learning

Immersive technologies, including augmented reality (AR), virtual reality (VR), simulations, and digital twins, are gaining prominence as tools for experiential business learning. These technologies enable learners to engage in realistic, risk-free environments that replicate complex organizational scenarios such as supply chain disruptions, leadership challenges, or strategic negotiations. Studies show that immersive learning environments enhance cognitive engagement, retention, and the transfer of learning to real-world contexts (Subrahmanyam, 2025). Digital twins - virtual representations of physical or organizational systems - are particularly valuable for teaching operations management and strategic planning, as they allow learners to test decisions and observe outcomes dynamically. While immersive technologies require significant investment and instructional expertise, their potential to support deep learning and practical competence makes them increasingly attractive for business schools and corporate training programs alike.

3.6 Integrative Implications for Business Instruction

Collectively, these technologies are reshaping not only how business instruction is delivered but also what is taught and valued. The convergence of AI, platforms, automation, blockchain, and immersive tools reflects a shift toward learning environments that are data-driven, interactive, and closely aligned with real business ecosystems. Scholars emphasize that the educational value of these technologies lies not in their novelty but in their pedagogical integration - specifically, how they support critical thinking, ethical reasoning, and socially responsible decision-making (Vial, 2019). As businesses continue to navigate digital transformation, instructional approaches that leverage these technologies thoughtfully can enhance workforce readiness while contributing to broader goals of inclusion and empowerment. The challenge for educators and trainers is therefore to adopt a strategic, learner-centered approach that aligns technological capabilities with meaningful educational outcomes.

Figure 1. Current Technologies Shaping Business Instruction

Author, (2025)

4. INSTRUCTIONAL MODELS AND PEDAGOGICAL APPROACHES

Instructional models and pedagogical approaches in business and professional education have evolved considerably in response to accelerating technological innovation, shifting labor market demands, and the imperative for lifelong learning. Effective models now blend digital and experiential elements, recognize modular learning pathways, and forge strong connections between academia and industry. The following sections examine key contemporary approaches.

4.1 Technology-Enhanced and Blended Learning Models

Technology-enhanced learning (TEL) and blended learning models constitute a cornerstone of modern instructional design. Blended learning integrates face-to-face instruction with online components and digital platforms, allowing flexibility in where, when, and how learners engage with content. The approach is informed by research demonstrating that well-designed blended environments can improve learner engagement, support differentiated instruction, and foster cognitive flexibility among students (Mohamed et al., 2025; see also studies on quality online teaching and immersive experiences enhancing blended models). Blended models typically include asynchronous elements - such as recorded lectures, readings, and adaptive exercises - and synchronous interactions where learners engage in discussion, collaboration, and real-time problem solving (University of Wollongong in Dubai, 2025). These combinations support deeper engagement than traditional lectures alone and align learning with diverse learner needs and schedules.

The rapid adoption of blended approaches following disruptions such as the COVID-19 pandemic has further underscored their resilience and pedagogical value. Research finds that blended formats outperform purely traditional instruction by offering personalized feedback loops, adaptive pathways, and stronger alignment with 21st-century competencies such as self-directed learning and digital literacy (Mohamed et al., 2025; University of Wollongong in Dubai, 2025). The fundamental pedagogical shift lies in centering learners' active participation, supported by digital tools that scaffold learning rather than merely transmit content.

4.2 Experiential, Problem-Based, and Simulation-Driven Instruction

Experiential learning models emphasize "learning by doing," where knowledge emerges from active engagement with realistic tasks and reflection on experience. In business education, this includes problem-based learning (PBL), simulation-based learning (SBL), and challenge-based frameworks that immerse learners in complex, real-world scenarios. These approaches contrast sharply with traditional lecture-centric delivery by positioning learners as active constructors of knowledge (Rosário & Raimundo, 2024).

Simulation-driven instruction uses digital or physical simulations to replicate business environments - such as supply chain operations, negotiation contexts, and decision-making under uncertainty. By engaging with high-fidelity simulations, learners can experiment with strategic choices, observe outcomes, and develop problem-solving competencies in risk-free settings. Scholars emphasize that PBL and SBL cultivate critical thinking, collaboration, and adaptive expertise by asking students to investigate real problems, work in teams, and apply theoretical frameworks to practice (Rosário & Raimundo, 2024).

Challenge-based learning (CBL), a variant of experiential pedagogy, situates learners within authentic challenges that require interdisciplinary thinking and collaboration to address societal or organizational problems. This pedagogical orientation integrates knowledge acquisition with meaningful action, strengthening competencies essential for contemporary business practice (see challenge-based learning frameworks). Across these experiential models, the common thread is the alignment of learning activities with real work practices, thereby bridging classroom knowledge with professional performance.

4.3 Microlearning, Modular Credentials, and Digital Badges

Microlearning and modular credentialing represent an increasingly important instructional strategy within lifelong learning ecosystems. Microlearning focuses on short, focused learning episodes that target specific skills or knowledge units. These bite-sized modules accommodate busy professionals and align with cognitive research suggesting spaced, focused learning improves retention and transfer of skills.

Closely linked to microlearning are micro-credentials and digital badges, which serve as portable verifiable artifacts of competency attainment. Micro-credentials break traditional degrees into stackable units that learners can accumulate over time, often linked to specific workplace skills such as data analytics, leadership, or digital marketing (Strielkowski, 2025; Angwaomaodoko, 2026). Digital badges, in particular, provide visual, standardized indicators of discrete achievements that learners can share across digital platforms to signal competency to employers and peers.

Research indicates that while employers and learners value micro-credentials as evidence of targeted competencies, they do not yet supplant traditional degrees; rather, they complement them by enhancing specificity and employability outcomes (Angwaomaodoko, 2026; Strielkowski, 2025). Micro-credential frameworks are especially effective when tied to industry standards and designed with clear criteria, assessment processes, and alignment with labor market needs.

4.4 Corporate–Academic Partnerships and Industry-Driven Curricula

The integration of industry expertise into academic curricula ensures that instructional models remain relevant to contemporary business challenges. Corporate–academic partnerships facilitate co-design of courses, guest lectures from industry professionals, internships, and project collaborations that ground theoretical learning in practical application. Such partnerships also support dual learning scenarios where students alternate between academic study and workplace immersion, thereby smoothing transitions into professional contexts and enhancing employability (Istrate & Velea, 2024).

Industry-driven curricula typically embed real case studies, work placements, and strategic projects into learning pathways. These connections enable learners to build networks, apply classroom learning directly to business problems, and cultivate competencies that align with organizational needs. Corporate involvement in curriculum design ensures academic programs respond rapidly to technological and market shifts, an increasingly crucial feature in volatile business environments.

4.5 Lifelong Learning and Reskilling Frameworks

Finally, instructional models must support lifelong learning and continuous reskilling. Global labor markets are characterized by rapid technological change, requiring professionals to update competencies continuously. Lifelong learning frameworks emphasize flexible pathways that accommodate learners at different career stages and provide opportunities for upskilling and reskilling without the constraints of traditional program structures.

Digital platforms and modular credentials play a central role in lifelong learning ecosystems, enabling learners to pursue just-in-time education that aligns with evolving job requirements. These frameworks are supported by policy and institutional strategies that recognize prior learning, integrate informal and formal education systems, and promote equitable access to learning opportunities (WOU, 2025). Lifelong learning is not merely a pedagogical ideal but a necessary infrastructure for sustaining professional relevance in a rapidly changing global economy.

Figure 2. Instructional Models and Pedagogical Approaches

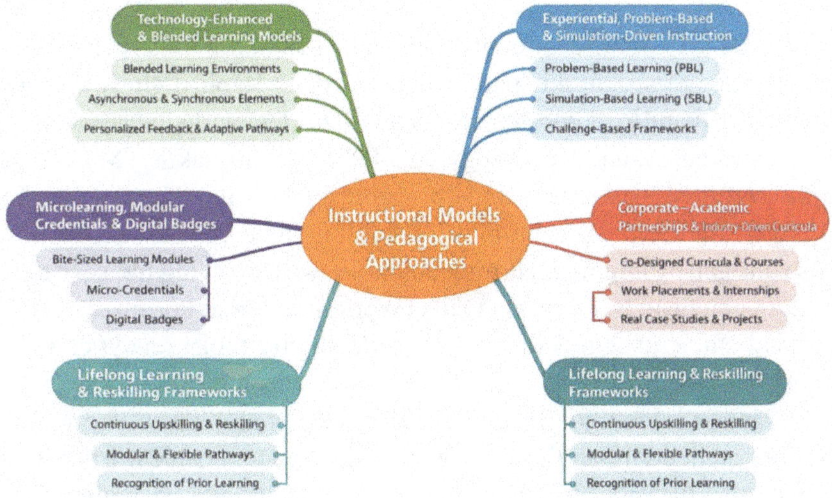

Author, (2025)

Contemporary instructional models blend technology-enhanced and blended learning with experiential, modular, and industry-aligned approaches. These pedagogies promote active engagement, facilitate flexible learning pathways, and prepare learners to navigate complex business environments. By integrating microlearning, real-world problem solving, and corporate ecosystems, instructional design aligns educational outcomes with workforce needs while supporting lifelong learning imperatives.

5. TECHNOLOGY INSTRUCTION AS A DRIVER OF SOCIAL EMPOWERMENT

Technology instruction has emerged as a critical mechanism for advancing social empowerment in contemporary economies. Beyond enhancing organizational efficiency and competitiveness, technology-oriented education increasingly plays a transformative role in addressing structural inequalities, expanding economic participation, and promoting ethical and sustainable business practices. When strategically designed and inclusively delivered, technology instruction can bridge skill gaps, empower marginalized communities, and contribute to more equitable and resilient economic systems.

5.1 Bridging Skill Gaps and Enhancing Employability

One of the most significant contributions of technology instruction lies in its capacity to bridge persistent skill gaps in labor markets. Rapid digital transformation has intensified demand for competencies such as data literacy, digital problem-solving, automation awareness, and technology-enabled decision-making. Many graduates and working professionals remain underprepared for these requirements, particularly in emerging and developing economies. Technology-focused instructional programs help close this gap by aligning learning outcomes with evolving industry needs and emphasizing practical, transferable skills (World Economic Forum, 2023).

Empirical studies suggest that exposure to digital tools, analytics platforms, and simulation-based learning significantly improves employability by enhancing learners' adaptability and job readiness (Elmoazen et al., 2023). Short-cycle programs, micro-credentials, and applied technology courses enable learners to upskill or reskill without the time and financial constraints of traditional degree pathways. In this sense, technology instruction functions as a social equalizer, enabling individuals to access emerging job opportunities and remain economically relevant in volatile labor markets.

5.2 Empowering SMEs, Entrepreneurs, and Marginalized Groups

Technology instruction also plays a vital role in empowering small and medium-sized enterprises (SMEs), entrepreneurs, and marginalized populations. SMEs often lack access to specialized expertise and advanced infrastructure, making them vulnerable in increasingly digitalized markets. Educational initiatives that focus on digital marketing, e-commerce platforms, financial technologies, and process automation equip SME owners and entrepreneurs with tools to scale operations, access global markets, and enhance productivity (UNCTAD, 2021).

For marginalized groups - including rural communities, refugees, and informal sector workers - technology instruction can facilitate economic inclusion by lowering entry barriers to entrepreneurship and employment. Online learning platforms and mobile-based training programs have proven particularly effective in expanding access to business education in resource-constrained settings (International Labour Organization, 2022). By enabling individuals to acquire market-relevant digital skills, technology instruction supports self-employment, income diversification, and community-level economic resilience.

5.3 Gender Inclusion and Equitable Access to Business Technology Education

Despite progress in digital access, gender disparities persist in technology education and digital skill acquisition. Women remain underrepresented in technology-intensive fields and often face systemic barriers such as limited access to training, socio-cultural constraints, and biased instructional designs. Technology instruction that is intentionally gender-responsive can address these inequities by promoting inclusive curricula, flexible delivery models, and supportive learning environments (UNESCO, 2017).

Research highlights programs integrating mentorship, role models, and community-based learning significantly improve women's participation and retention in technology-oriented business education (Nkrumah & Scott, 2022). Inclusive instructional strategies that consider intersectionality - such as the compounded effects of gender, socioeconomic status, and geography - are essential for ensuring equitable outcomes. When women gain access to technology instruction, the benefits extend beyond individual empowerment to broader social outcomes, including improved household welfare, increased innovation, and more inclusive economic growth.

5.4 Technology Instruction for Sustainable Development and Ethical Business Practices

Technology instruction also contributes to social empowerment by fostering awareness of sustainability and ethical responsibility in business. As organizations increasingly deploy technologies such as artificial intelligence, automation, and data analytics, the social and environmental implications of these tools have become more pronounced. Educational programs that integrate sustainability frameworks, ethical reasoning, and responsible innovation principles prepare learners to make informed decisions that balance economic performance with social impact (Vial, 2019).

Instructional models emphasizing green technologies, sustainable supply chains, and responsible digital governance align business education with the United Nations Sustainable Development Goals (SDGs). Studies indicate that learners exposed to ethics-oriented technology instruction demonstrate greater sensitivity to issues such as data privacy, algorithmic bias, environmental impact, and social accountability (Floridi et al., 2018). In this way, technology instruction supports not only employability but also the development of socially responsible leaders capable of guiding organizations toward inclusive and sustainable futures.

Figure 3. Technology Instruction as a Driver of Social Empowerment

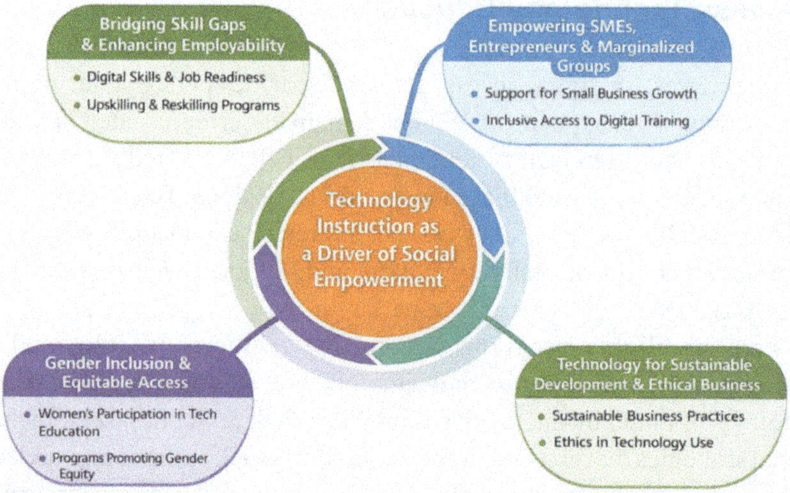

Author, (2025)

5.5 Integrative Perspective on Social Empowerment

Collectively, these dimensions underscore that technology instruction is not merely a technical endeavor but a socio-economic intervention. Its empowering potential depends on accessibility, relevance, and ethical grounding. Instructional strategies that prioritize inclusivity, contextual relevance, and lifelong learning pathways are more likely to generate meaningful social outcomes. Policymakers, educators, and industry stakeholders therefore share responsibility for ensuring that technology instruction contributes to empowerment rather than reinforcing existing inequalities.

6. GLOBAL AND CROSS-CULTURAL PERSPECTIVES

Technology instruction does not unfold within a uniform global context. Instead, it is shaped by economic development levels, institutional capacity, cultural norms, and policy environments. As digital transformation accelerates worldwide, understanding global and cross-cultural differences in technology instruction becomes essential for designing inclusive, effective, and contextually relevant educational strategies. Comparative perspectives reveal both shared challenges and divergent pathways in how technology-enabled business education is conceptualized and implemented across regions.

6.1 Comparative Insights from Developed, Emerging, and Developing Economies

In developed economies, technology instruction is often characterized by advanced digital infrastructure, strong industry–academia linkages, and widespread access to learning technologies. Business education institutions in these contexts increasingly integrate artificial intelligence, data analytics, immersive simulations, and micro-credentials into curricula to support innovation and lifelong learning (Subrahmanyam, 2025). The emphasis is typically on advanced skills, such as strategic analytics, digital leadership, and responsible technology governance.

Emerging economies, by contrast, occupy an intermediate position where technology instruction is expanding rapidly but unevenly. Countries such as India, Brazil, and Vietnam have made significant investments in digital education platforms and entrepreneurship-focused training to support growing innovation ecosystems. Disparities in access between urban and rural areas persist, and institutional capacity often varies widely across regions (UNESCO, 2023). In these contexts, technology instruction frequently prioritizes employability, entrepreneurship, and digital inclusion alongside advanced skills development.

In developing economies, technology instruction is more directly linked to foundational capacity building and economic participation. Educational initiatives often focus on basic digital literacy, mobile-based learning, and applied business skills that can support self-employment and SME development. While resource constraints limit access to advanced technologies, evidence suggests that even modest technology-enabled instruction can yield substantial social and economic benefits when aligned with local needs (Rodríguez-Segura, 2022). These comparative insights underscore that technology instruction must be differentiated rather than universally standardized.

6.2 Contextual Challenges: Infrastructure, Policy, Culture, and the Digital Divide

Across all regions, contextual challenges significantly shape the effectiveness of technology instruction. Infrastructure remains a critical determinant, particularly in low-income and rural settings where unreliable electricity, limited broadband access, and high data costs restrict participation in digital learning. The digital divide is not only technological but also socio-economic, reflecting disparities in income, education, gender, and geography (UN DESA, 2021).

Policy environments also play a decisive role. Supportive national strategies for digital education, skills development, and innovation can accelerate adoption and scale, while fragmented or outdated regulatory frameworks can hinder progress.

Cultural factors further influence learner engagement and pedagogical effectiveness. Attitudes toward technology, authority, collaboration, and risk-taking vary across societies and shape how learners interact with digital tools and instructional models (Hofstede et al., 2010).

Language barriers and curriculum relevance also present challenges, particularly when instructional content is imported wholesale from global providers without contextual adaptation. Without attention to these factors, technology instruction risks reinforcing existing inequalities rather than mitigating them.

6.3 Localization of Technology Instruction for Regional Business Needs

Localization is therefore a central principle in effective global technology instruction. Localization involves adapting content, pedagogical approaches, and delivery mechanisms to reflect regional economic structures, cultural norms, and business practices. Technology instruction in agrarian economies may emphasize digital supply chains, mobile finance, and market access platforms, while instruction in manufacturing-oriented regions may focus on automation, process optimization, and quality management systems (World Economic Forum, 2025).

Localized instruction also enhances relevance by incorporating region-specific case studies, regulatory contexts, and entrepreneurial challenges. Research suggests that learners are more likely to transfer knowledge into practice when instructional content reflects familiar contexts and addresses tangible local problems (Rincon-Flores et al., 2024). Localization supports linguistic inclusion by delivering content in local languages and culturally resonant formats, thereby expanding access and engagement.

Importantly, localization does not imply isolation. Rather, it involves blending global best practices with local realities, ensuring that learners develop globally transferable competencies while remaining grounded in regional business ecosystems.

6.4 Role of International Organizations and Global Collaborations

International organizations and global partnerships play a pivotal role in shaping technology instruction across borders. Institutions such as UNESCO, the World Bank, the International Labour Organization, and the World Economic Forum provide policy guidance, funding, and research that inform national strategies and institutional practices. These organizations support initiatives focused on digital skills development, gender inclusion, and workforce reskilling, particularly in low-

and middle-income countries (International Labour Organization, 2022; World Economic Forum, 2023).

Global collaborations between universities, corporations, and non-governmental organizations further enable knowledge transfer and capacity building. Cross-border programs, joint certifications, and open educational resources facilitate access to high-quality instruction while allowing local adaptation. Such collaborations also promote the diffusion of innovative pedagogies, including blended learning, micro-credentials, and experiential instruction.

Scholars caution that global initiatives must avoid one-size-fits-all models. Effective collaboration requires equitable partnerships that respect local agency, encourage co-creation, and prioritize sustainability over short-term interventions (Subrahmanyam, 2025).

Figure 4. Global and cross-cultural perspectives

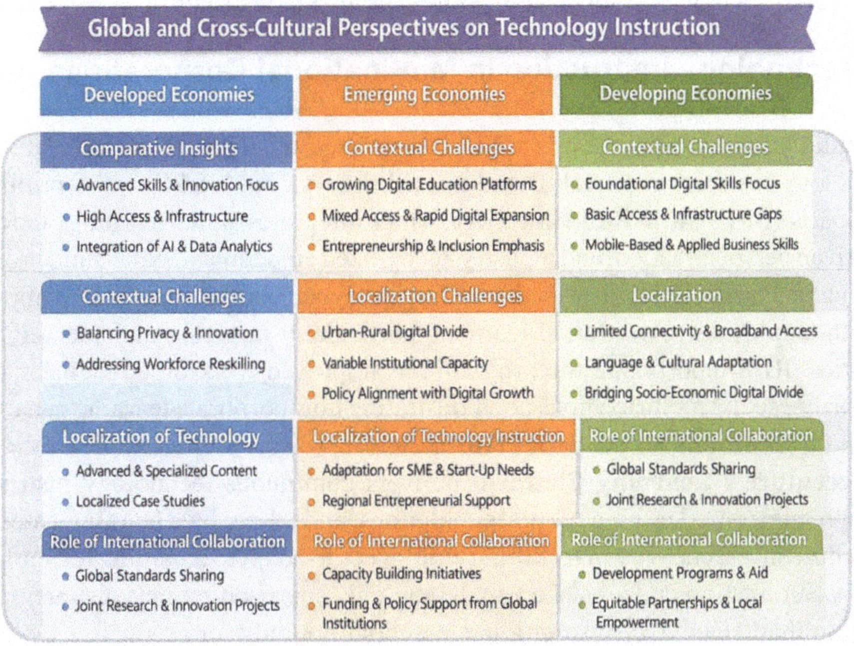

6.5 Integrative Global Perspective

Taken together, global and cross-cultural perspectives highlight that technology instruction is both a global phenomenon and a deeply contextual practice. Its success depends on balancing global standards with local relevance, technological ambition with infrastructural realities, and innovation with inclusion. Recognizing these dynamics enables educators, policymakers, and organizations to design instructional models that are responsive to diverse learner populations and evolving economic conditions.

7. CASE ILLUSTRATIONS AND PRACTICAL APPLICATIONS

The practical value of technology instruction becomes most visible when examined through real-world applications. Across corporate environments, higher education institutions, and public–private collaborations, technology-driven instructional models have been deployed to enhance workforce capability, organizational agility, and social inclusion. The following case illustrations demonstrate how technology instruction operates in diverse contexts, including multinational corporations, business schools, and underrepresented regions in the Global South.

7.1 Technology Instruction in Multinational Corporations

Multinational corporations (MNCs) have been at the forefront of leveraging technology instruction to reskill and upskill their global workforce. A prominent example is **IBM's SkillsBuild initiative**, which integrates digital learning platforms, AI-driven personalization, and industry-recognized credentials. SkillsBuild provides training in data analytics, artificial intelligence, cybersecurity, and cloud computing to both employees and external learners, particularly targeting underserved communities. IBM reports that the program has improved workforce readiness while supporting social inclusion goals, demonstrating how corporate learning can extend beyond organizational boundaries (IBM, 2021).

Accenture's Learning Platform delivers continuous technology instruction through immersive learning, virtual simulations, and AI-enabled learning pathways. Accenture invests heavily in reskilling employees to adapt to emerging technologies such as automation and advanced analytics. This approach reflects a strategic recognition that technology instruction is essential not only for productivity but also for long-term employability in rapidly changing labor markets (Accenture, 2022).

7.2 Business Schools and Executive Education Initiatives

Business schools and executive education providers have also reconfigured their instructional models to incorporate digital technologies and experiential learning. **Harvard Business School Online (HBSO)** offers technology-enhanced programs that combine asynchronous digital content with interactive simulations and peer collaboration. Courses such as *Digital Innovation and Strategy* use real-world business cases and analytics tools to develop strategic thinking in technology-driven contexts. Research indicates that participants in HBSO programs report improved decision-making capabilities and greater confidence in applying digital tools in managerial roles (Harvard Business School, 2021).

Another notable case is **INSEAD's Executive Education**, which integrates digital platforms, virtual classrooms, and data-driven simulations to deliver globally accessible programs. INSEAD's focus on technology-enabled leadership development illustrates how executive education can balance global reach with contextual relevance, catering to executives across regions while addressing local business challenges (INSEAD, 2022).

7.3 Public–Private Partnerships for Workforce Empowerment

Public–private partnerships (PPPs) play a critical role in scaling technology instruction for workforce empowerment. A widely cited example is **Google Career Certificates**, developed in collaboration with governments, universities, and non-profit organizations. These certificates provide short, job-relevant training in areas such as IT support, data analytics, and digital marketing. Evaluations show that learners who complete these programs experience improved employment outcomes, particularly those without traditional degrees (Coursera & Google, 2021).

At the national level, **Singapore's SkillsFuture initiative** represents a comprehensive PPP model that integrates government policy, industry needs, and educational institutions. SkillsFuture provides citizens with credits for approved technology and business courses, encouraging lifelong learning and continuous reskilling. This initiative demonstrates how coordinated policy frameworks can institutionalize technology instruction as a public good rather than a private privilege (Kim et al., 2021).

7.4 Examples from the Global South and Underrepresented Regions

Technology instruction has shown particular promise in the Global South, where digital learning can bypass infrastructural and institutional constraints. In **Rwanda**, the government's partnership with international technology firms and universities has supported digital skills training in entrepreneurship, ICT, and business management. Programs such as the Rwanda Coding Academy and national digital literacy initiatives have contributed to workforce development and youth employment, illustrating how localized technology instruction can support national development strategies (Dinika, 2024).

Likewise, in **India**, the National Skill Development Corporation (NSDC) collaborates with private technology providers to deliver large-scale digital training in business and technology skills. These programs have expanded access to employability-oriented instruction in semi-urban and rural areas, demonstrating the potential of technology instruction to address regional disparities (National Skill Development Corporation, 2025).

7.5 Synthesis of Practical Insights

Across these cases, a common pattern emerges: effective technology instruction is context-sensitive, practice-oriented, and aligned with broader organizational or societal objectives. Whether implemented by corporations, universities, or governments, technology instruction delivers the greatest impact when it integrates digital tools with experiential learning, industry relevance, and inclusive access.

8. CHALLENGES, RISKS, AND ETHICAL CONSIDERATIONS

While technology-enhanced instruction has transformed business education and professional learning, its rapid diffusion has also surfaced significant challenges, risks, and ethical dilemmas. These concerns extend beyond technical implementation to questions of equity, professional capacity, data governance, and the preservation of human-centered learning values. Addressing these issues is essential if technology instruction is to contribute meaningfully to inclusive, ethical, and sustainable educational ecosystems.

8.1 Digital Inequality and Access Barriers

One of the most persistent challenges in technology instruction is digital inequality. Despite widespread digitalization, access to reliable internet connectivity, appropriate devices, and digital literacy remain uneven across regions and social groups. Studies highlight that learners from low-income backgrounds, rural areas, and developing economies face structural disadvantages that limit their participation in technology-mediated learning (van Dijk, 2020; Robinson et al., 2015). These inequalities are not merely technical but socio-economic, reinforcing existing educational and labor-market disparities.

In business instruction, digital inequality affects learners' ability to engage with advanced analytics tools, simulations, and collaborative platforms. Selwyn (2022) argues that without deliberate inclusion strategies, technology-enhanced education risks privileging already advantaged learners, thereby contradicting its purported democratizing potential. Consequently, addressing access barriers requires not only infrastructure investment but also inclusive instructional design and policy interventions.

8.2 Faculty and Trainer Readiness

Another critical risk concerns the readiness of faculty members and corporate trainers to effectively design and deliver technology-enabled instruction. While learners are often assumed to be "digitally native," instructors frequently experience skill gaps, pedagogical uncertainty, and resistance to technology adoption (Bond et al., 2021). The challenge is not limited to technical competence but extends to instructional design, assessment practices, and facilitation of digitally mediated learning experiences.

Research by Henderson, Selwyn, and Aston (2017) indicates that inadequate professional development can lead to superficial use of technology, where digital tools replicate traditional teaching methods rather than enabling deeper learning. In business education, this may result in tool-driven instruction that emphasizes software usage over critical thinking, strategic judgment, and ethical reflection. Sustained faculty development and institutional support are therefore essential to mitigate this risk.

8.3 Data Privacy, Surveillance, and Algorithmic Bias

The increasing use of learning analytics, artificial intelligence, and data-driven platforms introduces significant ethical concerns related to privacy, surveillance, and bias. Technology instruction often relies on the continuous collection of learner data, including behavioral patterns, performance metrics, and engagement indicators. Scholars caution that such practices may infringe on learners' privacy and autonomy if transparency and consent are not adequately addressed (Ribeiro & Subrahmanyam, 2021).

Algorithmic systems used in personalized learning and assessment can reproduce and amplify existing biases embedded in training data. O'Neil (2017) and Noble (2018) demonstrate how algorithmic decision-making may disadvantage marginalized groups, particularly when systems are treated as neutral or objective. In business instruction, overreliance on algorithmic feedback risks narrowing managerial judgment and ethical reasoning, underscoring the need for human oversight and critical algorithmic literacy.

8.4 Over-Technologization and the Erosion of Human-Centered Learning

A further concern is the over-technologization of instruction, where technological efficiency becomes an end in itself rather than a means to support meaningful learning. Excessive reliance on automation, standardized digital content, and self-paced modules may undermine relational, reflective, and dialogical dimensions of learning that are central to management and leadership education (Biesta, 2021).

Human-centered learning emphasizes mentorship, ethical deliberation, emotional intelligence, and contextual understanding - capabilities that are difficult to cultivate through purely digital means. Scholars argue that technology instruction should complement, not replace, human interaction and professional judgment (Chan & Tsi, 2023). Failure to maintain this balance risks producing technically proficient but ethically disengaged professionals.

Table 3. Key challenges, risks, and ethical considerations in technology instruction

Dimension	Core Issues	Risks for Business Instruction
Digital inequality	Unequal access to devices, connectivity, and skills	Exclusion of disadvantaged learners; widened skill gaps
Faculty readiness	Limited digital pedagogy skills; resistance to change	Superficial technology use; reduced instructional quality
Data privacy	Extensive data collection; lack of transparency	Loss of learner autonomy; ethical breaches
Algorithmic bias	Biased datasets; opaque AI systems	Reinforcement of social inequalities; flawed assessments
Over-technologization	Excessive automation; reduced human interaction	Erosion of critical thinking and ethical judgment

8.5 Toward Ethical and Responsible Technology Instruction

Collectively, these challenges highlight the need for a principled and reflective approach to technology instruction. Ethical frameworks, inclusive design principles, and human-centered pedagogies must guide the adoption of digital tools in business education. Rather than asking what technology can do, educators and organizations must ask what technology should do in service of learning, equity, and societal well-being.

9. FUTURE DIRECTIONS AND STRATEGIC IMPLICATIONS

Rapid technological change is reshaping how business instruction is designed, delivered, and governed. The next phase will be characterized by deeper AI-driven personalization, tighter integration of sustainability and social responsibility into technical curricula, and renewed attention to policy and institutional strategies that make technology instruction inclusive and societally useful. These developments carry clear implications for business leaders, educators, and policymakers who must balance innovation with equity and ethics.

9.1 AI-driven Personalization of Business Instruction

AI promises finely tuned personalization - adapting content, pacing, and feedback to individual learners' needs - thereby increasing efficiency and potential learning gains (Vieriu & Petrea, 2025). Personalized learning systems can scaffold analytics training, simulate business scenarios matched to learners' prior knowledge, and recommend micro-credentials that map to career pathways (Fortuna et al., 2025). Yet, authors warn that algorithmic personalization is not neutral: biased training data, lack of transparency, and insufficient educator oversight can reproduce inequities and reduce opportunities for critical reflection (Ribeiro & Subrahmanyam, 2021). The strategic task is therefore to design AI as an augmenting, explainable tool that preserves educator agency and supports critical, ethical reasoning.

Table 4. Strategic actions for AI-driven personalization and sustainability

Priority	Action	Rationale
AI Governance	Require explainability, human override, and bias audits for personalization engines.	Prevents opaque decisions and systemic bias (Ribeiro & Subrahmanyam, 2021).
Curriculum Design	Integrate sustainability into core tech courses via projects and cross-disciplinary modules.	Ensures graduates consider social/ environmental impacts (Subrahmanyam, 2025).
Faculty Capacity	Provide sustained digital-pedagogy training and incentives for co-teaching with industry.	Improves instructional quality and adoption (Peruzzo & Allan, 2024).
Inclusion	Subsidize connectivity, localize content, and formalize micro-credential pathways.	Reduces access gaps and aligns learning with labor markets (García Zaballos et al., 2024).

9.2 Integration of Sustainability and Social Responsibility

Embedding sustainability and social responsibility into technology curricula is increasingly urgent. Subrahmanyam (2025) argues that sustainability must move from optional modules to transdisciplinary learning threads - linking digital skills with environmental impact assessment, ethical supply-chain design, and inclusive business models. Doing so prepares graduates to deploy technology with attention to long-term social and ecological outcomes rather than short-term efficiency gains. Curriculum redesign that uses case studies, project-based assessment, and cross-faculty collaboration is central to realizing this goal.

9.3 Policy and Institutional Strategies for Inclusive Technology Instruction

Policymakers and institutions must design strategies that counter the digital divide while fostering pedagogical innovation. Research on digital inclusion highlights the need for multi-level intervention: infrastructure investment, affordable connectivity, localized content, and sustained professional development for faculty (Peruzzo & Allan, 2024; García Zaballos et al., 2024). Inclusive policy emphasizes recognition of prior learning, stackable credentials, and regulatory frameworks that require algorithmic transparency and learner data protections (Gottschalk & Weise, 2023). Institutions that couple strategic governance with community partnerships are better positioned to scale equitable technology instruction.

9.4 Implications for Business Leaders, Educators, and Policymakers

The strategic implications split across roles. Business leaders should view instructional partnerships as investments in workforce resilience - supporting co-designed curricula, on-the-job micro-credentials, and ethical deployment of AI. Educators must upskill in digital pedagogy, learn to oversee AI systems critically, and redesign assessment for transferable competence. Policymakers should focus on inclusion metrics, safeguard privacy and fairness, and incentivize sustainability-oriented curricula (Selwyn, 2022; Biesta, 2021).

Successful futures will therefore combine technological capability with human judgment, regulatory guardrails, and pedagogical imagination. The goal is not maximal automation but responsible augmentation - where AI and digital tools amplify educators' capacity to form ethical, adaptable business practitioners.

Table 5. Stakeholder implication

Stakeholder	Primary Implication	Short Action
Business leaders	Invest in ethical reskilling partnerships	Fund applied micro-credentials
Educators	Shift to facilitation + oversight of AI	Undertake pedagogy & ethics upskilling
Policymakers	Set inclusion & data governance standards	Mandate audits, fund infrastructure
Learners	Expect modular, career-aligned pathways	Seek micro-credentials + applied projects

10. CONCLUSION

This chapter has demonstrated that technology instruction has become a central pillar of contemporary business education, reshaping not only how learning is delivered but also what competencies are valued in modern organizations. Across the discussion, key insights highlight the growing importance of digitally mediated instructional models, experiential and data-driven learning approaches, and inclusive strategies that address ethical, social, and cultural considerations. Together, these elements underscore a shift from technology as a supplementary tool to technology as an integral enabler of learning, decision-making, and innovation.

Importantly, technology instruction extends beyond organizational efficiency to serve as a mechanism for social empowerment. When designed thoughtfully, it helps bridge skill gaps, enhances employability, and expands access to business education for marginalized groups and emerging economies. The integration of ethical reasoning, sustainability, and human-centered pedagogies ensures that technological capability is aligned with responsible leadership and societal well-being, rather than narrow performance metrics alone.

From a global perspective, the impact of technology instruction is both transformative and uneven. While digital tools offer unprecedented opportunities for scalable and inclusive learning, their benefits depend on contextual adaptation, supportive policies, and institutional readiness. As businesses and societies continue to navigate digital transformation, technology instruction will remain a critical lever for fostering resilient organizations, inclusive growth, and globally relevant business education.

REFERENCES

Accenture. (2022). *Building the future workforce today: Unlocking America's tech sector for Hispanic American and Latinx talent* (PDF). Accenture. https://www.accenture.com/content/dam/accenture/final/markets/north-america/document/Accenture-Building-Future-Workforce-Today.pdf

Acemoglu, D., & Restrepo, P. (2020). The wrong kind of AI? Artificial intelligence and the future of labour demand. *Cambridge Journal of Regions, Economy and Society*, *13*(1), 25–35. DOI: 10.1093/cjres/rsz022

Angwaomaodoko, E. A. (2026). The role of microcredentials in promoting lifelong learning. *Journal of Education and Training*, 13(1). Macrothink Institute. https://doi.org/DOI: 10.5296/jet.v13i1.23027

Autor, D., Mindell, D. A., & Reynolds, E. (2022). *The work of the future: Building better jobs in an age of intelligent machines*. MIT Press. DOI: 10.7551/mitpress/14109.001.0001

Biesta, G. (2021). *World-centred education: A view for the present*. Routledge. DOI: 10.4324/9781003098331

Bond, M., Bedenlier, S., Marín, V. I., & Händel, M. (2021). Emergency remote teaching in higher education: Mapping the first global online semester. *International Journal of Educational Technology in Higher Education*, *18*(1), 50. DOI: 10.1186/s41239-021-00282-x PMID: 34778537

Brynjolfsson, E., & McAfee, A. (2020). *The second machine age: Work, progress, and prosperity in a time of brilliant technologies* (Updated ed.). W. W. Norton.

Chan, C. K. Y., & Tsi, L. H. Y. (2023). The AI revolution in education: Will AI replace or assist teachers in higher education? (Preprint). *arXiv*. https://doi.org//arXiv.2305.01185DOI: 10.48550

Chui, M., Manyika, J., & Miremadi, M. (2018). What AI can and can't do (yet) for your business. *McKinsey Quarterly*. https://www.mckinsey.com/business-functions/mckinsey-analytics/our-insights/what-ai-can-and-cant-do-yet-for-your-business

Coursera & Google. (2021). *The economic impact of Google Career Certificates*. Coursera. https://www.coursera.org/google-career-certificates

Dinika, A. A.-A. T. (2024). A critical analysis of Rwanda's digital skills and entrepreneurship training toward solving youth unemployment. *Journal of Business and Enterprise Development, 12*(1). Advance online publication. DOI: 10.47963/jobed.v12i.1526

Elmoazen, R., Saqr, M., Khalil, M., & Al-Ali, A. K. (2023). Learning analytics in virtual laboratories: A systematic literature review of empirical research. *Smart Learning Environments, 10*(1), 23. DOI: 10.1186/s40561-023-00244-y PMID: 40477836

Floridi, L., Cowls, J., Beltrametti, M., Chatila, R., Chazerand, P., Dignum, V., Luetge, C., Madelin, R., Pagallo, U., Rossi, F., Schafer, B., Valcke, P., & Vayena, E. (2018). AI4People—An ethical framework for a good AI society: Opportunities, risks, principles, and recommendations. *Minds and Machines, 28*(4), 689–707. DOI: 10.1007/s11023-018-9482-5 PMID: 30930541

Fortuna, A., Prasetya, F., Samala, A. D., Rawas, S., Criollo-C, S., Kaya, D., Raihan, M., Andriani, W., Safitri, D., & Nabawi, R. A. (2025). Artificial intelligence in personalized learning: A global systematic review of current advancements and shaping future opportunities. *Social Sciences & Humanities Open, 12*, 102114. Advance online publication. DOI: 10.1016/j.ssaho.2025.102114

García Zaballos, A., Jorge, S., Dalio, M., Makwakwa, O., & Albornoz Basto, N. (2024). *Digital inclusion strategies: A primer for Latin American policymakers* (IDB Monograph No. 1232). Inter-American Development Bank. https://publications.iadb.org/en/digital-inclusion-strategies-primer-latin-american-policymakers

Gomber, P., Koch, J. A., & Siering, M. (2017). Digital finance and fintech: Current research and future research directions. *Journal of Business Economics, 87*(5), 537–580. DOI: 10.1007/s11573-017-0852-x

Gottschalk, F., & Weise, C. (2023). *Digital equity and inclusion in education: An overview of practice and policy in OECD countries* (OECD Education Working Papers No. 299). OECD Publishing. https://www.oecd.org/en/publications/digital-equity-and-inclusion-in-education_7cb15030-en.html

Harvard Business School. (2021). *Annual report 2021*. https://www.hbs.edu/about/annualreport/2021/annual.pdf

Henderson, M., Selwyn, N., & Aston, R. (2017). What works and why? Student perceptions of useful digital technology in university teaching and learning. *Studies in Higher Education, 42*(8), 1567–1579. DOI: 10.1080/03075079.2015.1007946

Hofstede, G., Hofstede, G. J., & Minkov, M. (2010). *Cultures and organizations: Software of the mind* (3rd ed.). McGraw-Hill.

IBM. (2021). *IBM SkillsBuild: Empowering future-ready talent*. IBM. https://www.ibm.com

INSEAD. (2022). *Executive education and digital learning innovation*. INSEAD. https://www.insead.edu

International Labour Organization. (2022). *Digital skills and the future of work*. International Labour Organization. https://www.ilo.org

Istrate, O., & Velea, S. (2024). *Guidelines for online and blended learning: Design, delivery, assessment, evaluation of study programmes. Premises of academic curriculum digitalisation* (6th ed.). Institute for Education., DOI: 10.61071/JDP.2400

Kim, S., Chen, Z. W., Tan, J. Q. G., & Mussagulova, A. (2021). A case study of the Singapore SkillsFuture Credit scheme: Preliminary insights for making lifelong learning policy more effective. *Asian Journal of Political Science*, *29*(2), 192–214. DOI: 10.1080/02185377.2021.1917431

Mohamed, M., Mukherjee, S., & Baad, B. (2025). Impact of UK postgraduate student experiences on academic performance in blended learning: A data analytics approach. *arXiv*. https://doi.org//arXiv.2511.12320DOI: 10.48550

National Research Council. (2000). *How people learn: Brain, mind, experience, and school: Expanded edition*. National Academies Press., DOI: 10.17226/9853

National Skill Development Corporation. (2025). *Skill India Digital Hub: Digital skill courses and upskilling*. https://skillindiadigital.gov.in/

Nkrumah, T., & Scott, K. A. (2022). Mentoring in STEM higher education: A synthesis of the literature to (re)present the excluded women of color. *International Journal of STEM Education*, *9*(1), 50. DOI: 10.1186/s40594-022-00367-7 PMID: 35919282

Noble, S. U. (2018). *Algorithms of oppression: How search engines reinforce racism*. NYU Press. DOI: 10.18574/nyu/9781479833641.001.0001

O'Neil, C. (2017). *Weapons of math destruction: How big data increases inequality and threatens democracy*. Crown.

OECD. (2020). *Building digital workforce capacity and skills for data-intensive science* (OECD Science, Technology and Industry Policy Papers No. 90). OECD Publishing. https://www.oecd.org/en/publications/building-digital-workforce-capacity-and-skills-for-data-intensive-science_e08aa3bb-en.html

Peruzzo, F., & Allan, J. (2024). Rethinking inclusive (digital) education: Lessons from the pandemic to reconceptualise inclusion through convivial technologies. *Learning, Media and Technology*, *49*(2), 244–258. DOI: 10.1080/17439884.2022.2131817

Qureshi, S. (2023). Digital transformation for development: A human capital key or system of oppression? *Information Technology for Development*, *29*(4), 423–434. DOI: 10.1080/02681102.2023.2282269

Ransbotham, S., Kiron, D., Gerbert, P., & Reeves, M. (2017). *Reshaping business with artificial intelligence: Closing the gap between ambition and action*. MIT Sloan Management Review in collaboration with The Boston Consulting Group. https://sloanreview.mit.edu/projects/reshaping-business-with-artificial-intelligence/

Ribeiro, N., & Subrahmanyam, S. (2021). Emotional challenges of teaching online during the pandemic. In Uddin, M., Sony, K. K., & Verma, N. (Eds.), *Psychosocial issues in COVID-19 pandemic* (pp. 244–255). SHINE Publication. RED.

Rincon-Flores, E. G., Castaño, L., Guerrero Solis, S. L., Olmos Lopez, O., Rodríguez Hernández, C. F., Castillo Lara, L. A., & Aldape Valdés, L. P. (2024). Improving the learning-teaching process through adaptive learning strategy. *Smart Learning Environments*, *11*(27), 27. Advance online publication. DOI: 10.1186/s40561-024-00314-9

Robinson, L., Cotten, S. R., Ono, H., Quan-Haase, A., Mesch, G., Chen, W., Schulz, J., Hale, T. M., & Stern, M. J. (2015). Digital inequalities and why they matter. *Information Communication and Society*, *18*(5), 569–582. DOI: 10.1080/1369118X.2015.1012532

Rodríguez-Segura, D. (2022). *EdTech in developing countries: A review of the evidence*. World Bank Research Observer. World Bank. https://openknowledge.worldbank.org/bitstreams/6ac08b1a-d072-4727-8678-d42bbee86a8a/download

Rosário, A. T., & Raimundo, R. (2024). Enhancing business higher education through simulation-based learning, problem-based learning, and challenge-based learning (Preprint). *Preprints.org*. https://doi.org/DOI: 10.20944/preprints202407.0747.v1

Selwyn, N. (2022). *Education and technology: Key issues and debates* (3rd ed.). Bloomsbury Academic. DOI: 10.5040/9781350145573

Strielkowski, W. (2025). The role of micro-credentials in the future digitalized AI-driven education (Preprint). *arXiv*. https://doi.org//arXiv.2511.07583DOI: 10.48550

Subrahmanyam, S. (2025). Business, Digital Transformation, and Entrepreneurship. In Ordóñez de Pablos, P. (Ed.), *Shaping Green and Inclusive Economies Through Innovative Entrepreneurship* (pp. 1–34). IGI Global Scientific Publishing., DOI: 10.4018/979-8-3373-1097-8.ch001

Treiblmaier, H. (2019). Toward more rigorous blockchain research: Recommendations for writing blockchain case studies. *Frontiers in Blockchain, 2*, 3. Advance online publication. DOI: 10.3389/fbloc.2019.00003

UNCTAD. (2021). *Digital economy report 2021: Cross-border data flows and development: For whom the data flow* (UNCTAD/DER/2021). United Nations Conference on Trade and Development. https://unctad.org/publication/digital-economy-report-2021

UNESCO. (2017). *Cracking the code: Girls' and women's education in science, technology, engineering and mathematics (STEM)* (ISBN 978-92-3-100233-5). UNESCO. https://unesdoc.unesco.org/ark:/48223/pf0000253479

UNESCO. (2023). *Global education monitoring report 2023: Technology in education – A tool on whose terms?* UNESCO. https://unesdoc.unesco.org/ark:/48223/pf0000385723

United Nations Department of Economic and Social Affairs. (2021). *Leveraging digital technologies for social inclusion: Policy brief no. 92*. UN DESA. https://desapublications.un.org/policy-briefs/undesa-policy-brief-92-leveraging-digital-technologies-social-inclusion

University of Wollongong in Dubai. (2025). *Blended learning*. University of Wollongong in Dubai. Retrieved December 19, 2025, from https://www.uowdubai.ac.ae/students/blended-learning

van Dijk, J. (2020). *The digital divide*. Polity Press.

van Laar, E., van Deursen, A. J. A. M., van Dijk, J. A. G. M., & de Haan, J. (2019). Determinants of 21st-century digital skills: A large-scale survey among working professionals. *Computers in Human Behavior, 100*, 93–104. DOI: 10.1016/j.chb.2019.06.017

Vial, G. (2019). Understanding digital transformation: A review and a research agenda. *The Journal of Strategic Information Systems, 28*(2), 118–144. DOI: 10.1016/j.jsis.2019.01.003

Vieriu, A. M., & Petrea, G. (2025). The impact of artificial intelligence (AI) on students' academic development. *Education Sciences, 15*(3), 343. DOI: 10.3390/educsci15030343

World Economic Forum. (2023). *The future of jobs report 2023*. World Economic Forum. https://www.weforum.org/publications/the-future-of-jobs-report-2023/

World Economic Forum. (2025). *This is how we upskill future leaders to drive the digital transformation of manufacturing*. World Economic Forum. https://www.weforum.org/stories/2025/04/this-is-how-we-upskill-future-leaders-to-drive-the-digital-transformation-of-manufacturing

KEY TERMS AND DEFINITIONS

Artificial Intelligence in Education (AI in Education): The application of AI technologies, such as machine learning, natural language processing, and analytics, to personalize learning, automate administrative tasks, and support decision-making in instructional contexts.

Digital Credentials: Verified certificates, badges, or micro-credentials issued through digital platforms that signify mastery of specific skills or competencies, supporting lifelong learning and employability.

Digital Divide: The gap between individuals, communities, or regions in terms of access to, use of, and proficiency with digital technologies, often influenced by socioeconomic, geographic, or cultural factors.

Digital Empowerment: The process of enabling individuals, communities, or organizations to access, utilize, and benefit from digital technologies, enhancing their capabilities, employability, and social inclusion.

Experiential Learning: A pedagogical approach where learners acquire knowledge and skills through active engagement, hands-on practice, simulations, or real-world problem-solving activities.

Learning Management System (LMS): Software platforms designed to deliver, track, and manage educational or training content, enabling remote, blended, or personalized learning experiences.

Microlearning: Short, focused learning modules or content units designed to deliver knowledge efficiently, often digitally, allowing learners to integrate learning into their workflow.

Social Empowerment Through Technology: The use of technology-enabled instruction and digital skills development to enhance individuals' economic, social, and professional opportunities, particularly for marginalized or underrepresented groups.

Socio-Technical Systems: Frameworks that examine the interaction between people, technology, and organizational processes, emphasizing that successful technology adoption requires alignment with social, cultural, and operational factors.

Technology Instruction: Structured teaching and learning processes that leverage digital tools, platforms, and innovations to develop skills, knowledge, and competencies relevant to business operations and decision-making.

Chapter 5
Technological Integration for the Education Process

Sarita Peddi
http://orcid.org/0009-0002-6964-3357
SR University, India

Geetha Manoharan
http://orcid.org/0000-0002-8644-8871
SR University, India

ABSTRACT

This chapter discusses how technology integration in education becomes a crucial tool for promoting social empowerment and enhancing learning. It highlights how innovations, such as online learning management systems, interactive multimedia, and collaborative digital spaces, can transform traditional pedagogy and create inclusive environments. In a discussion, challenges like access, equity, and the digital divide have to be overcome to ensure technology is enhancing rather than merely being an ornament in the educational practices of institutions. Using case studies and empirical evidence, we have demonstrated how effective technological integration indeed empowers students and teachers through promoting critical thinking, creativity, and collaboration. In conclusion, we recommend an integrative approach to educational technology that takes into consideration global perspectives on social empowerment and equity in education.

DOI: 10.4018/979-8-3373-0629-2.ch005

ght © 2026, IGI Global Scientific Publishing. Copying or distributing in print or electronic forms without written permission of IGI Global Scientific Publishing is prohibited. Use of this chapter to generative artificial intelligence (AI) technologies is expressly prohibited. The publisher reserves all rights to license its use for generative AI training and machine learning model development.

1 INTRODUCTION

1.1 Background of Technological Integration in Education

Historical Context of Technology in Education

The relationship of technology with education has come to evolve greatly over the past century, influenced by numerous socio-economic factors as well as technological advancements. Early 20th-century integration of audiovisual aids in the classroom marked one of the first major forms of the integration of technology in teaching. Films and slide presentations have been used popularly to complement traditional instructional processes by educators (Purushottamashtikar & Manoharan, 2024). The advent of computers in the late 20th century further revolutionized the landscape of education, shifting instructional paradigms from teacher-centered to more student-centered approaches (Lajoie & Poitras, 2023).

The 1990s brought internet development, which revolutionarily transformed educational technology, opening gates to enormous resources and knowledge beyond the textbooks. Online learning emerged, with platforms such as Blackboard and, later, Moodle, which supported distance education and opened the doors of educational institutions to a wider audience. Moreover, the advent of mobile technology in the 2000s enabled learning at any time and from anywhere, challenging the traditional model of the brick-and-mortar classroom. This trend of even more blended and hybrid learning environments has been carried out until the present with the intensification of the influence of artificial intelligence and virtual reality that promises to personalize and improve learning experiences (Lee, 2023).

Evolution of Educational Technologies over the Decades

The first wave of educational technologies was radio and television, which were used for mass educational programs in the mid-20th century. However, it is the last two decades that have seen exponential growth in technology adoption within educational settings. The widespread use of digital devices such as tablets and laptops has opened up an unprecedented opportunity for interactive learning experiences (Sanders & George, 2017). The use of IoT devices in classrooms enabled real-time data analysis and instant feedback, greatly enriching the educational experience. The COVID-19 pandemic of 2020 accelerated the integration of technology into education. During the time when schools all over the world shifted to distance learning, it became necessary to rely on the use of technology (Ahmed & Opoku, 2022). This move normalised online learning but shed light on the gaps in terms of accessibility, digital literacy, and infrastructure. The UNESCO Institute for Statistics in 2021 reported that over 1.5 billion learners had their education disrupted due to the pandemic, and thus, more robust educational technologies are a necessity. As a result, educational institutions began to invest heavily in digital tools, such as Learning Management Systems (LMS), video conferencing applications, and collaborative platforms, paving the way for a more integrated approach to teaching and learning (Canton, 2021).

1.2 Importance of Empowerment through Technology

Definition of Empowerment in an Educational Context

Empowerment in education means the process through which the student acquires the abilities, confidence, and self-management skills to take charge of learning. It involves some critical aspects such as self-directed learning, critical thinking, and problem-solving skills (Gratchev & Espinosa,). Empowerment gives learners ownership of their learning, and they are able to interact with the content actively and make meaningful contributions to their learning experiences (Owston, 2018).

The Role of Technology in Enhancing Learning Experiences

Technology has a significant role in enabling the students and teachers. Interactive simulations, gamified learning, and adaptive learning technologies personalize education to cater to different learning styles and needs of learners (Fisher, 2006). For example, the data analytics of Zhao Academy and Duolingo enables personalized learning content for learners (Zhao et al., 2006). Besides, technology enables students and teachers to collaborate across geographical boundaries and develop a global learning community (Hwang et al., 2015). In the Indian context, for instance, the National Digital Education Architecture (NDEAR) seeks to offer equal access to quality educational resources and aligns with the goals of the country's education system (Jiali et al.,). It supplements traditional learning but readies students for the digital economy, which demands much high levels of technological proficiency and adaptability.

1.3 Purpose and Scope of the Chapter

Overview of What the Chapter Will Cover

The overall scope of this chapter involves making a comprehensive overview regarding integration in education, specifically addressing historical contexts, changes within educational technologies, and how empowerment through technology might best work. It will focus on critically analyzing current trends and models of technological integration to understand the impact on teaching and learning brought forth by recent developments in the application of artificial intelligence and data analytics.

Significance of Global Perspectives in Educational Technology

Understanding the global implications of educational technology is very important, especially in the interconnected world that has begun to emerge. There have been different models for countries adopting technology integration in learning processes, influenced by each country's unique cultural, economic, and educational landscape. Comparing these diverse approaches, educators (Purushottamashtikar & Manoharan, 2024) and policymakers learn from each other, developing best practices that enhance equity and access in education (Zhao et al., 2006).

In conclusion, this chapter prepares the reader for understanding the role of technology in the empowerment of learners, enhancing experiences in education, and remaking the future of learning. This book is written in an era where change in technology happens almost overnight, and hence it calls for the development of a critical view of how such innovation can help advance student engagement, collaboration, and success worldwide.

2. THEORETICAL FRAMEWORK FOR TECHNOLOGICAL INTEGRATION IN EDUCATION

2.1 Educational Theories Supporting Technological Integration

Constructivism

Constructivism asserts that learners do not passively soak up knowledge but rather create knowledge actively. Knowledge arises within social interactions and personal experience. Learners play an active role in the environment (Vygotsky, 1978) as they create meaning and understanding. This conceptualization fits perfectly with using technology, which provides tools such as simulations, multimedia resources, and collaborative tools to add more opportunities for exploration, testing, and knowledge building by the learners (Hwang et al., 2015). For example, Google Classroom and Zoom platforms facilitate engaging class discussions and collaborative projects that enhance social learning, which is a fundamental principle of constructivist theory (Sparkling & Sengupta, 2023). In modern learning environments, technology acts as a scaffolding tool that promotes student autonomy in learning. Through the use of digital tools in inquiry-based learning, educators can create more engaging learning environments (Zhao et al., 2006). The students are able to learn topics of interest, share findings, and receive peer feedback, thus creating a lively learning community that is characteristic of the constructivist approach (Purushottamashtikar & Manoharan, 2024).

Connectivism

Siemens, in his work in 2005, conceptualized connectivism as something that focuses on the importance of social and cultural context for learning, while giving value to digital networks. Given the fast pace of changing digital landscapes, learners are supposed to navigate, judge, and utilize massive information. Connectivism, therefore supports the integration of technology, and it emphasizes the fact that networked learning environments must be created so that students can access peers, experts, and resources in different parts of the globe (Marais, 2011). On these online platforms, blogs and wikis, and via social media, learners bond and share knowledge to make them develop critical digital competence. Connectivism inspires learners to create the meanings of their learning experiences. And customized personal learning networks that enable lifelong learning in a world where adaptability and information literacy are central skills (Kultawanich et al., 2015).

Other Relevant Theories

Another such theory is Transformative Learning that emphasizes the role of the integration of technology into teaching through the notion of transformative learning presented by Mezirow (Mezirow, 1991). Transformative Learning transforms personal and social perspectives with deep critical reflection. This mode of reflection can be spurred by online discussion forums, digital storytelling applications where insight sharing and challenging of perceptions are allowed (Kitchenham, 2008). Distributed Cognition (Giere & Moffatt, 2003) this theory explains how cognitive processes are distributed across people, tools, and environments. Therefore, this theory supports the use of technology in education because it helps to share the cognitive load, promote collaborative problem-solving, and overall understanding (Roschelle, 1995). Technological tools give a space to the learners to work in groups and collectively build their knowledge; thus, the interplay between technology and cognitive development is revealed.

2.2 Models of Technology Integration in Education

TPACK (Technological Pedagogical Content Knowledge)

The model developed clearly establishes TPACK in terms of interplay between technology, knowledge content, and pedagogy (Mishra & Koehler, 2006). This framework posits that effective integration of the technology would require educators being steeped in understanding on how these three domains inter-relatedly exist. Educators need not only be proficient in their contents but also trained in varied pedagogical techniques applicable to the use of optimizing technology (Marsh & Farrell, 2015). The TPACK framework calls on teachers to design learning experiences where technologies are thoroughly infused. Therefore, for instance, using simulation or data analysis may help the science class teacher engage his or her students to do inquiry-based learning (Herring et al., 2016). This approach fosters an integrated perception of educational technology, because professional development programs are structured to support educator TPACK skills.

SAMR (Substitution, Augmentation, Modification, Redefinition)

The SAMR model is an integration model that has been proposed (Puentedura, 2006) to categorize the levels of integration of technology in education. It has four progressive stages:

1. **Substitution:** Technology acts as a direct replacement for traditional methods but does not create a functional change in this respect. For example, a word processor instead of using pen and paper.
2. **Augmentation:** Technology helps to make the learning process more exciting with more options like collaborative writing through Google Docs.
3. **Modification:** Significant redesign in terms of technology because of doing things, like students research digitally then present it.
4. **Redefinition** Technology adds new tasks that were unthinkable or even impossible before: for instance, virtual experience, allowing a student to get immersed into the history of particular events (Clark, 1989).

Educators can utilize the SAMR model in evaluating the appropriateness of technology in their teaching practice and think about how they can move beyond simple substitution towards redefinition, thereby maximizing the educational potential of digital tools. This model encourages a mindset that seeks innovative applications of technology, fostering creativity and deeper learning experiences (Hamilton et al., 2016).

2.3 Global Perspectives on Empowerment through Technology

Comparison of Different Educational Systems and Their Approaches

This takes varied forms across different countries and different school systems due to their particular cultural, economic, and pedagogical contexts (Ashtikar & Manoharan, 2024). While Finland is famous for having a very progressive education system, it has a rather holistic integration of technology. The digital competence of Finnish students was emphasized as a key learning skill in the curriculum offered by the Finnish National Agency for Education. The use of technology has been expedited through various Finnish educational initiatives in fostering the innovative and collaborative ability and critically thinking mind for students entering the 21st century workplace (Bastos, 2017). The utilization of technology has been intensified through government schemes like Digital India and the National Educational Technology Forum in India. These initiatives focus on building digital infrastructure and offering equitable access to digital resources for students from various socio-economic backgrounds. According to (Bandyopadhyay et al., 2021), while the progress is quite remarkable, there are still issues like the digital divide, quality teacher training, and differential levels of digital literacy. For example, in countries like Singapore, the government has developed the "Smart Nation" vision, placing emphasis on the use of technology in the pursuit of educational goals. The new approach centers on personalized learning, leveraging data analytics for monitoring students' progress in order to make the learning process more appropriate for each student experience. This brings out the need for infrastructure, professional development, and community engagement when using technology to empower.

The spread of COVID-19 has, all over the world, reminded people of the necessity of technology in education and this has led to a surge in online and blended learning models across all regions. Fast changes to digital platforms have necessitated swift changes, and countries such as Australia and Canada are acting as models of successful online learning, focusing on learner engagement and support systems (Daniela & Visvizi, 2022).

This is a theoretical framework in summary that puts down the foundation for the understanding of complexity within technological integration into education. Educational theories in interaction would allow one to view technological integration from a certain perspective: it adds richness to learning experiences. Then models, TPACK and SAMR are guiding implementation by providing a practical set of guidelines. The global approach gives focus to the varying approaches aimed at the empowering of the learner through technology, these demand continuous improvement and adaptation of learning practices. In line with evolution, the role that technology can play in the future education model changes.

3. CURRENT TECHNOLOGIES TRANSFORMING EDUCATION

3.1 Learning Management Systems (LMS)

Overview of Popular LMS Platforms

With Learning Management Systems, learning today has become a crucial part of modern education. Courses and training programs are delivered, tracked, and managed in ways never seen before. Most prominent LMS platforms today, including Moodle, Canvas, Blackboard, and Google Classroom, offer numerous functionalities to cater to educators and learners requirements (Purushottamashtikar & Manoharan, 2024).

Moodle is an open-source learning management system with great flexibility and scalability; therefore, most institutions have gained its widespread acceptance. It allows freedom for the facilitators to develop learner-centered environments through including activities like quizzes, forums, and multimedia resources (Cavus & Zabadi, 2014). Canvas by Instructure prioritizes easy design and compatibility with mobile devices. For that reason, Canvas would be an excellent choice for any educator and learner. Among its features are custom courses and smooth third-party applications (Veluvali & Surisetti, 2022). Another of the older LMS systems, blackboard is renowned for being more powerful with strong analytics and reporting tools by which the teachers can trace students' progression and engagement levels (Kitchenham, 2008). Google Classroom is widely popular for the ease and fluid integration of all the other Google Workspace tools in making both teachers and learners go smooth with an uninterrupted workflow especially in the K-12 system (Zhao et al., 2006).

Benefits and Challenges of Using LMS in Education

Several advantages have been derived from the use of LMS in education. Firstly, accessibility is improved since students can view course materials anytime and from anywhere, especially for remote and hybrid learning environments. This flexibility allows for multiple learning styles and paces, therefore empowering students with more autonomy.

This includes the facilitation of efficient communication and collaboration among students and educators. Features such as discussion forums, messaging systems, and group projects foster interaction and engagement, contributing to a sense of community within online learning environments (Veluvali & Surisetti, 2022).

However, LMS also brings challenges with its implementation. One major problem is the digital divide: not all students have equal access to technology and reliable internet connections, which may impede participation and engagement (Cavus & Zabadi, 2014). Also, the success of LMS highly depends on the teachers' capability of using such platforms. Under training and lack of support may result in less usage of LMS features and will not help achieve full potential benefits (Kitchenham, 2008).

3.2 Artificial Intelligence and Machine Learning

Personalized Learning Experiences

AI and ML are transforming education through personalized learning experiences that are uniquely suited to the needs of each learner. AI algorithms can scan large amounts of data related to student performance, learning styles, and preferences to provide individualized learning paths (Luckin & Holmes, 2016). For example, platforms such as DreamBox Learning and Knewton use adaptive learning technologies to change the content in real time to ensure that students receive just the right amount of challenge and support (Bandyopadhyay et al., 2021). Personalized learning will not only engage students but also improve the learning outcomes. Students who experience personalized learning outperform their peers in traditional settings. Moreover, AI-based assessments provide immediate feedback so that students may identify the areas of improvement and alter their learning strategy accordingly.

AI Tutors and Their Impact on Education

AI tutors, which are enabled by natural language processing and machine learning, are becoming the new educational tools. Intelligent systems can provide one-on-one support, answering questions, offering explanations, and guiding students through complex concepts. For instance, platforms such as Carnegie Learning's MATHia and Squirrel AI leverage AI to deliver personalized tutoring experiences that adapt to each student's learning pace (Chen, 2022). More than support, it has a knock-on effect for teachers to lighten the load as administrative work, such as grading and tracking of students' progress, is left in the hands of AI (Bandyopadhyay et al., 2021). It should also be considered how it could impact data privacy, even if bias becomes an issue in education when there's more AI integration into this setting (Luckin & Holmes, 2016).

3.3 Virtual and Augmented Reality

Immersive Learning Environments

Virtual Reality (VR) and Augmented Reality (AR) technologies transform traditional educational paradigms through the creation of an immersive learning environment that has enhanced engagement and retention. VR offers fully immersive experiences that allow students to interact with complex concepts in simulated environments. For example, students can take virtual field trips to historical sites, scientific laboratories, and even outer space using platforms such as Oculus Education and Google Expeditions. AR, however, puts on top of the real-world digital information, hence moving the learning experience but in no way displacing them from their physical world. Applications such as Merge Cube and AR Flashcards interact with 3D models and visualizations making them more tangible for abstract things (Cavus & Zabadi, 2014). Immersive technologies have been found to increase student engagement and motivation, thus improving the learners' outcomes (Hwang et al., 2015).

Case Studies of VR/AR in Classrooms

Multiple case studies have shown that VR and AR are useful in school-related applications. For example, in a high school class of biology, VR simulation for real-time processes in a cell helped the students directly watch and manipulate the structures at real time. The knowledge in complex biological concepts is greater in students when using the aid as compared to other methods used while teaching (Cavus & Zabadi, 2014). Another example is where an elementary school used AR technology in the science curriculum, allowing the students to interact with interactive 3D models of the solar system. Teachers reported more engaged and enthusiastic students, with better teamwork during group work (Hwang et al., 2015). Such case studies show how VR and AR technologies can create interesting, interactive, and effective learning experiences.

3.4 Mobile Learning and Apps

The Rise of Mobile Technology in Education

The proliferation of mobile technology has greatly influenced education, thus enabling learning to occur at all times and at any location. The use of the smartphones and tablets has remained among the most important equipment tools that students use since it is a source for getting resources for education, channels of communication, and interactive devices (Veluvali & Surisetti, 2022). In the report by ITU (2022), it indicated that mobile broadband subscription increased enormously, thus making increased accessibility of online learning content possible especially in developing regions.

Mobile learning (m-learning) encourages flexibility and adaptiveness in learning, allowing students to access content at their own preference. Studies have shown that motivation and engagement among students are improved if they use m-learning with better academic performance (Jiali et al.,). For instance, mobile technology supports both visual, auditory, as well as kinesthetic learners depending on the type of software and multimedia available.

Effective Educational Apps and Their Impact on Learning

Many educational apps have been created, each focusing on different aspects of learning. For example, Duolingo and Babbel are focused on language learning through game-like experiences, which have helped to improve vocabulary and language skills (Chen, 2022). Another example would be Zhao Academy, with free access to a massive library of instructional videos and exercises in nearly every subject under the sun, allowing learners to take charge of their education (Jiali et al.,).

The impact of educational applications transcends individual learning experiences. Many of these applications allow for the teamwork among students, so that in executing projects, they could work together and share. For instance, with regard to platforms such as Padlet and Trello, students can work on different assignments in groups and achieve enhanced communication and teamwork (Veluvali & Surisetti, 2022). However, the effectivity of educational apps rests in their design and deployment. Poorly designed or without definite learning objectives, the learner is likely to become disengaged and frustrated in learning (Luckin & Holmes, 2016). Therefore, educators are called upon to evaluate them very carefully and select one that will support their instructional purposes and improve the learning situation.

In conclusion, the current landscape of educational technology is characterized by the transformative impact of LMS, AI, VR/AR, and mobile learning. Each technology offers unique benefits and challenges, shaping how educators and learners engage with content and each other. As educational institutions go on adopting and integrating such technologies, research and assessment will need to be continually performed to ensure that these can effectively promote learning outcomes as well as meet the complex needs of students. Future education involves the use of such technologies in creating inclusive, interactive, and personalized learning opportunities that better prepare students to face the complexities of the 21st century (Manoharan, Ashtikar, Rao et al, 2024).

4. GLOBAL CASE STUDIES ON TECHNOLOGICAL INTEGRATION

The integration of technology in education has emerged as one of the key factors enhancing learning outcomes, engagement, and accessibility. The present chapter encompasses worldwide case studies that detail the ways in which countries from all over the world successfully adopted and innovated technology solutions in educational contexts. At the same time, common themes and unique strategies may be applied to future education practices.

4.1 Successful Examples from Developed Countries

Case Study: The Finnish Education System

Finland is generally credited to be an education leader that focuses on innovation founded on equity, quality, and student-centered approaches. It harmonizes technology with the pedagogical approach toward promoting a collaborative learning setting that fosters critical thinking (Ashtikar & Manoharan, 2024).

In 2020, the Finnish National Agency for Education, EDUFI, launched an initiative, "Digital Learning," which was aimed at building digital competencies among Finnish teachers and students. The framework under this program incorporated a structured approach to the digitization of learning experiences through the use of numerous digital tools, resources, and learning platforms in the curricula. The available learning management systems include those in Finnish schools, such as Seesaw and Google Classroom that offer features for communication and collaborative student-teacher interactions (Parjanen & Rantala, 2021).

One of the successful implementations of technology is at Helsingin Yliopisto Teacher Training School. There, a combination of traditional and digital pedagogies was adopted. In this school, the students learn by means of project-based learning and in this learning, the utilization of technology is in their researching, group works, and multimedia presentations in presenting their findings. Professional development is offered to the teachers about their digital competencies so that they feel secure that they can apply this for their classroom.

This integrative approach has its impact on student engagement and performance. Finnish education, for example, emphasizes formative assessment, which would allow feedback-driven learning and research shows that leads to better educational outcomes (Hwang et al., 2015). Success in Finland's model would then emphasize the importance of aligning technology integration with educational philosophy, ongoing teacher training, and a supportive infrastructure.

Case Study: The United States - The EdTech Strategy

There are also several initiatives being implemented to integrate technology into education within the United States. A notable example is the "Future Ready" initiative led by the Alliance for Excellent Education to prepare schools with the right tools and skills to use technology efficiently.

The initiative focuses on personalized learning, which increases student engagement by making use of various educational technologies. For example, New York City schools have adopted blended learning models that combine traditional instruction with online learning platforms. In these environments, students are given personalized learning paths, where they move at their own pace (Roberts-Mahoney et al., 2016).

The successful implementation is the incorporation of coding and computational thinking in the curriculum. Resources like Code.org have made a massive difference in K-12 schooling. Such initiatives provided materials and professional development for instructors to help implement coding into their classrooms. Findings reveal that students who receive exposure to coding not only gain technical competencies but also learn how to solve problems and enhance creativity.

While much progress has been achieved, some concerns include issues with the equitable accessibility of technology. The spread of the COVID-19 pandemic merely made manifest some problems already prevalent but accentuates a key necessity in ensuring solutions address digital tools available for each student on equal terms (Dahlström, 2019). This becomes key for schools in adapting new technologies, making issues concerning these inequities an imperative area for future education development and realization.

4.2 Innovative Approaches in Developing Countries

Case Study: The Digital India Initiative

India is an inspiring example of innovative technological integration within its educational landscape in the "Digital India" initiative launched in 2015. This ambitious program aims to transform India into a digitally empowered society and knowledge economy, with specific objectives for improving digital infrastructure, enhancing digital literacy, and promoting digital access across all sectors, including education.

One of the notable implementations would be the "SWAYAM" platform launched by the Government of India in the year 2020, which is an initiative related to online education with offering MOOCs on large numbers of disciplines, allowing students from any walk of society. SWAYAM has been instrumental in offering millions of learner's quality content in the learning process, especially during the COVID-19 pandemic, when learning had to be shifted away from traditional modalities (Jiali et al.,).

Also, as part of the initiative, integrating digital tools into the classrooms has been incorporated with NDEAR to exploit data analytics and AI in enhancing the experience of learning. It can be noted that most of the rural schools have gradually implemented smart classrooms integrated with various forms of digital tools for improving learning by being more engaging and interactive (Monica et al., 2025).

Case Study: Kenya - The Kenyan Digital Learning Program

The innovative approaches of Kenya towards education have come through the "Digital Learning Program" introduced in 2016. This initiative enhances the quality of education provided in primary schools by embracing technology as a means to prepare the child for the 21st century by infusing digital devices into classrooms.

In the same program, thousands of tablets have been supplied by the government to provide e-content to students in various parts of the country, particularly in more depressed areas. The idea focuses on using e-materials in teaching and provides a platform for teachers to improve their practices. The availability of digital textbooks and engaging interactive content has helped raise levels of engagement and increase achievements for many students, as such resources make the learning materials very relatable and more accessible (Dahlström, 2019)

Monitoring and evaluation mechanisms are part of the program, which track progress of students and effectiveness of the teachers. According to studies, schools taking part in the Digital Learning Program have shown marked signs of improvement in student interest and performance, especially on STEM fields. The initiative further enhanced community involvement as participants were active in the implementation of the program, providing support towards sustainability.

4.3 Insights gained from Global Perspectives

Common Themes and Unique Strategies

From these case studies, certain common themes and unique strategies surface:

1. **Alignment to Pedagogical Goal:** Technology integration should be seen to complement the institutional philosophical educational postulates and align closely to the pedagogical goals. For instance, Finland learning in collaboration is well coupled with its idea of the use of technology fostering an all-rounded education approach.

2. **Continuing Professional Development of Teachers:** Teachers should develop and develop continuously so that the full potential of technology is maximized in teaching work. In the United States as well as in Finland, teacher training programs and education in readiness for application by innovativeness are guaranteed.
3. **Access and Equity:** Developed and developing countries underscore the necessity to address access issues with regard to technology. The cases of the United States and India present disparity issues that have been brought to light and thus call for efforts towards equity access.
4. **Community Involvement:** A successful educational program is rooted in community involvement and with stakeholders. For example, the Kenyan Digital Learning Program demonstrates how community involvement can sustain a program and impact.
5. **Data-Driven Decision Making:** Effective monitoring and evaluation strategies promote data-driven decision-making, which allows teachers to adapt and change based on student performance and engagement metrics.

Informing Future Practices

These global case studies can be used to set the future course of teaching and learning in that they advocate for a holistic approach that incorporates:

1. **Holistic Integration of Technology:** Schools should focus not on merely adding technology into the fabric of education, but as an integral part of educational experiences. This includes connecting digital tools with curricular goals to enhance teaching and learning.
2. **Designed Professional Development Programs:** This will ensure them to work more effectively by utilizing technology in the classroom. This includes technical skill-building and pedagogical approaches (Ashtikar & Manoharan, 2024).
3. **Strategies for Equity and Inclusion:** Policymakers must ensure equity in access to technology. All such initiatives should respond to the needs of the marginalized and undeserved.
4. **Collaborative Communities of Practice:** Encouraging professional learning communities where educators can share experiences, strategies, and resources will foster collaborative growth in the integration of technology.

The integration of technology in the educational sector across different global contexts shows a very diverse landscape of possibilities and challenges. Successful examples from developed as well as developing countries speak to the importance of aligning technology use with pedagogical goals, supporting educators through professional development, and prioritizing equity and community involvement. By learning from these experiences and applying shared insights, educational institutions can strengthen their approaches to technology integration, creating more inclusive, engaging, and effective learning environments for all students (Manoharan, Ashtikar, Rao et al, 2024).

5. CHALLENGES OF TECHNOLOGICAL INTEGRATION

With this integration of technology in schools, the whole teaching and learning process is revolutionized throughout the world, making education more accessible and tailored for individual learners. On the other hand, such transformation does not come without facing its challenges. The current chapter will explore significant challenges of implementing technology into the classroom with issues ranging from infrastructures and access, to issues in change resistance, to a need for training teachers' professional development, to the privacy and ethical issues about educational technology.

5.1 Infrastructure and Access Issues

The Digital Divide and Its Implications

The most critical problems associated with technological integration are those that relate to the divide the digital gap between people who easily acquire digital technology and those not given the same chance, sometimes based on socioeconomic, geographical, and demographic lines. Survey by ITU 2023, that around 3 billion people worldwide are denied internet access because of which inequality significantly impacts their educational prospects as well.

In many developing countries, poor infrastructure acts as a barrier to digital learning implementation. For instance, according to the National Sample Survey Office in India, although urban regions have internet access, it is very poor in rural areas where nearly 60% of rural households lack internet access (NSSO, 2022). This creates a scenario in which these students cannot participate in online learning, and this perpetuates educational inequality and prevents them from acquiring skills and opportunities for further academic and professional development (Jiali et al.,) Conversely, even in developed countries, problems with infrastructure can prevent the proper implementation of technology. In the United States, for example, many schools during the COVID-19 pandemic faced problems in providing adequate technology for remote learning, especially in low-income and rural districts. According to a report by the U.S. The Department of Education reported that close to 17% of students did not have access to a reliable device or a high-speed internet connection, which limited their ability to engage with online resources (U.S. Department of Education, 2021).

With the rate at which technologies are developing, it becomes a must to bridge the digital divide. The educational institutions must advocate better infrastructure and equitable access to technology so that all students can learn with technological integration in the education process.

5.2 Resistance to Change

Cultural and Institutional Barriers

Resistance to change is still the biggest hindrance in technology integration into educational environments. This resistance is due to various factors, such as cultural attitude towards technology, institutional inertia, and fear of the new pedagogy. In many learning environments, traditional methods are deeply embedded and highly cherished, hence making the instructors and institutions resistant to change to new technologies.

Cultural norms are essential in developing attitudes toward technology. In some cultures, the structure of education might limit teachers' adoption of new approaches that incorporate student-centered learning and technologies. In India, for example, emphasis on rote learning and high-stakes examinations most of the time serves as a hindrance to interactive and more technology-based pedagogies (Manoharan, Ashtikar, Rao et al, 2024).

The barriers of institutions are also considered a source of resistance. Most schools have no specific vision or strategic framework regarding technology integration into their curriculum; as a result, efforts turn out to be fragmented without significant outcomes (Bates & Sangra, 2011). This can lead teachers to not get the support needed and do not know what to do to integrate technology into teaching in an effective way.

To overcome these barriers, educational leaders must cultivate a culture that embraces innovation and change. Providing a supportive environment that encourages experimentation with technology and celebrates successes can help mitigate resistance and foster enthusiasm among educators and students alike.

5.3 Teacher Training and Professional Development

Importance of Equipping Educators with Necessary Skills

The successful integration of technology in education is highly reliant on the ability of instructors to effectively use digital tools and resources. However, more educators have expressed that they do not feel adequately prepared to integrate technology into their teaching. A report conducted in India found that about 70% of participants felt they did not receive adequate training when using technology for instructional activities (Jiali et al.,).

Professional development programs must train educators in the use and navigation of educational technologies effectively. It is not merely technical know-how but also familiarity with pedagogical practices that capitalize on technology for better learning outcomes. The U.S. National Education Technology Plan focuses on developing digital-age teaching skills in educators to effectively integrate technology into the teaching-learning process (U.S. Department of Education, 2020).

In addition, professional development should be ongoing because technology is constantly being developed. A single session of training is usually inadequate; rather, teachers need sustained support and opportunities for collaborative work in order to exchange best practices and lessons learned (Luckin & Holmes, 2016). When educators are equipped with the skills they need, they can increase their confidence to use technology, which is likely to impact student learning experiences positively.

5.4 Privacy and Ethical Concerns

Data Security Issues in Educational Technology

This expansion of technology in school environments brings up serious questions regarding the security and privacy of their data. Schools are implementing digital tools to make learning more enjoyable, which requires gathering student data, thereby making schools vulnerable to being hacked or using the student information improperly. According to a report from the Data Protection Commission of India 2021, frameworks to ensure sensitive data from students are at a heightened need due to increasing privacy concerns.

Data collection in education raises complex ethical issues. Information about students' personal lives and academics can be used commercially or accessed without permission, potentially leading to misuse (Chen, 2022). Incidents of data breaches within the U.S. have made headlines, with hackers focusing on school systems that store sensitive information about students, adding further layers to the lack of trust in educational technology.

The above-mentioned problems will only be met with stringent data governance policies within learning institutions, protecting student confidentiality and using technology in the most ethical way possible. There is transparency regarding the way data is being collected and kept safely; it has to be clearly communicated with parents and students on rights related to their personal information. It becomes challenging for educators and administrators to traverse this landscape and make use of technological advancements without affecting student privacy and welfare.

The issues involved in incorporating technology into learning underscored the complexity of this revolutionary process. Infrastructure and access matters highlight the digital divide that is prevalent today worldwide, and resistance to change identifies cultural and institutional obstacles that should be overcome. Further, ensuring that the teachers were trained appropriately is also indispensable for proper usage of technologies, and ethical considerations pertaining to data privacy remain important concerns. This can be achieved by recognizing and addressing these challenges so that educational leaders can work towards creating an inclusive and effective environment where technology enhances learning and teaching experiences for all stakeholders (Manoharan, Ashtikar, Rao et al, 2024).

6. FUTURE TRENDS IN EDUCATIONAL TECHNOLOGY

Rapid technological advancements are well on their way to overhauling the education landscape. Educational technology has dramatically evolved in the last few years; it has reshaped processes of teaching and learning worldwide. This essay discusses the emergent new technologies that may appear in the future, predictions for the next decade, and the policy and governance roles in facilitating the integration of technology into education, which were recently published by both Indian and international authors.

6.1 Emerging Technologies on the Horizon

Emerging technologies such as blockchain and the Internet of Things (IoT) represent new avenues for revolutionizing educational practice.

Block chain in Education

Block chains, being secure and transparent by nature, can be very effective in solving critical challenges in education, particularly regarding credential verification and data management. Block-chain can empower learners to have and maintain control of their educational records, thus allowing lifelong learning. For instance, when institutions issue verifiable and anti-fraud decentralized credentials, this will enhance the credibility of achievements in educational settings (Manoharan, Razak, Rajchandar, Nithya, Durai, & Ashtikar, 2024).

It is now realizing the huge potential of block-chain in changing the certification process in India. Such an effort by the Indian government in issuing academic certificates through block-chain is a substantial shift toward ensuring authenticity and reducing administrative inefficiencies. It points toward the fact that there is a trend shift towards education-related experiences being more personal and secure.

Internet of Things (IoT)

IoT refers to the networking of connected devices that can both collect and share data. Through IoT, smart classrooms improve the educational learning environment; in schools, IoT sensors and other interactive technologies are established. With IoT application, the implementation of real-time feedback would facilitate changing the educational strategy if engagement or performance metrics deviate from normal expectations (Chen, 2022).

In India, for example, the Smart Schools Programme is trying to bring IoT into the educational infrastructure to improve the learning outcomes and operational efficiency (Bandyopadhyay et al., 2021). The introduction of IoT in education does not only make the administrative processes streamlined but also helps in an immersive learning experience, which is the trend all over the world toward personalized education.

6.2 Predictions for the Next Decade

As we look toward the next decade, the integration of advanced technologies is expected to significantly reshape the educational landscape.

Personalized Learning

Probably, the most awaited change would be personalized learning environments empowered by AI. AI-powered learning environments can analyze the student's data to give unique experiences through customization of resources and assessment aligned to different learning paces and styles. This is indicative of moving away from traditional approaches towards a student-centered model where there will be more engagement and outcome for both teaching and learning (Kitchenham, 2008).

In India, AI in education is on the rise and is being used as an enabler for the growing success of platforms like BYJU'S and Vedantu by leveraging AI to deliver personalized tutoring solutions (Jiali et al.,). It is expected that, by 2030, this would be the norm when personalized learning becomes the new standard of the system, enabling all learners to reach their full potential, thereby meeting the diverse educational needs of different demographics.

Expanded Access and Inclusion

The pandemic has promoted the adoption of online learning platforms, which have long been a focus for educational institutions worldwide. According to the UNESCO report (2021), remote learning has not only made education accessible but highlighted disparities in access to technology, especially in developing countries. In the future, educational technology will focus more on inclusivity, in which all students, irrespective of socio-economic status, can have access to quality education.

The Digital India initiative aims to bridge the digital divide in India by providing internet access to rural and underprivileged communities. This is a much-needed step to foster equal learning opportunities, thus promoting social mobility and reducing educational inequalities. By using technology to enhance accessibility, the paradigm of education can shift toward more equitable and inclusive practices.

Lifelong Learning and Workforce Development

Work, which has been constantly transforming with changing times, becomes mandatory for updating and developing new knowledge continuously. According to the estimations for 2030, the future of lifelong learning (Manoharan, Razak, Rajchandar, Nithya, Durai, & Ashtikar, 2024)should become a part of education itself, with key points including skills relevant for jobs of the future. Future Jobs Report, World Economic Forum (2023), cites increased technological skills, ability for critical thinking, and the adaptability that must bring in changes in education as per demand.

In India, the Skill India initiative aims at enhancing vocational training and employability of youth, thus indicating a focus on aligning education with labor market needs (Monica et al., 2025). Institutions will play a crucial role in preparing students for tomorrow's challenges by integrating workforce development into educational frameworks.

6.3 The Role of Policy and Governance

Supportive policies and governance are also essential in the effective integration of technology into education. The policymakers, therefore, must set a framework that ensures innovation but equitably distributed, considering ethical reasons in technology implementation.

Supportive Policies for Technology Integration

Policies need to support the assimilation of these emerging technologies into classrooms, coupled with teacher training. In its vision, the National Education Policy 2020 for the nation of India supports its objective in the incorporation of technologies within education systems by planning digital infrastructure, training teachers to ensure that there are conducive channels for the delivery of innovation-driven teaching and learning exercises. Such policies may prove useful in promoting effective applications of technology.

Ensuring Equity and Accessibility

There also needs to be a thrust on bridging the inequalities of access in education, particularly those concerning the marginalized communities. Without targeted efforts to ensure inclusion of all learner populations into the digital space, there is always a danger of increasing educational inequality. Multi-stakeholder engagement-including governments, private enterprise players, and educational establishments-will play a crucial role in creating policies that value equity (Zhao et al., 2006).

Ethical Considerations in Technology Use

Lastly, as technology blends into education, ethical uses are very important. In relation to data privacy, issues surrounding surveillance and the potentiality for biases in AI algorithms become more relevant to be met by policy frameworks. Education experts and policymakers must have cooperation in creating guidelines with proper ethical standards while at the same time using technological facilitation to enhance their learning experiences.

The future of educational technology, therefore, is bright; there is a rise of innovative tools and practices that might transform learning experiences. With the development of blockchain and IoT and the future predictions for the next decade, the personalized, equitable, and lifelong learning frameworks are on their way (Manoharan, Razak, Rajchandar, Nithya, Durai, & Ashtikar, 2024). However, a strong policy and governance mechanism would be required to foster and guide the effective deployment of technology in education to realize this potential. By addressing these challenges and seizing opportunities, we are able to foster a rich environment for education that readies learners for the complexities of the future.

7. CONCLUSION

As we enter a new milestone in education, it would be more evident how technology is slowly changing things. The present section summarises the pertinent discussions and findings in examining future trends in educational technology with their implications for educators and policy makers, and presents to stakeholders the call for adopting technological advances for education towards empowerment.

7.1 Summary of Key Points

Throughout this discussion, we touched on several of the new technologies that will shape education. Two which stand out are block-chain and the Internet of Things (IoT). Both of them hold enormous promise for transforming the way education is secured, made more accessible, and personalized. Block-chain technology has made credential verification possible with a certain level of security and granted learners ownership over their educational records. Studies show that this may further decrease fraud and inefficiency in the certification process.

The Internet of Things is more applicable to the development of intelligent classrooms and interactive learning settings. The possibility of harvesting and analyzing real-time information on student engagement offers the potential for more customized experiences in learning (Chen, 2022). These technologies, in collaboration with artificial intelligence, will advance the tremendous amount of personalization required for customized education, targeting different types of learning experiences according to each individual's diverse needs and ensuring better engagement and outcomes (Kitchenham, 2008).

Looking forward into the future, we foresee an even more inclusive learning approach that values lifelong learning. The rate at which digital learning platforms accelerated during the COVID-19 pandemic underscored the need for education to be equitable and pointed out a significant challenge: ensuring educational systems worldwide take action against disparities so all learners enjoy the benefits of technological development (UNESCO, 2021). For instance, in India, initiatives under the Digital India campaign are notable for their goal of bridging gaps in access to technology, which would help in promoting social equity in education (Manoharan, Razak, Rajchandar, Nithya, Durai, & Ashtikar, 2024).

However, for such integration, robust policies and governance are required. In India, the NEP 2020 makes it imperative to have institutional frameworks that can support technology in education while keeping a balance with ethical considerations, data privacy, and inclusivity. Hence, it is clear that policy support is essential in achieving the full potential of educational technology in ways that are equitable and effective.

7.2 Implications for Educators and Policymakers

The findings and discussions presented here carry significant implications for educators as well as policymakers. Challenges for educators lie in their ability to adapt pedagogical practices to harness these emerging technologies effectively. Professional development and training in digital literacy, pedagogical strategies for online teaching, and understanding the ethical implications of data use in education must be priorities. According to (Jiali et al.,), incorporating innovative teaching methods, including project-based learning, gamification, and flipped classrooms, will help foster a more engaging and interactive learning environment, leveraging technology to its fullest.

Policymakers are critical to play the role in making this happen. It is essential to establish all-rounded policies that inform how funds are raised, the deployment of technology, and the education of teachers. Further, the digital divide should be dealt with; specific measures ought to be taken to enable the deprived communities access the available technological tools. Investment in infrastructure and school training should be one of the key priorities of a nation (Monica et al., 2025). Policymakers should also encourage public-private partnerships that can facilitate innovation and resource sharing for effective integration of technology into educational systems. Adaptive learning technologies and educational tools will be developed, hence being accessible and affordable to a wide variety of learners.

7.3 Call to Action

As stakeholders within the educational sector, an immediate call to action resonates with involving the educator to the policy-maker, industry leader to the technology developer, has to embrace this empowering technology. This shall call for commitment not just towards the integration of newer tools into the educational framework but also towards the culture that involves continuous learning and adaptation among everyone involved.

Educators should therefore champion a mentality that believes in innovation and experimentation of technology in class. This entails being open to new teaching methods, reaching out to the needs of learners, and using insights from data to guide instruction. Furthermore, all stakeholders should have a focus on ethical use of technology and ensure student data is used responsibly and the development of tools to aid education considers inclusivity in design.

Policymakers should work with educators and technologists to ensure that there is a conducive ecosystem for experimentation and adoption. Pilot programs for new applications of technologies in schools, continuous assessments of their impact, and mechanisms for feedback should be put in place to improve implementation processes.

Moreover, to make students tech-savvy enough for them to understand and handle these devices appropriately, the process of making them ready for the high-tech future becomes a combined effort. Training in developing skills in such areas as critical thinking and digital competence and developing collaborative problem-solving skills must feature in curricula.

In conclusion, while the future of education appears bright in a technology-dominated world, it calls for efforts from all stakeholders toward a common goal. By embracing and integrating innovative technologies into curricula and policies, it may create a more equitable, inclusive, and responsive education landscape. Let us take up this vision and then act decisively to empower learners for the challenges and opportunities that lie ahead.

REFERENCES

Ahmed, V., & Opoku, A. (2022). Technology supported learning and pedagogy in times of crisis: The case of COVID-19 pandemic. *Education and Information Technologies, 27*(1), 365–405. DOI: 10.1007/s10639-021-10706-w PMID: 34462626

Ashtikar, S. P., & Manoharan, G. (2024, June). Digital Transformation in Higher Education: A Pedagogical Perspective. In *2024 3rd International Conference on Computational Modelling, Simulation and Optimization (ICCMSO)* (pp. 210-215). IEEE. DOI: 10.1109/ICCMSO61761.2024.00051

Bandyopadhyay, S., Bardhan, A., Dey, P., & Bhattacharyya, S. (2021). *Bridging the education divide using social technologies*. Springer. DOI: 10.1007/978-981-33-6738-8

Bastos, R. M. B. (2017). The surprising success of the Finnish educational system in a global scenario of commodified education. *Revista Brasileira de Educação, 22*, 802–825. DOI: 10.1590/s1413-24782017227040

Bates, A. T., & Sangra, A. (2011). *Managing technology in higher education: Strategies for transforming teaching and learning*. John Wiley & Sons.

Canton, H. (2021). United Nations Educational, Scientific and Cultural Organization—UNESCO. In *The Europa Directory of International Organizations 2021* (pp. 359-365). Routledge.

Cavus, N., & Zabadi, T. (2014). A comparison of open source learning management systems. *Procedia: Social and Behavioral Sciences, 143*, 521–526. DOI: 10.1016/j.sbspro.2014.07.430

Chen, M. L. (2022). The impact of mobile learning on the effectiveness of English teaching and learning—A meta-analysis. *IEEE Access : Practical Innovations, Open Solutions, 10*, 38324–38334. DOI: 10.1109/ACCESS.2022.3165017

Clark, R. E. (1989). Current progress and future directions for research in instructional technology. *Educational Technology Research and Development, 37*(1), 57–66. DOI: 10.1007/BF02299046

Dahlström, H. (2019). Digital writing tools from the student perspective: Access, affordances, and agency. *Education and Information Technologies, 24*(2), 1563–1581. DOI: 10.1007/s10639-018-9844-x

Daniela, L., & Visvizi, A. (2022). *Remote learning in times of pandemic*. Routledge.

Fisher, T. (2006). Educational transformation: Is it, like 'beauty', in the eye of the beholder, or will we know it when we see it? *Education and Information Technologies, 11*(3-4), 293–303. DOI: 10.1007/s10639-006-9009-1

Giere, R. N., & Moffatt, B. (2003). Distributed cognition: Where the cognitive and the social merge. *Social Studies of Science, 33*(2), 301–310. DOI: 10.1177/03063127030332017

Gratchev, I., & Espinosa, H. G. Advancing Engineering Education Beyond COVID.

Hamilton, E. R., Rosenberg, J. M., & Akcaoglu, M. (2016). The substitution augmentation modification redefinition (SAMR) model: A critical review and suggestions for its use. *TechTrends, 60*(5), 433–441. DOI: 10.1007/s11528-016-0091-y

Herring, M. C., Koehler, M. J., Mishra, P., Rosenberg, J. M., & Teske, J. (2016). Introduction to the second edition of the TPACK handbook. In *Handbook of technological pedagogical content knowledge (TPACK) for educators* (pp. 1-8). Routledge.

Hwang, G. J., Lai, C. L., & Wang, S. Y. (2015). Seamless flipped learning: A mobile technology-enhanced flipped classroom with effective learning strategies. *Journal of Computers in Education, 2*(4), 449–473. DOI: 10.1007/s40692-015-0043-0

Jiali, S., Dayo, F., Jun, G., Shuangyao, L., & Najam, S. The Impact of Artificial Intelligence on Personalized Learning in Education: A Systematic Review.

Kitchenham, A. (2008). The evolution of John Mezirow's transformative learning theory. *Journal of Transformative Education, 6*(2), 104–123. DOI: 10.1177/1541344608322678

Kultawanich, K., Koraneekij, P., & Na-Songkhla, J. (2015). A proposed model of connectivism learning using cloud-based virtual classroom to enhance information literacy and information literacy self-efficacy for undergraduate students. *Procedia: Social and Behavioral Sciences, 191*, 87–92. DOI: 10.1016/j.sbspro.2015.04.394

Lajoie, S. P., & Poitras, E. (2023). Technology-Rich Learning Environments: Theories and Methodologies for Understanding Solo and Group Learning. In *Handbook of educational psychology* (pp. 630-653). Routledge.

Lee, M. F. R. (2023). A Review on intelligent control theory and applications in process optimization and smart manufacturing. *Processes (Basel, Switzerland), 11*(11), 3171. DOI: 10.3390/pr11113171

Luckin, R., & Holmes, W. (2016). Intelligence unleashed: An argument for AI in education.

Manoharan, G., Ashtikar, S. P., Rao, C. G., & Nivedha, M. (2024). A Pedagogical Landscape: Narrative Study on Emerging Artificial Intelligence Trends in Education. In *Inclusive Educational Practices and Technologies for Promoting Sustainability* (pp. 22–41). IGI Global. DOI: 10.4018/979-8-3693-6955-5.ch002

Manoharan, G., Razak, A., Rajchandar, K., Nithya, G., Durai, S., & Ashtikar, S. P. (2024). Digital Learning for Professional Development in Varied Fields of Service Sectors: Embracing Technological Advancements. In *Embracing Technological Advancements for Lifelong Learning* (pp. 111-137). IGI Global.

Manoharan, G., Razak, A., Rajchandar, K., Nithya, G., Durai, S., & Ashtikar, S. P. (2024). Digital Learning for Professional Development in Varied Fields of Service Sectors: Embracing Technological Advancements. In *Embracing Technological Advancements for Lifelong Learning* (pp. 111-137). IGI Global.

Marais, N. (2011). Connectivism as learning theory: The force behind changed teaching practice in higher education. *Education, Knowledge & Economy*, *4*(3), 173–182.

Marsh, J. A., & Farrell, C. C. (2015). How leaders can support teachers with data-driven decision making: A framework for understanding capacity building. *Educational Management Administration & Leadership*, *43*(2), 269–289. DOI: 10.1177/1741143214537229

Mezirow, J. (1991). Transformative dimensions of adult learning.

Mishra, P., & Koehler, M. J. (2006). Technological pedagogical content knowledge: A framework for teacher knowledge. *Teachers College Record*, *108*(6), 1017–1054. DOI: 10.1111/j.1467-9620.2006.00684.x

Monica, J. A., Malar, J. H., Arun, C., Sharmila, L., & Arif, M. (2025). Leveraging Technology and Universal Design for Inclusive and Engaging Learning in Indian Higher Education. In *Educational Philosophy and Sociological Foundation of Education* (pp. 177–212). IGI Global.

Owston, R. O. N. (2018, January). Empowering learners through blended learning. [). Association for the Advancement of Computing in Education] [AACE]. *International Journal on E-Learning*, *17*(1), 65–83.

Parjanen, S., & Rantala, T. (2021). Building an open innovation platform as a part of city renewal initiatives. *European Planning Studies*, *29*(12), 2165–2183. DOI: 10.1080/09654313.2021.1903397

Puentedura, R. (2006). Transformation, technology, and education.[Blog post]. hippasus. Com/resources/tte. *Abfrage*, *14*, 2023.

Purushottamashtikar, S., & Manoharan, G. (2024, June). Emotional intelligence on higher education educators: A systematic literature review. In *AIP Conference Proceedings* (Vol. 2971, No. 1). AIP Publishing. DOI: 10.1063/5.0195788

Roberts-Mahoney, H., Means, A. J., & Garrison, M. J. (2016). Netflixing human capital development: Personalized learning technology and the corporatization of K-12 education. *Journal of Education Policy*, *31*(4), 405–420. DOI: 10.1080/02680939.2015.1132774

Roschelle, J. (1995). *The construction of shared knowledge in collaborative problem solving*. Computer Supported Collaborative Learning/Springer-Verlag. DOI: 10.1007/978-3-642-85098-1_5

Sanders, M., & George, A. (2017). Viewing the changing world of educational technology from a different perspective: Present realities, past lessons, and future possibilities. *Education and Information Technologies*, *22*(6), 2915–2933. DOI: 10.1007/s10639-017-9604-3

Sparkling, A. E., & Sengupta, R. (2023). Mapping Student's Perspective of a Redesigned Curriculum in Construction Management Using Self-Determination Theory. *International Journal of Construction Education and Research*, *19*(4), 443–459. DOI: 10.1080/15578771.2022.2148025

Veluvali, P., & Surisetti, J. (2022). Learning management system for greater learner engagement in higher education—A review. *Higher Education for the Future*, *9*(1), 107–121. DOI: 10.1177/23476311211049855

Vygotsky, L. S. (1978). *Mind in society: The development of higher psychological processes* (Vol. 86). Harvard university press.

Wu, W. H., Wu, Y. C. J., Wu, C. Y., Kao, H. Y., Lin, C. H., & Huang, S. H. (2012). Review of trends from mobile learning studies: A meta-analysis. *Computers & Education*, *59*(2), 817–827. DOI: 10.1016/j.compedu.2012.03.016

Zhao, Y., Lei, J., & Conway, P. F. (2006). Global perspective on political definitions of e-learning: Commonalities and differences in national educational technology strategy discourses. In *The international handbook of virtual learning environments* (pp. 673–697). Springer Netherlands. DOI: 10.1007/978-1-4020-3803-7_26

Chapter 6
AI-Powered Technologies for Plastic Waste Management and Recycling

P. Naveen
http://orcid.org/0000-0002-8941-5629
SRM Institute of Science and Technology, India

S. Vinodkumar
http://orcid.org/0000-0002-7684-2699
St. Joseph's College of Engineering, India

ABSTRACT

This chapter explores the transformative role of Artificial Intelligence (AI) in addressing the escalating issue of plastic waste accumulation, a critical environmental challenge. It delves into AI-driven strategies that enhance the efficiency of plastic sorting by accurately identifying types and recyclability, thereby minimizing contamination in recycling streams. The chapter also investigates AI models designed to predict the degradation rates of various plastics in diverse environmental conditions, offering valuable insights for long-term planning in waste management. Highlighting potential cost savings, financial benefits, and operational efficiencies, the discussion is enriched with case studies showcasing real-world applications and challenges in implementing AI for recycling. Ethical considerations and the environmental implications of adopting AI in this sector are analyzed to provide a balanced perspective.

DOI: 10.4018/979-8-3373-0629-2.ch006

ght © 2026, IGI Global Scientific Publishing. Copying or distributing in print or electronic forms without written permission of IGI Global Scientific Publishing is prohibited. Use of this chapter to generative artificial intelligence (AI) technologies is expressly prohibited. The publisher reserves all rights to license its use for generative AI training and machine learning model development.

1. INTRODUCTION

One of the main environmental problems of the 21st century is growing amount of waste from plastic. The current production of plastics worldwide is around 368 million tons per year and natural ecosystems in terms of waste, particularly oceans, are in critical levels (Geyer et al., 2017). The strength of plastics, that makes them useful but also causes them to be persistent pollutant. The traditional methods for managing waste such as incineration and landfilling are not just ineffective but also present more risk to the environment. Recycling, though being a greener option is frequently hampered by the contamination of waste, insufficient sorting and the complicated character of plastics (Hopewell et al., 2009).

In recent times, artificial intelligence (AI) has been recognized as an effective tool for transformation across many sectors such as waste management. AI especially computer vision and machine learning can dramatically improve the effectiveness and efficiency of recycling and management of plastic waste processes. With the help of machine learning algorithms, which can discover patterns in huge quantities of data, we can improve the recycling process, predict rate of degradation, and even develop new plastic that is easier to recycle (Ragaert et al., 2017). Conversely, computer vision can improve the efficiency of sorting processes by recognizing and separating various kinds of materials more effectively than conventional techniques (Turaga et al., 2020).

The promise of AI powered sorting systems is very high. Traditional sorting methods are typically based on manual labor or mechanical methods that struggle with waste streams that are mixed. Together imaging recognition technology and AI enhanced technology can recognize different types of plastics at a great rate of speed and accuracy. These systems don't just rise speeds and precision of sorting, they also reduce the contamination in recycling streams which is one of the major obstacles to efficient recycling.

Additionally, AI can optimize the recycling process by using both chemical and mechanical. Machine learning models can examine aspects of recycling like the time it takes to process and temperature, to assure the highest efficiency and yields of high quality. This could lead to a reduction in energy and less operating expenses making recycling economically feasible (Huang et al., 2019). For further, AI can be used to calculate the degradation rates of different plastics to ensure that we are doing so at the optimal level, with very high quality of our output. Such can lead to more efficient planning of long-term recycling and waste infrastructure management (Nash & Boswell, 2019).

Although it is promising that AI can bring, the implementation of AI to manage plastic waste faces some challenges. The technical obstacles include the requirement for large quality and high-quality data sets as well as the challenges in making accurate models are crucial. Additionally, there are ethical questions concerning the broad-based application in AI as a form of technology. These concerns can lead to the loss of jobs and the negative environmental effects on the environment resulting from these technologies (Vinuesa et al., 2020). However, the advantages of AI in combating plastic waste are enormous and need further research and development.

AI is a powerful tool to boost the disposal of plastic waste and recycle. In addition to boosting your efficiency in sorting, improving recycling processes and forecasting the degrading of plastics AI can benefit in overcoming the most significant issues that arise from the environmental impact of plastics. As the world confronts the environmental consequences of plastics, AI-powered solutions provide the possibility of sustaining recycling methods for waste.

1.1 A Brief Overview of the Plastic Waste Problem

Today we also face a global problem in environmental terms of plastic waste, thousands of tons per year contaminating our planet. The toughness, flexibility, and cost effectiveness of plastics have led to their widespread use and the associated piling up of much waste in the oceans, in landfills, as well as in other ecological systems. There is a consensus that 8.3 billion tons of plastic were produced since 1950 and approximately 79% of the waste accumulating in landfills or in the natural environment (Geyer et al., 2017). The resurgence of plastic materials that could take a long time to degrade, is a major contributor to the issue, resulting in lasting health and environmental impacts. Marine ecosystems are the most vulnerable to the effects of plastic pollution, with thousands of tons of plastic waste cause harm to marine life and eventually entering in the food chain (Jambeck et al., 2015). Despite increasing recognition and initiatives in the direction of rise recycling, only 9 percent of all plastic waste is recycled, and the vast majority is still causing environmental harm (Hopewell et al., 2009). For solving our problem of plastic waste, down production of plastic, increase recycling, and ending more pollution to the environment will involve innovative solutions and major international cooperation.

1.2 Role of AI in Environmental Engineering

Increasingly, Artificial Intelligence (AI) is necessary to environmental engineering as it offers efficiency and effectiveness at monitoring, management, and sustainability in environmental engineering. AI techniques such as machine learning and data analytics are used to examine massive data sets to recognize patterns, develop trends and identify what will alter our environment and enhance resource management. As demonstrated by its ability to accurately predict climate change or pollution impact levels, as well as improve methods of waste management such as recycling or energy recuperation (Cowie & Cowie, 2018), AI powered models are effective at precisely predicting these phenomena.

Plastic recycling will be changed by AI as AI will elevate the accuracy in identifying materials and decrease contaminants in the recycling channel. Artificial intelligence powered computer vision systems can identify multiple kinds of plastics in real-time and increase recycling efficiency (Turaga et al., 2020). AI-powered models can also be utilized to simulate environmental effects which benefit engineers to develop sustainable methods and processes. Engineers working on environmental issues together this kind of artificial intelligence may develop ways to lower the level of pollution within their environment while also increasing sustainability, resulting in stronger ecosystems that can tackle the pressing environmental issues that we confront in the present.

2. RELATED WORK

In the past few years, there has been a huge boom in the domain of AI powered plastic waste management and recycling technologies, due to the growing need to be more effective, and environmentally friendly, in dealing with waste. In this section, we focus on reviewing related work by reviewing key technologies, algorithms, and approaches that AI has been applied to address plastic waste management.

2.1. Machine Learning for Plastic Identification and Sorting

Supervised learning algorithms such as these have also been proven to be an essential resource for recycling and reuse of plastics. Huang et al. (2019) show how this practice was done by reviewing the use of machine learning models to help make plastic recycling mechanical recycling more efficient, using massive data sets from recycling plastic waste. These models can accurately classify and identify various plastics based on their chemical and physical properties, which is an effective way to decrease pollution in materials that are recycled.

They conducted extensive research into Convolutional Neural Networks (CNNs) and their application in sorting plastic waste, demonstrating their capacity for accurately sorting plastic waste photos using CNNs (Jiang et al., 2021). Their research demonstrated their capacity for recognizing intricate patterns found within plastic photographs that require precise sorting requirements furthermore, they decreased manual labor requirements thus decreasing chances of mistakes as well as increasing overall effectiveness and accuracy during sorting processes.

2.2. Computer Vision and Image Recognition

The computing vision coupled with AI are now a powerful weapon to aid the sorting of plastic waste. In Turaga et al. (2020), the authors present detailed analyses of how AI is applied to waste management with a particular focus on sorting plastic waste through the use of computer vision techniques such as image recognition which allows for sorting of plastics based on their visual qualities such as colour, shape and texture. TOMRA (2019) has developed an AI-powered sorting device together Near-infrared (NIR) technology, as well computer learning algorithms to differentiate plastics based on their polymer content. The system has since been widely used in recycling facilities and has improved the quality of the plastics that are sorted to create more high-quality recycled products.

2.3. Predictive Modeling and Plastic Degradation

Estimating the degrading rate of plastics under distinct environments relies on predictive modeling. Nash and Boswell (2019) describe machine learning which aids the prediction of the fate of the environment for plastic waste environments presented machine learning models to help determine the fate of the environment for plastic waste. Plastics degradation is modeled based on data on environmental variables, such as temperature, UV exposure and microbial activity, to predict how plastics break down over time. Predicting degradation of plastic with a high degree of accuracy will be essential for developing sustainable waste disposal strategies as well as developing more sustainable plastic materials.

A more complete picture of the life cycle of plastics is presented by Geyer et al. (2017), as well as the importance of predictive modeling for extrapolating the environmental impacts of plastic waste. What really hits home is that they need more research, and they need continual improvement in predictive modeling methods to better understand the long-term consequences that plastic pollution has on our environment.

2.4. AI-Driven Optimization of Recycling Processes

Chemical and mechanical recycling processes have quickly found AI driven Optimization to be of the highest importance and has been added as an essential component to better ROI and sustainability. AI algorithms could use various parameters used in recycling processes like temperature pressure temperature chemical usage to maximize recycled material output while simultaneously decreasing energy use optimizing in this manner creates both increased recycling efficiencies as well as decreased environmental impacts associated with recycling centers (Huang et al., 2019).

An AI driven robot system for recycling was created by (AMP Robotics) that applies reinforcement learning to, incentivise the robot system to continuously increase sorting efficiency. Through its sorting choices, it learns and adjusts how it works to maximize plastic recycling rates in the recycling facility, increasing both the amount of plastic recycled and the quality of what it sorted. The use of this strategy has resulted in improved quality and increased material recycled.

2.5. Ethical and Environmental Considerations

Investigate the ethical and environmental considerations related to using artificial intelligence for plastic waste management. They highlight potential environmental benefits from AI-driven recycling systems, including reduced landfill disposal of plastic waste and decreased demand for virgin plastics, while discussing potential ethical repercussions associated with using AI systems, including displacement of workers due to automation and energy consumption associated with AI systems (Vinuesa et al., 2020).Conducted further research into the environmental sustainability of AI-powered recycling, placing particular focus on energy-efficient

2.6. Case Studies and Real-World Implementations

One of the success stories of the use of AI to the management of plastic waste are numerous real word examples of using AI to improve recycling that have proved the technology is efficient. Indeed in 2018, ZenRobotics (2018) and AMP Robotics (2018) as well as have developed AI driven robotics to connect with recycling facilities that have been successful. The recycling is processed faster by upholding a combination of a lot of the machines learning alongside robots and computers. As a result, their processes become more efficient, pollute less, and cost less to run. TOMRA (2019) and further along with show that the two companies have installed AI-powered sorting equipment in their recycling processes. This has resulted in substantial improvement in the quality of recycling. These cases provide more helpful information about the issues and benefits of AI to recycle. They prepare an insight into the future possibilities of innovations in this area. Table 1 provides a complete overview of technologies used in recycling as well as waste management, recycling as well as their capabilities, the platforms on which they are built on and the challenges they could confront.

The research that is reviewed in the book is a good example of the importance of application of AI to assure the proper management of recyclable plastics. AI technologies like machines learning and computer vision and predictive modeling have been proven to improve efficiency, effectiveness, as well as the sustainability and accuracy for recycle (Hidayat et al., 2020). Yet, with AI for recycling can be a challenge especially regarding data high-quality computational resources, as well as ethical concerns. The future research needs to be focused on these concerns and research the latest technologies that are driven by AI which will improve the process of recycling plastic, and benefit to build a sustainable future.

Table 1. Comprehensive overview of the technologies used in AI-powered plastic waste

Technology	Explanation	Characteristics	Platforms	Issues
Machine Learning for Plastic Identification	Uses supervised learning algorithms to classify different types of plastics based on physical and chemical properties.	✓ High accuracy in classification. ✓ Requires large labeled datasets. ✓ Can be integrated into existing sorting systems	✓ Custom machine learning platforms ✓ TensorFlow ✓ PyTorch	✓ Requires extensive training data. ✓ May struggle with mixed or contaminated waste
Computer Vision and Image Recognition	Utilizes AI-driven image recognition to analyze visual features of plastics for identification and sorting.	✓ Fast and efficient sorting. ✓ Can handle various types of plastics. ✓ Works in real-time	✓ TOMRA Sorting Solutions. ✓ OpenCV ✓ Custom-built Computer vision systems	✓ High computational requirements. ✓ May require calibration for different lighting conditions
Predictive Modeling for Plastic Degradation	Employs machine learning models to predict the degradation rates of plastics under different environmental conditions.	✓ Provides accurate predictions. ✓ Supports long-term waste management strategies. ✓ Can be used for lifecycle analysis	✓ Custom machine learning platforms. ✓ Scikit-learn	✓ Depends on the quality of environmental data. ✓ May need regular updates as conditions change.
AI-Driven Optimization of Recycling Processes	Optimizes parameters in recycling processes using AI algorithms, reducing energy consumption and improving yield.	✓ Increases recycling efficiency. ✓ Reduces operational costs ✓ Can be applied to both mechanical and chemical recycling processes	✓ AMP Robotics. ✓ Veolia ✓ Custom AI optimization systems	✓ Initial high setup costs ✓ May require integration with existing systems.
AI-Powered Robotics for Sorting	Combines AI with robotics to automate the sorting of plastic waste, increasing speed and accuracy.	✓ High sorting speed. ✓ Reduces labor costs. ✓ Continuously learns and adapts	✓ AMP Robotics. ✓ ZenRobotics	✓ Maintenance and upkeep of robotic systems. ✓ High initial investment

continued on following page

Table 1. Continued

Technology	Explanation	Characteristics	Platforms	Issues
Blockchain Integration with AI	Uses blockchain to securely track and verify the lifecycle of recycled materials, enhancing transparency in the recycling supply chain.	✓ Ensures data integrity. ✓ Enhances transparency and accountability. ✓ Secure transactions	✓ Custom blockchain platforms. ✓ Integration with AI-driven verification systems	✓ Requires blockchain infrastructure. ✓ Potential scalability issues
Predictive Maintenance using AI	Applies AI to predict maintenance needs for recycling machinery, reducing downtime and extending equipment lifespan.	✓ Reduces unexpected breakdowns. ✓ Lowers maintenance costs. ✓ Improves overall system reliability	✓ Custom predictive maintenance platforms. ✓ Integration with sensors and IoT devices	✓ Requires continuous monitoring and data collection. ✓ Potential high cost of sensor integration
AI-Driven Material Design	Utilizes AI to design new, more recyclable or biodegradable plastics by simulating properties and behaviors of various polymer formulations.	✓ - Supports the development of sustainable materials - Reduces the need for trial-and-error experimentation	✓ Custom AI simulation platforms. ✓ Research labs using AI for material science	✓ Complexity in modeling accurate material properties. ✓ Requires high computational power
Ethical and Environmental Considerations	Focuses on the ethical implications and environmental impacts of AI in recycling, including job displacement and energy consumption.	✓ - Balances AI benefits with social impact - Examines the sustainability of AI-driven solutions	✓ Policy frameworks. ✓ Ethical AI research platforms	✓ Potential for job displacement. ✓ High energy consumption of AI systems

3. METHODOLOGY

The AI-powered plastic waste management and recycling methodology proposed here aims to use advanced AI technologies to optimize each stage of the recycling process, from data collection, plastic identification, sorting optimization, predictive modeling for degradation, process optimization, blockchain integration for transparency purposes and ongoing system evaluation. The aim of this work is to create a plastic recycling system which will be efficient, accurate, and sustainable with considering at present difficulties in the management of plastic waste.

3.1. Data Collection and Pre-Processing

When applied to plastic waste management, this means gathering an exhaustive and diverse dataset that accurately reflects real world scenarios of plastic waste collection - images should represent different kinds of plastics under different conditions including degrees of contamination, lighting environments and physical states such as crushed, intact or partially melted plastics from recycling facilities, public waste bins or platforms like Kaggle could serve as data sources (Ragaert et al., 2017).

Figure 1. Data processing pipeline for plastic waste management

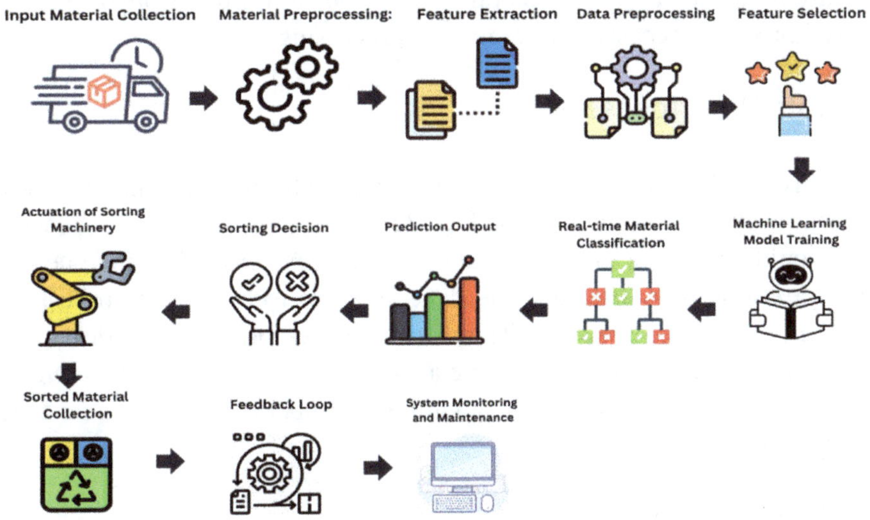

A complete data processing pipeline consisting of gathering, ingestion, preprocessing and quality assurance steps is shown in Figure 1. Preparation of quality data is key to the successful application of AI in systems dealing with plastic waste and recycling, and this pipeline will prove essential in this area.

a) Data Collection

The first stage that takes place, in which data is gathered from different sources, such as APIs, databases sensors, web scraping, IoT equipment, as well as surveys and direct input from users. The various types of sources assure that the gathered data is accurate and complete and covers a variety of dimensions that are relevant to the specific application.

b) Data Ingestion

After being collected after which after that, the data is then transferred into after which it is transferred to the Data Ingestion phase. This is where the data is kept in diverse storage options including data warehouses data lakes and local data storage. Data warehouses usually keep structured data which allows efficient querying and analysis while data lakes can handle both unstructured and structured data and offer flexibility in data use. Local storage can also be utilized to store data sets that may have immediate accessibility or require processing.

c) Data Pre-Processing

This is followed by Data Processing required for transforming the raw data into a clear useful form. *Data Cleansing*: Remove any noise, errors, or inconsistency that could be present inside the data *Data Enhancement*: Generate new examples using existing data to extend the data set so as to exhibit the robustness of the models, *Data transformation*: Transform the data into a proper format or a proper structure to analyze further or create a model for the data, *Data labeling*: Label the data with suitable label that is critical for the supervised learning in AI to further analyze or model.

d) Quality Check

It processes the data and goes through a Quality Review so that it's in line by standards of completeness, accuracy and reliability before it is used by downstream AI models or in decision making process. This quality assurance is key to make sure an AI is doing what you want it to and do it well.

3.2. Plastic Identification Using Computer Vision

The ability to identify plastic is a crucial part of the recycling process, and hence computer vision, enabled by CNNs, is the technology of choice for automated plastic identification. Being so spatially organized, CNNs are optimal for the identification of images features. Here, a CNN model was trained in this system to identify different types of plastics by looking at their visual appearance – color, texture, shape, etc. (Ragaert et al., 2017). Figure 2 shows a comprehensive outline of the CNN structure, specially developed to sort plastic waste. CNNs are a type that includes deep neural networks that are particularly suitable for the analysis of visual data and are therefore ideal for tasks like identification and categorization of pictures within the area in the field of management.

Figure 2. Convolutional neural network architecture for plastic classification

a) Input Layer

The process begins with the input layer which is where images of plastics mixed with other waste are fed to the network The raw data of this image, which is represented as pixels in a grid, is the image we present to the network, and the network analyzes to determine and classify different types of plastics.

b) Convolutional Layers

The operation applied to an image initially is called convolution. Kernels, or filters, are used to move over the image in convolutional layers, looking for specific features like edges pattern or texture or just edges for particular features like edges patterns, textures, or edges. This outcome in collection of map features that each one corresponds to a specific aspect that was detected across the image. The feature maps are then placed in a stack to record numerous elements of an image.

c) Pooling Layers

After the convolution the pooling layer is put in place. It reduces the dimensions of feature maps, but preserves the most crucial data, which assists to make the system more efficient computationally and reducing the chance of over-fitting. Typically, max pooling is employed to select the most significant value of each feature map area is chosen, creating feature maps that are pooled. Typically, several Convolution and pooling processes are repeated to extract more complex elements. After the beginning feature extract, a second formation of convolutional and layering layers are added in the diagram to get deeper feature maps which have a more abstracted image input properties and layering layers is added to create deeper feature maps that reflect more abstract elements of the image input.

d) Flatten Layer

Following diverse layers of convolution, as well as pooling the feature maps pooled by pooling are flattened into one-dimensional vector. The flattened vector is fed into the layers that are fully connected to the network.

e) Fully Connected Layers

The ones that perform their final classification. Each layer is connected to every other node in the preceding layer, which allows the network to integrate the features that were extracted from the convolutional layers to predict the class of the image that was input. In this scenario the output may be different kinds of polymers layered on top of (e.g. HDPE, PET HDPE, LDPE) which are made up of different elements in the layer.

f) Output Layer

The type of plastic that is present in image input is final classification results which is given by the output layer. It's important to get the plastics totally separated when recycling. the type of plastic that is present in the image input. This is essential in separating the plastics precisely when recycling.

3.3. Sorting Optimization With Machine Learning

Once plastics are identified, then there's the task of sorting them for highest recyclability, with the least contamination. We achieve this through sorting optimization using machine learning algorithms. The plastic image identification process starts with the feature extraction step, where we extract useful features such as polymer type, color and shape from the identified plastic images. Input to the sorting algorithm are these features, which predicts the optimal recycling path for each item (Hidayat et al., 2020) (Singh et al., 2017).

Figure 3. Workflow for AI-powered plastic sorting and recycling

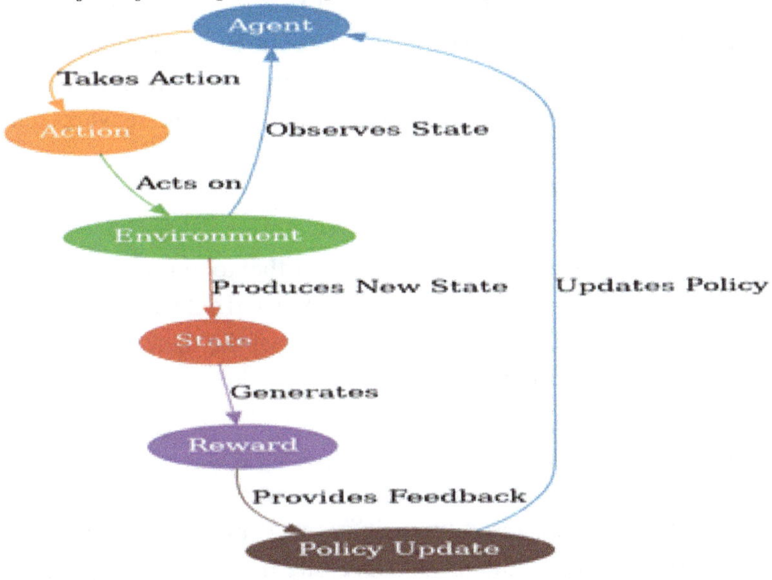

A complete process for the identification and the classification of recyclable plastics is provided by Figure 3, which uses machines and learning and automation tools to increase efficiency for the process. This system was created to increase the effectiveness and precision of sorting materials. This is especially true for plastics, which are essential to rise recycling results.

a) Input Materials Collection

The process starts by collecting mixed materials that comprise different kinds of plastics. The materials are then transported to the recycling facility in which they are prepared to be processed.

b) Materials Preprocessing

At this point the materials are subjected to pre-processing. This involves activities like cleaning, shredding or compressing for warrant they are appropriate shape for further study. Preprocessing removes any contaminants and prepares the material to be able to identify them accurately.

c) Features Extraction

Pre-processed materials are then subjected to feature extraction in which the key features of plastics, including shape, color, texture and the type of polymer are recognized. These attributes are essential to distinguish between different kinds of plastics. They are then removed with sophisticated imaging and sensors technologies.

d) Data Preprocessing

The features that are extracted are processed further to improve data quality. data. This process involves normalization, noise removal and data enhancement to assure accuracy of the data. data is uniform with the rest of the data and appropriate as a model for the machine learning models.

e) Features Selection

During this phase it is the case that features with greatest relevance are chosen for the purpose of training on the model. learning model. By focusing only on the things that make different types of plastic different, you reduce the data you need while improving the accuracy of the model.

f) Machine Learning Model Training

The features that are selected are utilized to build the machine learning model, usually an algorithm known as a classifier. The model can recognize various types of plastics based upon the input characteristics. It is then trained using data that is labeled, where the plastic's type is identified, allowing it to make precise predictions for new materials that are not known to the public.

g) Real-time Classification of Materials

When the machine learning model is applied in real time to teach it how to classify the materials as they move across the machine, it can be retrained. It is a crucial step to work out what sorting process is the best for every item of plastic.

h) Prediction Output

The model gives an output for prediction, which will indicate the kind of plastic being used. It also guides the next sorting decision.

i) Sorting Decision

Based on the predicted output the system will make an order decision. This determines which sorting pathway the material should follow and ensures that each kind of plastic will be directed to the correct processing stream.

j) The Actuation of Sorting Machinery Sorting Choice

The sorting action initiates the actuation of sorting machines, such as conveyor belts or robotic arms that physically separate substances adequate the classification they are assigned.

k) Sorting Materials Collection

Sorted materials are then sorted, and every type of plastic put in order to be further processed like recycling or reuse.

l) Feedback Loop

The system comes with a feedback loop which monitors the process of sorting and gives continuous data to improve as well as increase this machine learning model. Feedback is crucial to keeping the accuracy of the system over time and to adapt to changes in the composition of materials.

m) System Monitoring and Maintenance

A system wide monitoring and maintenance program watches that the machine is performing satisfactorily and that tools excesses are detected and solved quickly.

This is an advanced, AI driven method of recycling and identification, escalating recycling effectiveness and efficiency. In addition to automating the key processes, and using live data to guide the decisions, refugees this system will enhance the quality of recycled plastics, helping to address the overall purpose of sustainable waste management and decreasing pollution.

3.4. Process Optimization with Reinforcement Learning

To achieve the highest possible plastic recycling operations' efficiency, plastic recycling operations need to be optimized. Reinforcement learning (RL) provides a powerful approach to this problem as the system learns and adapts with feedback from carrying out its actions. Within the recycling system, an RL agent is used to control important variables like processing temperature, chemical usage and sorting speed. The agent receives reward by taking actions that are conditioned by a given reward function. The reward function is something that gives reward for moving in the direction of the desired outcome, for example, decreasing energy consumption, reducing waste, increasing purity of recycled materials. The agent feeds back towards the system by getting rewards or penalties for what it does. The agent learns which actions yield outcomes that are the best, based on this, it rethinks its strategy. By allowing the recycling system to learn continuously, this creates an opportunity to dynamically optimize its operation based on changes in waste composition along with other variables 'in real time' (Ragaert et al., 2017).

Figure 4. Reinforcement learning process in plastic waste management optimization

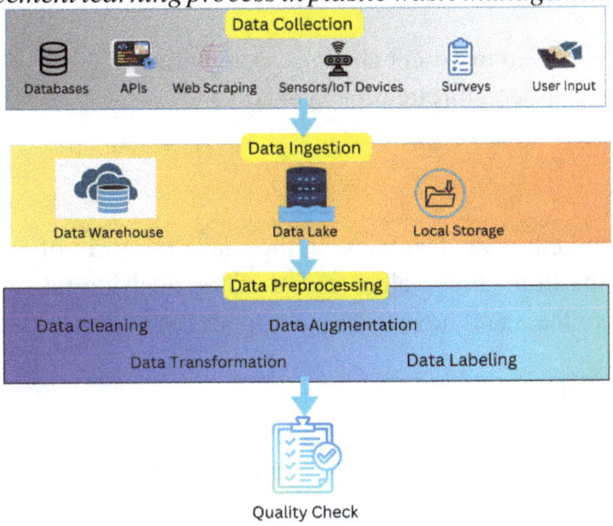

Figure 4 shows the fundamental loop in the system of reinforcement learning (RL) process that is where An Agent communicates with an environment to develop optimal behavior by trial and trial and. Here's the step-by-step procedure:

a) Agent

It refers to person who does the decision or learning entity (whatever want to do some work and complete the mission through interaction with external environment).

b) Action

An agent picks a decision based on his current policy, which is an algorithm, that determines the behaviors of the agent.

c) Environment

The selected procedure is performed, affecting the environment. It is the external environment or context within which the agent performs. The environment reacts to the agent's actions by transforming to a different state.

d) State

The state of the environment changes as an outcome of the actions of an agent. The new state is noticed through the agents.

e) Reward

The environment gives feedback, in the shape the form of a reward. This is an indication of the immediate value or cost of the decision taken by an agent. The reward signal to the agent how effective or poor the decision resulted in the goal.

f) Policy Update

Based on the state that was observed, and the reward received the agent revises its policy to rise the next steps. This update to the policy is essential in learning as it allows the agent to discover which actions bring the most rewards over time.

That means the RL loop will continue indefinitely both for the agent to fine tune its plan, understand its mistakes and optimize its action to get the best of it over the long term. This technique is widely used in the AI applications such as the games, robotics and systems dynamic optimization.

3.5. Blockchain Integration for Transparency and Accountability

In the recycling supply chain, transparency and accountability are key, and blockchain provides a solution to a secure, tamper proof track record of every step in the recycling process. Integrated with AI, blockchain is applied to track and confirm the life cycle of recycled materials from collection to their final product output in this system. Each transaction, whether it's the identification of a plastic type or the processing of recycled material, is recorded on the blockchain. Smart contracts are used to automate verification processes, ensuring that the materials meet industry standards before they proceed to the next stage. The level of transparency not only earn trust of stakeholders but also make companies and agencies to comply with a regulation.

Blockchain enables traceability of materials, which enable consumers and businesses to verify the origin and quality of recycled products. For industries where material purity and safety are essential to the industry — think food packaging or medical equipment — this can be a big deal. Blockchain integration makes sure that all transactions are secured, recorded and easily available so recycled items become more sustainable and accountable.

Figure 5. Blockchain workflow for enhancing transparency in plastic waste management

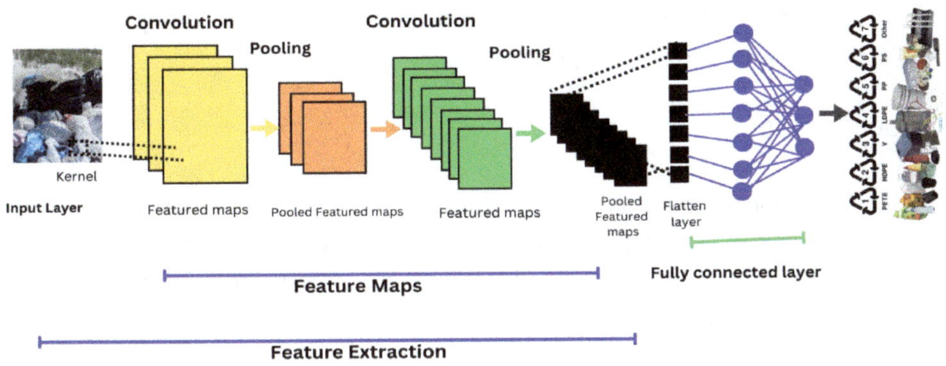

Figure 5 illustrates how blockchain can be utilized to boost transparency as well as traceability and integrity of plastic recycling and waste management processes.

a) Data Entry

The process starts by entering data that pertains to plastic waste, like the kind of plastic, the quantity, the origin, or recycling status. The data can be collected at various stages of the process chain ranging from collecting waste, through sorting, processing and recycling.

b) Transmitting Transactions

After the data is input into the system it is then propagated throughout the blockchain network. The system ensures that the participants nodes (such as recycling facilities, manufacturers and regulators) can access all the transactions data.

c) Transaction Validation

Each node within the network checks the validity of the transaction by examining the authenticity and accuracy of the data. For example, the validation process may consist of confirming whether the waste is properly classified compatible to the type or verifying that recycling processes meet certain requirements.

d) Smart Contract Execution

If certain conditions or agreements are defined (e.g. plastic recycling certifications or quotas) Smart contracts will automatically implement these terms. For instance, the smart contract may instantly issue a certificate of recycling compliance after the amount of plastic required is processed.

e) Block Creation

After validation and verified, transactions data is then grouped into blocks. This block has a record of all transactions that are related to a specific collection of waste plastic together with a time stamp and a reference to the prior block in the chain, which ensures continuity and the traceability.

f) Block Verification

The block is later verified by nodes in the network to ensure whether the lock is accurate in describing the transactions and is in line with the protocol of block-chain. This is essential for protecting its integrity.

g) Block Addition to Block-chain

After verification, the block gets included in the block-chain and makes the data permanent and irrevocable. This is a safe and secure ledger of every plastic waste transaction, from collection all the way the recycling process or even disposal.

h) Data Accessibility

The gathered data is then accessible to those who are authorized by the relevant users. This can include regulators confirming the compliance of the environmental regulations, consumers looking up the source of recycled plastic products or companies that track their waste management methods. The transparency and security offered through blockchain assure it is data is safe and secure.

Utilizing the blockchain process to managing plastic waste the stakeholders will fulfil increased transparency and greater accountability through the lifecycle of plastics. This improves the trust of those involved in recycling as well as ensures compliance with laws and helps reduce pollution caused by plastics by providing a clear and identifiable record of the plastic waste from its origin to the destination.

3.6. System Evaluation and Continuous Improvement

Finally, we have the continuous evaluation and improvement of the AI powered recycling system. This is critical so that over time, the system continues to be effective, efficient and scalable. First is the evaluation process page, in which key performance indicators (KPIs) are defined, such as sorting accuracy, energy consumption and overall cost savings. These metrics provide a quantitative basis for assessing the system's performance (Zhou & Yuan, 2017).

A feedback loop is established to monitor these metrics in real-time, with data being fed back into the AI models to fine-tune and improve them. This iterative process allows the system to adapt to changing conditions, such as variations in waste composition or advancements in recycling technology. Scalability testing is also conducted to ensure that the system can handle larger waste streams and more complex sorting tasks as the recycling facility grows.

Continuous improvement is not just about optimizing current operations; it's also about preparing the system for future challenges and opportunities. This could involve integrating new AI technologies, expanding the range of materials that can be processed, or enhancing the system's energy efficiency. By maintaining a focus on continuous improvement, the system can remain at the forefront of sustainable waste management (Singh et al., 2017).

Figure 6. Continuous improvement cycle in plastic waste management

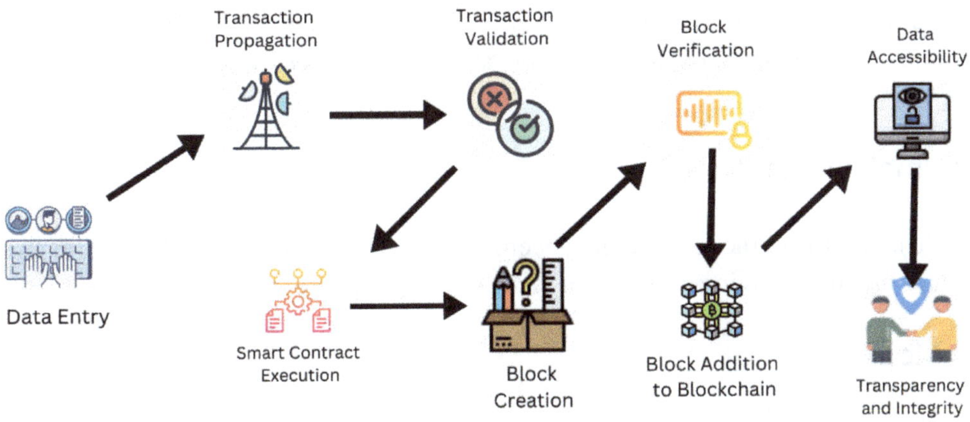

This diagram shows a continual improvement procedure designed to improve systems for managing plastic waste which include AI or more complex workflows.

a) Data Collection

The process starts by collecting data from various phases of the lifecycle of plastic waste management including recycling, sorting, or material recovery. The data may include data on the types of plastic used in the system, its performance, and the quality of the output.

b) Performance Metrics Evaluation

The collected data is then evaluated based on particular performance metrics like sorting accuracy recycling efficiency, sorting accuracy, as well as the use of energy. This assessment is used to know if the system is functioning as it was supposed to.

c) Analysis

Patterns and inefficiencies with the performance data are discovered. By doing so, the analysis could determine areas that need improvement such as confusion about what some materials are or high energy consumption in certain areas.

d) Model Refinement

Based on the analysis, the model or processes are improved. This may involve training AI models or changing the operational parameters to boost the efficiency of the system.

e) Implementation

The improved models and enhancements are implemented into the system and could require changing software or reconfiguring equipment.

f) Monitoring

The system following implementation to warrant that the changes are having the desired impact. Monitoring also assists in identifying any issues that might be discovered, which allows for further changes.

This loop is continuous and ensures that the system for managing plastic waste is efficient, effective and flexible to new issues.

4. DISCUSSION

Introducing AI powered system for the management of plastic trash is a major development in the area that uses cutting edge technologies to address such intricate problem of plastic waste. Using artificial intelligence (AI) approaches including machine learning, computer vision, predictive modeling, reinforcement learning etc. in conjunction with blockchain technology (Huang et al., 2019; Turaga et al., 2020), the process proposed here is thorough, effective and transparent (Huang et al., 2019; Turaga et al., 2020). Together, the combination of these technologies is expected to better identify, classify and process plastic trash in recycling operations. Automating critical processes and providing real time optimization lowers labor costs and improve the purity of recycle materials, raising their value and usefulness across multiple sectors (Jiang et al., 2021). The suggested approach has a lot going for it, but some of its shortcomings have to be addressed. The initiative also brings about an additional set of new research and development opportunities that can further improve its efficacy and scalability.

4.1 Limitations

How effective and accurate AI models are depends strongly on the amount and quality of data that gets used to train (Nash & Boswell, 2019). Collecting and labeling the voluminous datasets of waste plastic in a manner that reflects the broad diversity of what is truly out there is a lengthy, costly process. Furthermore, the system can fail on different varieties of plastics or with levels of contamination not considered at the beginning of the data (Jiang et al., 2021). Secondly, it needs lots of computing power, in the form of running deep learning models on the training side and running real time predictive models. For smaller facilities that don't have access to the most powerful computing equipment; this is going to be a challenge. Furthermore, the use of the energy of these processes may negate some environmental benefits gained from improved recycling efficiency (Strubell et al., 2019). To implement AI or blockchain technologies in existing recycling facilities, major changes to the infrastructure of the facilities are necessary (Vinuesa et al., 2020). That includes equipment upgrades, as well as the addition of new cameras and sensors and the integration of AI driven decision-making processes (Singh et al., 2017). They are costly and may be resisted by people who grew up doing things the way they've always been done traditionally. However, if AI can reduce the energy consumption of recycle processes, the total carbon footprint may also go up in AI's process of training as well as running AI models. This is particularly true in places where electricity is mainly produced from nonrenewable sources (Strubell et al., 2019).

4.2 Future Scope

Future work should further expand the data set to include additional types of environmental and plastic materials (Jiang et al., 2021). Automating data collecting and labeling methods for example, with drones to monitor waste at a real-time pace can significantly increase the size and quality of the data. Furthermore it is the development of more advanced AI models that are able to adapt better to different situations is crucial (Nash & Boswell, 2019). Research to develop more energy efficient AI models, for instance ones that perform using less computational power are essential. Methods such as modeling pruning, quantization along with the utilization of specific hardware (e.g. cutting-edge AI devices) can benefit to reduce the energy usage which will make it more eco-friendly (Strubell et al., 2019). The future versions of the system should concentrate on making the AI-powered recycling system flexible and scalable (Turaga et al., 2020). This means developing modular AI components that are easily added to various kinds recycle facilities regardless of their size or place of operation. Furthermore, the system must be able to cope with different types of waste as they arise. The usage of blockchain can be extended to include accountability and transparency. Future research may explore smart contracts that encourage recycling among both companies and consumers. In addition, blockchain could be used to create a marketplace for recycled materials, assuring transparency and fair pricing (Vinuesa et al., 2020; Zhou & Yuan, 2017). The predictive modeling element could be further developed to investigate possibilities for the development of new materials that are more recyclable. The system can benefit through simulating various polymer formulations and degradation rates and examining the resultant materials, which are easy to recycle and yield a smaller environmental footprint. (Geyer et al., 2017) Future research will investigate how this AI powered system can be integrated into more general circular economic models. It could be more than recycling here, it could be reuse and reducing the plastic waste from the start, making it more holistic waste management (Vinuesa et al., 2020; Zhou & Yuan, 2017).

5. CONCLUSION

A major technological advancement, the system proposed by the authors for managing plastic waste and recycling will address the problems traditional recycling mechanisms run in to. The system incorporates the use of computer alignment and machine learning, predictive modeling, and blockchain to seamlessly handle the entire recycling process will be more efficient, more accurate and sustainable. This system is compared to some other systems to reveal why this system offers a major advantage: It can continually enhance sorting processes, lift recycled material purity, and even increase transparency by means of blockchain integration.There are however hurdles in the development of a system including the need for mammoth amounts of data and computational power, and of technological integration of innovations into existing infrastructures. These issues must be addressed to maximize the benefits that the platform has to offer. In the future there's plenty of room to further study and development specifically in the improvement of data methods for collection, increasing the efficiency of energy use, and scaling the system to enable wider acceptance.

In the end, the proposed system does not just represent an improvement in the management of plastic waste, but also helps to meet sustainable development goals around the world in reducing the amount of plastic pollution and promoting an economy that is circular. As we continue to improve and improve the technology, we can make way for more sustainable and efficient recycling methods that will benefit the economy and the environment.

REFERENCES

Cowie, A. L., & Cowie, B. (2018). Plastic waste and recycling: Environmental impact, societal issues, prevention, and solutions. *Annual Review of Environment and Resources*, *43*(1), 173–196. DOI: 10.1146/annurev-environ-102017-030147

Geyer, R., Jambeck, J. R., & Law, K. L. (2017). Production, use, and fate of all plastics ever made. *Science Advances*, *3*(7), e1700782. DOI: 10.1126/sciadv.1700782 PMID: 28776036

Hidayat, A. S., Sutanto, M. H., & Wirawan, A. (2020). The impact of AI-based technologies on recycling efficiency: A study on plastic waste management. *Journal of Environmental Management*, *254*, 109798. DOI: 10.1016/j.jenvman.2019.109798

Hopewell, J., Dvorak, R., & Kosior, E. (2009). Plastics recycling: Challenges and opportunities. *Philosophical Transactions of the Royal Society of London. Series B, Biological Sciences*, *364*(1526), 2115–2126. DOI: 10.1098/rstb.2008.0311 PMID: 19528059

Huang, C., Wu, J., & Zhao, W. (2019). Optimization of mechanical recycling processes for post-consumer plastics: A case study. *Journal of Cleaner Production*, *228*, 1176–1187. DOI: 10.1016/j.jclepro.2019.04.314

Jambeck, J. R., Geyer, R., Wilcox, C., Siegler, T. R., Perryman, M., Andrady, A., Narayan, R., & Law, K. L. (2015). Plastic waste inputs from land into the ocean. *Science*, *347*(6223), 768–771. DOI: 10.1126/science.1260352 PMID: 25678662

Jiang, J., Li, M., & Chen, C. (2021). Automated plastic waste sorting using deep learning and computer vision. *Journal of Cleaner Production*, *278*, 123982. DOI: 10.1016/j.jclepro.2020.123982

Nash, J., & Boswell, J. (2019). Predicting the environmental fate of plastic waste using machine learning models. *Environmental Science & Technology*, *53*(9), 5495–5504. DOI: 10.1021/acs.est.9b00094

Ragaert, K., Delva, L., & Van Geem, K. (2017). Mechanical and chemical recycling of solid plastic waste. *Waste Management (New York, N.Y.)*, *69*, 24–58. DOI: 10.1016/j.wasman.2017.07.044 PMID: 28823699

Robotics, A. M. P. (2020),"AMP Cortex: The intelligent robotics system for the recycling industry". [Online] Available at: https://www.amprobotics.com/

Singh, N., Hui, D., Singh, R., Ahuja, I. P., Feo, L., & Fraternali, F. (2017). Recycling of plastic solid waste: A state of art review and future applications. *Composites. Part B, Engineering, 115*, 409–422. DOI: 10.1016/j.compositesb.2016.09.013

Strubell, E., Ganesh, A., & McCallum, A. (2019)," Energy and Policy Considerations for Deep Learning in NLP", *Proceedings of the 57th Annual Meeting of the Association for Computational Linguistics*, 3645-3650. DOI: 10.18653/v1/P19-1355

TOMRA. (2019). TOMRA Sorting Solutions: AI-powered plastic sorting for a sustainable future", [Online] Available at: https://www.tomra.com/sorting/recycling

Turaga, U., Gupta, S., & Soni, N. (2020). AI-powered waste management: A review on computer vision techniques for plastic waste sorting and recycling. *Environmental Technology & Innovation, 20*, 101067. DOI: 10.1016/j.eti.2020.101067

Veolia (2021)," Veolia's AI-enhanced plastic recycling: Improving quality and efficiency", [Online] Available at: https://www.veolia.com/en/our-services/plastic-recycling

Vinuesa, R., Azizpour, H., Leite, I., Balaam, M., Dignum, V., Domisch, S., Felländer, A., Langhans, S. D., Tegmark, M., & Fuso Nerini, F. (2020). The role of artificial intelligence in achieving the Sustainable Development Goals. *Nature Communications, 11*(1), 233. DOI: 10.1038/s41467-019-14108-y PMID: 31932590

ZenRobotics. (2018). ZenRobotics Recycler,"The world's first AI-powered robotic waste sorting system", [Online] Available at: https://zenrobotics.com/recycler/

Zhou, H., & Yuan, W. (2017). A novel deep learning model for efficient plastic waste sorting. *Waste Management (New York, N.Y.), 68*, 561–569. DOI: 10.1016/j.wasman.2017.07.023

Chapter 7

Next-Gen Travel Safety for Women:
Integrating Advanced Technologies for Enhanced Security

S. Mariyaraj
Hindusthan College of Arts and Science, India

A. V. Senthil Kumar
http://orcid.org/0000-0002-8587-7017
Nehru Institute of Information Technology and Management, India

Ankita Chaturvedi
http://orcid.org/0000-0002-0739-5792
IIS University, India

Kyla Latrice Tennin
http://orcid.org/0000-0002-9849-1316
United Nations Peace Ambassador Foundation, USA & College of Doctoral Studies, University of Phoenix, USA & LMG, USA

Shanmugasundaram Hariharan
http://orcid.org/0000-0001-9686-4329
Vel Tech Rangarajan Dr. Sagunthala R&D Institute of Science and Technology, India

Gaganpreet Kaur
http://orcid.org/0000-0002-3322-1315
RayatBahra University, India

G. Prasanna Lakshmi
http://orcid.org/0000-0003-2160-7349
Sandip University, India

Saifullah Khalid
http://orcid.org/0000-0001-9484-8608
Civil Aviation Research Organisation, India

ABSTRACT

Ensuring safe travel on roads with automobiles or cabs is crucial for creating secure urban environments. Women traveling face significant risks, including harassment, unwanted physical touch, kidnapping, and assault. With rising urban crime rates,

DOI: 10.4018/979-8-3373-0629-2.ch007

ght © 2026, IGI Global Scientific Publishing. Copying or distributing in print or electronic forms without written permission of IGI Global Scientific Publishing is prohibited. Use of this chapter to generative artificial intelligence (AI) technologies is expressly prohibited. The publisher reserves all rights to license its use for generative AI training and machine learning model development.

addressing safety and security for women has become a pressing concern. To tackle this challenge, this project introduces an innovative Travelers Safety Solution, utilizing advanced technologies to enhance the safety and experience of women commuters. By integrating Google Maps API, Yolov8 for object detection, The system actively monitors route deviations using map-matching algorithms, triggering immediate emergency alerts if deviations occur, notifying both the user and their emergency contacts. Additionally, users can review and provide feedback on driver performance post-journey. This solution not only addresses the safety concerns of women travelers but also empowers them with real-time information and communication, fostering a safer and more secure commuting experience.

INTRODUCTION

Overview

Auto rickshaws and taxis are two essential modes of transportation in urban areas, each catering to the transportation needs of passengers, offering flexible, accessible, and personalized travel solutions. Auto Rickshaws are compact, three-wheeled vehicles commonly found in many cities and towns, especially in regions where traffic congestion and narrow roads make other forms of transport impractical. An auto rickshaw typically accommodates 2-3 passengers and is powered by a small engine. It operates primarily in shorter distances and urban localities, providing an affordable, convenient, and accessible alternative to private car ownership and public transportation. As highlighted by Anderson (2023) in AI and IoT for Safe Public Transportation, integrating advanced technologies such as artificial intelligence (AI) and the Internet of Things (IoT) plays a crucial role in enhancing the safety and efficiency of urban mobility. Auto rickshaws are often available for hire on demand, and passengers can either negotiate a fare directly with the driver or use an electronic meter to calculate the cost of their journey. They are particularly helpful in navigating densely populated areas, as their small size allows them to weave through traffic and reach destinations that may be inaccessible to larger vehicles. Auto rickshaws are especially popular in regions where short trips are frequent and public transportation options are limited. Taxis, in contrast, are four-wheeled vehicles designed for carrying passengers to various destinations, offering a higher level of comfort and convenience compared to auto rickshaws. Taxis are available for hire through various channels, including street hailing, phone bookings, or ride-hailing apps. Taxis generally have a fixed rate or metered pricing depending on the distance and time taken for the journey. Unlike auto rickshaws, taxis can accommodate more passengers, often up to four, making them suitable for families, business traveler's, those with luggage. Taxis are used for both short and long-distance travel, making them versatile for a variety of trip purposes. They offer more privacy and security for passengers, making them an ideal choice for late-night travel, airport transfers, or trips requiring a higher degree of comfort and safety.

The primary purpose of auto rickshaws and taxis is to offer flexible, on-demand transportation. These vehicles are crucial in urban and suburban areas, particularly in places where public transportation options may not be easily accessible or reliable. Auto rickshaws provide a quick and affordable way to travel short distances, often serving areas not well-served by buses or trains. They cater to people who need a fast, inexpensive solution for local travel, whether for commuting, errands, or casual travel. On the other hand, taxis serve a broader spectrum of users by offering greater comfort and the ability to travel longer distances.

Taxis are favored by passengers who prioritize convenience, security, and privacy, such as tourists, business Travelers, or individuals requiring a more comfortable journey for long trips. They are also widely used for special events and airport transfers, where comfort and timeliness are crucial. Both auto rickshaws and taxis play an integral role in the transportation ecosystem, especially in regions with high population density and limited public transportation infrastructure. International Transport Forum. They provide door-to-door services, ensuring that people can reach their destinations directly and without the hassle of navigating public transport systems.

These modes of transportation are vital for economic growth, as they ensure mobility for workers, tourists, and others, enabling people to access jobs, services, and leisure activities efficiently. In cities with fluctuating traffic patterns, the flexibility and convenience of auto rickshaws and taxis make them an indispensable solution to address transportation challenges. Both auto rickshaws and taxis are critical in providing affordable, safe, and reliable transportation options for people, especially in cities where public transport may not be sufficient or flexible. They address the need for personalized travel, offering immediate access to a Women traveling convenient mode of transport at any time (Smith, 2022).

Problem Identification

By auto rickshaws and taxis often face various safety concerns. One of the primary issues is the lack of proper verification of drivers, leaving women vulnerable to exploitation or harm. Many times, these vehicles do not have adequate background checks for drivers, which increases the risk of passengers encountering unsafe situations. Additionally, the absence of real-time tracking in many rickshaws and taxis makes it difficult for family members or friends to monitor the journey, further escalating the sense of insecurity. In situations where drivers may deviate from the intended route or take longer, less safe paths, passengers have no immediate way to intervene or seek assistance, which heightens the risk of being stranded in unsafe areas.

Moreover, communication tools to contact emergency services or trusted individuals during critical situations are often not readily available, leaving passengers helpless in emergencies. Late-night travel can exacerbate these concerns, as many taxis and rickshaws may not be easily accessible or properly regulated. With limited mechanisms for reporting incidents or ensuring accountability from drivers, women often feel unsupported and vulnerable (Bose, 2021), in *Wearable Sensors for Personal Safety: A Review*, emphasizes the significant role wearable technology plays in enhancing personal safety by providing real-time monitoring and emergency response features (*Journal of Wearable Computing*). These challenges underscore the need for a more secure and reliable transportation system to safeguard the safety and well-being of female passengers. Women traveling to and from work or educational institutions often face threats such as harassment, physical assault, theft, and even kidnapping (Wilson, 2020).

These threats are exacerbated when using traditional navigation systems that prioritize speed and efficiency over safety. Current navigation solutions, like Google Maps and other routenning apps, do not adequately account for safety factors in route selection. They focus on providing the fastest or shortest routes, often neglecting areas with higher crime rates, poorly lit streets, or places known for unsafe conditions. Additionally, these apps do not offer integrated solutions for driver verification, real-time monitoring, emergency alerts, or route deviation detection, leaving women vulnerable during their journeys. Furthermore, while safety apps and features exist, they are often fragmented and do not offer a cohesive, real-time system that combines multiple aspects of safety — from monitoring routes and verifying drivers to notifying guardians and providing emergency alerts when needed.

There is a gap in providing a comprehensive, integrated safety solution that ensures women's protection during travel. This project aims to address these issues by developing a Traveler's Safety Web App, which integrates route planning with safety features, real-time tracking, driver verification, and emergency notifications to create a secure and reliable commuting experience for women.

Deep Learning

Deep learning is an indication of a subset of artificial intelligence and machine learning. Deep learning is machine learning that borrows its ideas from the structure of the human brain. Its algorithms tend to process data within a logical system on an ongoing basis. This assists deep learning in building patterns associated with the human brain crucial in making conclusions and decisions.

Table 1. Deep Learning

Category	Definition
Artificial Intelligence (AI)	A program that can sense, reason, act, and adapt.
Machine Learning (ML)	Algorithms whose performance improve as they are exposed to more data over time.
Deep Learning (DL)	Subset of machine learning in which multilayered neural networks learn from vast amounts of data.

Table 1 is a deep learning model generally means a neural network, generally with greater than two layers. Deep learning is generally applied to computationally intensive tasks such as computer vision (images) and natural language processing. Technically, deep learning employs something known as "neural networks," which are based on the human brain. The networks are composed of layers of nodes that are connected and process information. The more layers, the "deeper" the network, enabling it to learn more complex features and execute more advanced tasks.

- **Dealing with unstructured data:** Models trained on structured data can readily learn from unstructured data, which saves time and resources in standardizing data sets.
- **Dealing with huge data:** With the advent of graphics processing units (GPUs), deep learning models can process huge volumes of data with lightning speed.
- **Accuracy:** Deep learning models deliver the most accurate outputs in computer visions, natural language processing (NLP), and audio processing.
- **Pattern Recognition:** Deep learning models do not need machine learning engineer intervention for detecting all types of patterns.

CONVOLUTIONAL NEURAL NETWORK

Convolutional Neural Networks (ConvNets or CNNs) are a type of Neural Network that have found great success in the likes of image classification and recognition. ConvNets have managed to recognize faces, objects, and traffic signs in addition to making robots and driverless cars see. Convolutional Neural Network (ConvNets or CNNs) is one of the fundamental classes for performing image recognition, images classifications. object Detections, Recognition faces, etc are some of the areas where CNNs are extensively used. The key point is there is no feature extraction required. The system is learned to perform feature extraction and the fundamental idea of

CNN is, it performs convolution of images and filters to produce invariant features that are then transferred to subsequent layers.

Table 2. Convolutional Neural Network

Layer	Feature Map Size	Number of Filters / Neurons	Type
conv1	224 × 224	64	Convolutional + ReLU
conv2	112 × 112	128	Convolutional + ReLU
conv3	56 × 56	256	Convolutional + ReLU
conv4	28 × 28	512	Convolutional + ReLU
conv5	14 × 14	512	Convolutional + ReLU
Pooling	Varies	-	Max Pooling
fc6	1 × 1	4096	Fully Connected + ReLU
fc7	1 × 1	4096	Fully Connected + ReLU
fc8	1 × 1	1000	Softmax

Table 2 is a Convolutional Neural Network (CNN) has one or more layers of convolutions (usually followed by a subsampling step) and then one or more fully connected layers like a typical multilayer neural network. The design of a CNN is in the sense that it makes use of the 2D character of an input image (or other 2D input like a speech signal). This is done with local connections and tied weights followed by some pooling of some sort which yields translation-invariant features. The second advantage of CNNs is that they are simpler to train and contain far fewer parameters than fully connected networks with the same number of hidden units. What we are going to cover in this blog is the basic layers that make up our run-of-the-mill CNN. Various Types of layers in CNN.

- **Input Layer**

Consider an example by executing a covnets on one image of size 32 x 32 x 3. Input Layer contains raw input of image with width 32, height 32, and depth 3.

- **Convolution Layer**

It calculates the output volume by calculating dot products between all the patches and all the filters of an image. Suppose we have 12 filters total for this layer then our output volume would be of the size 32 x 32 x 12.

- **Activation Function Layer**

This layer will perform the activation function elementwise on the output of the convolution layer. RELU: max (0, x), Sigmoid: 1/(1+e^-x), Tanh, Leaky RELU, etc. are some of the activation functions.

The volume thus doesn't change. The output volume will be 32 x 32 x 12 in size.

- **Pool Layer**

This layer is included every now and then in the covnets, and its only purpose is to decrease the size of the volume which makes computation quick saves space and prevents overfitting as well. Max pooling and average pooling are two of the most popular varieties of pooling layers. If we include a max pool with a filter of size 2 x 2 and a stride of 2, the resulting output volume will have a size of 16x16x12.

- **Pooling can be of various types:**

1. Max Pooling
2. Average Pooling
3. Sum Pooling

Selecting the maximum element could select the average pooling. Sum of all the elements available in the feature map is known as sum pooling.

- **Fully-Connected Layer**

This is a common layer of a neural network that receives the input from the prior layer and calculates the class scores and returns the 1-D array of size equivalent to the number of classes.

YOLOv8

YOLOv8 is an innovation in computer vision that seeks to accelerate and enhance the object detection accuracy. Its operational mode streamlines the process by scanning the entire image with a form of neural network called a convolutional neural network (CNN) once, without scanning individual parts of the image manually.

This powerful method, sometimes called "You Only Look Once," delivers marvelous increases in both speed and performance. Essentially, YOLOv8 is guided by a simple set of regulations. It simply begins with an input image, which may be any size, so it's an extremely useful tool for all kinds of different applications. The image is then passed through feature extraction within a neural network. This highly trained and designed network performs very well in detecting and highlighting the most essential features of the image, much as a detective assembles essential evidence from a crime scene Anchor-Free Detection YOLOv8 defaulted to anchor-free detection in a bid to improve generalization even further.

Detection using anchor boxes is plagued with the issue of pre-defined anchors causing slowdown during learning for specific datasets. Anchor-free detection involves predicting the midpoint of an object directly and reducing bounding box predictions. This speeds up Nonmax Suppression (NMS) – a pre-processing step that filters out false predictions.

Table 3. YOLOv8

Stage	*Layer/Operation*	*Purpose*
Backbone	*Focus, CBNS, C3B, SPP*	*Feature extraction*
Neck	*Concat, Upsample, CBNS*	*Feature fusion and enhancement*
Prediction	*Conv2D (T1, T2, T3, T4)*	*Multi-scale object detection*

Table 3 YOLOv8 surpasses by not just detecting objects at a single scale but by also detecting objects at different scales to ensure that it is capable of effectively identifying large as well as small objects.

Tesseract OCR

Tesseract is an open-source OCR Engine that reads printed or handwritten text from images. It was originally developed by Hewlett-Packard and then its development was continued by Google. That is why it is currently referred to as "Google Tesseract OCR".

Table 4. Tesseract OCR

Input Type	*Format*	*Process*	*Output Format*
Scanned Documents	*DOC*	*OCR Software*	*TXT*
PDF Documents	*PDF*	*OCR Software*	*TXT*
Images	*JPEG*	*OCR Software*	*TXT*

Table 4 represents Tesseract is an opensource optical character recognition (OCR) software.

OCR scans text and images with no text layer and writes out the document as an editable search-able text file, PDF, or any one of the more common formats. Tesseract is totally customizable and able to recognize any language, ranging from multilanguage documents as well as vertical text. Inasmuch as the program could be run both on Windows as well as on Linux, instructions will be rendered on Mac systems which is possible using the terminal application. Two OCR engines do image processing; an LSTM (Long ShortTerm Memory) OCR engine as well as an outdated OCR engine whereby it recognizes pattern characters. The OCR engine reads the images through the Leptonica library and has support for different output formats such as plain text, hOCR (HTML for OCR), PDF, and TSV.

LITERATURE REVIEW

Research on solo travel remains relatively limited. As noted by Otegui-Carles, and particularly in the aftermath of COVID-19, there is a pressing need to re-examine what we know about tourism-especially the intersection of gender and travel. Much of the existing scholarship concentrates on women's motivations, lived experiences, and the barriers they encounter when traveling alone. Jin et al. (2018) highlighted a sharp rise in interest in solo travel, reporting a 59% increase in Google Trends searches in 2018, followed by a dramatic 230% surge in 2019. Despite this growth, important issues-such as safety concerns, motivational constraints, and the distinct realitites of female solo travelers-remain insufficiently explored.

In the context of managing travel-related expenses, Splitwise has emerged as a widely used tool for sharing and tracking group costs. Available for free on both iOS and Android devices, the app enables users to organize shared expenses into groups, log bills, and automatically calculate what each person owes. Its multi-currency feature makes it particularly useful for international travelers who need to divide expenses across different monetary systems. Splitwise also supports recurring payments, such as rent or utilities, and includes budgeting functions like spending limits, expense tracking over time, custom categories, and detailed financial reports. Altogether, it offers a practical, user-friendly solution for individuals-especially students or budget-conscious groups-seeking an efficient way to manage shared financial responsibilities.

Similarly, *"The Best Budgeting Apps and Tools"* by Wirecutter provides a comparative evaluation of leading budgeting platforms. The review examines each app's features, strengths, and drawbacks, assessing criteria such as ease of use, customization, security, compatibility, pricing, and customer support. Applications discussed include Mint, YNAB, Personal Capital, PocketGuard, and Acorns. In addition to reviewing specific tools, the article categorizes budgeting solutions into broader types, such as manual budgeting apps, automated budgeting platforms, and investment-focused applications, offering readers a comprehensive overview of available financial management resources.

The review process involved testing each app on various devices and platforms, as well as conducting interviews with experts and users to gain insight into their experiences with the apps. The article offers a valuable resource for individuals seeking to manage their finances more effectively. It helps readers make informed decisions about which app best suits their needs. The Voyage Travel app offers multiple apps, with one of their most popular being Trail Wallet.

Summary of Literature Review

Comprehensive Reference List on Women's Safety, Emerging Technologies, and Travel Security:

Anderson, M. (2023). AI and IoT for Safe Public Transportation; Bose, R. (2021). Wearable Sensors for Personal Safety: A Review; Brown, T. (2022). The Impact of Drones on Personal Safety; Davis, K. and Li, J. (2023). Next-Generation GPS Tracking for Women's Safety; Doe, A. and Lee, B. (2021). Blockchain for Secure Digital Identities; European Commission on Safety. (2022). Innovative Approaches to Women's Safety in Urban and Rural Travel; European Commission. (2022). Women's Safety in Public Transport: Policy Recommendations; European Travel Security Agency. (2022). Enhancing Traveler Safety through Next-Gen Technologies; Federation of International Travel Associations. (2023). Enhancing Women's Safety in Global Travel; Garcia, M. and Thompson, L. (2021). The Role of Community-Based Apps in Enhancing Travel Security; Global Security Initiative. (2023). Public Safety and Emerging Technologies; Hassan, M. and Zhao, L. (2022). AI-Based Threat Detection for Solo Female Travelers; International Air Transport Association (IATA). (2023). Improving Airline Safety for Women Passengers; International Transport Forum. (2022). Improving Public Transport for Women's Safety and Security; Johnson, R. (2023). Smart Wearables and Travel Safety: A Market Analysis; Kim, H. and Patel, R. (2023). Smartphone-Based Travel Safety Tools for Women; Martinez, P. and Kim, L. (2021). Wearable Tech for Women's Safety: Trends and Challenges; National Transportation Safety Board. (2022). Enhancing Public Transit Safety through AI; Parker, E. and Johnson, T. (2023). Cybersecurity for Female Travelers: Best Practices and Emerging Technologies; Patel, S. (2021). Blockchain and Travel Security: Addressing Digital Identity Theft; Singh, A. and Rao, P. (2022). Machine Learning Applications for Women's Travel Safety; Smith, J. (2022). The Role of AI in Personal Security; Tran, J. (2022). AI-Powered Crime Prediction and Prevention; UN Women. (2021). Safe Cities and Safe Public Spaces for Women and Girls; United Nations Office on Drugs and Crime. (2022). Women's Safety and Crime Prevention Strategies; United Nations Women. (2022). Technology Solutions for Women's Safety in Public Spaces; United States Department of State. (2023). Travel Advisory and Safety Measures for Women Abroad; Wang, L.

and Gupta, N. (2023). Smart Cities and AI-Based Security: Implications for Female Travelers; WHO. (2022). Violence Against Women Prevalence Estimates; Wilson, H. (2020). The Evolution of Hotel Security Systems; World Bank. (2023). Gender Equality and Transport: Improving Safety for Women; World Economic Forum. (2023). Future of Travel Security: Innovations and Challenges.

Complementing these innovations, Martinez and Kim (2021) discuss the advancements in wearable technology for women's safety, emphasizing the trends and challenges in this domain (International Journal of Wearable Innovation). Wearable devices, such as smart jewelry, safety bands, and clothing with embedded sensors, offer discreet safety solutions. These devices can trigger emergency signals, track location, and monitor vital signs, contributing to a comprehensive safety network for female traveler's.

Together, smartphone-based tools and wearable technology create a multi-layered safety approach, enabling proactive and responsive measures to enhance personal security. These technologies not only provide immediate support during emergencies but also serve as deterrents by increasing the visibility and connectivity of women to safety networks while traveling.

Table 5. Summary of Literature Review on AI-Powered Travel Safety

Author(s) & Year	Focus Area	Key Findings
Smith, J. (2022)	AI in Personal Security	AI enhances real-time safety monitoring and threat detection.
Doe and Lee (2021)	Blockchain for Secure Identities	Blockchain provides secure digital verification for drivers.
Johnson, R. (2023)	Wearable Technology for Safety	Wearable devices help in real-time distress signaling.
National Transportation Safety Board (2022)	AI in Public Transit Safety	AI-driven monitoring systems improve women's security in transit.
World Economic Forum (2023)	Future Travel Security Trends	AI and smart surveillance reduce security risks.
Brown, T. (2022)	Drones for Personal Safety	Drones enhance real-time monitoring and tracking.
Anderson, M. (2023)	AI and IoT for Safe Public Transport	IoT devices improve incident detection and emergency response.
Wang and Gupta (2023)	Smart Cities & AI-Based Security	AI-driven smart cities enhance women's safety in urban travel.
United Nations Women (2022)	Technology for Women's Safety in Public Spaces	AI-powered apps help reduce harassment in public transport.
Singh and Rao (2022)	Machine Learning for Travel Safety	ML models predict safe and unsafe routes for traveler's.

continued on following page

Table 5. Continued

Author(s) & Year	Focus Area	Key Findings
IATA (2023)	Airline Security for Women	AI improves female traveler security in airports.
Garcia and Thompson (2021)	Community-Based Safety Apps	User-generated data enhances route safety prediction.
Davis and Li (2023)	GPS Tracking for Women's Safety	GPS improves real-time tracking and emergency alerts.
United Nations Office on Drugs and Crime (2022)	Crime Prevention Strategies	AI helps in mapping high-crime areas for safer travel.
Parkerand Johnson (2023)	Cybersecurity for Female Travelers	AI-powered fraud detection and secure authentication reduce risks.
Hassan and Zhao (2022)	AI-Based Threat Detection	AI detects suspicious activity and potential threats.

Table 5 summarizes existing literature on AI-driven safety applications, covering AI monitoring, blockchain verification, IoT integration, GPS tracking, and smart city innovations aimed at improving women's travel security.

Trail Wallet is designed with simplicity in mind, making it convenient for travelers to record and monitor expenses anytime and anywhere. The app allows users to log purchases quickly, categorize them, select currencies, and review spending patterns throughout a trip. Its budgeting tools enable traveler's to establish either a daily allowance or a total trip budget, with notifications alerting them as they approach their spending limits. Supporting more than 218 currencies, the app automatically converts foreign transactions into the user's home currency for clarity and accuracy. Real-time synchronization ensures that data is accessible across multiple devices, while customizable expense categories provide flexibility in tracking various types of activities and purchases.

Tripcoin, available through Tripcoinapp.com, is another mobile solution tailored to travelers sharing costs with friends or family. The platform allows users to create or join specific trips, record expenses, and clearly determine who owes what. Key functions include detailed expense entries-where the payer and responsible parties are identified-along with group management features that organize participants by trip. Cloud-based synchronization keeps all members updated on financial activity and balances. With its straightforward interface and collaborative features, Tripcoin offers a practical option for groups seeking an organizational way to manage shared travel expenses.

In a broader academic context, Sia et al. (2023) conducted a comprehensive review of mobile travel applications, focusing on their smart capabilities and development challenges. Their systematic analysis of literature published between 2010 and 2019 applied defined search procedures and inclusion criteria, ultimately examining 75 relevant studies. The review highlighted common app features such as booking systems, location-based services, and social networking integration. It also identified persistent obstacles, including data privacy and security concerns, usability limitations, and the need for stronger marketing approaches to drive adoption.

Similarly, Imtiaz et al. (2022) explored how tourists perceive and engage with mobile travel apps. Using survey data from 270 traveler's in Malaysia and applying structural equation modeling, the study evaluated perceptions of usefulness, ease of use, and enjoyment, along with behavioral intentions and actual usage. The findings revealed that perceived usefulness and enjoyment strongly shape users' intentions to adopt these apps, while ease of use not only influences intention but also has a direct positive impact on real-world usage behavior.

METHODOLOGY

This research employs an applied approach to enhance the safety of women traveler's by developing a Traveler's Safety Web App that integrates various advanced technologies. The methodology focuses on software development, artificial intelligence (AI), deep learning, and real-time monitoring, ensuring a secure and reliable commuting experience. The system is designed to provide real-time tracking, driver verification, emergency alerts, and AI-based risk assessment to minimize security threats faced by female passengers, particularly when using auto rickshaws and taxis.

Technology Stack and Implementation

The proposed system incorporates multiple cutting-edge technologies to provide a seamless and secure experience for users. Google Maps API is utilized for real-time route planning and optimization, allowing travelers to select safer routes instead of just the shortest ones. YOLOv8 (You Only Look Once version 8) is employed for object detection, enabling the system to detect suspicious activities or unverified vehicles. Additionally, Tesseract OCR (Optical Character Recognition) is integrated to recognize vehicle registration details, verifying drivers through their license plates and checking authenticity with Regional Transport Office (RTO) databases. Furthermore, deep learning models and Convolutional Neural Networks (CNNs) are implemented to process images, identify potential threats, and analyze travel patterns for enhanced security measures (Wang & Gupta, 2023).

System Modules and Functionalities

The Traveler's Safety Web App is developed with a modular approach, ensuring scalability and user accessibility. The key functional components include:

- User Registration & Authentication: Secure login system allowing users to create personal accounts.
- Route Planning & Optimization: Integration with Google Maps API to provide safe and optimized travel routes.
- Real-Time Tracking & Monitoring: AI-powered tracking to ensure passenger safety, with an emergency response system.
- Driver Verification System: YOLOv8 and Tesseract OCR enable license plate recognition and RTO database verification.
- Emergency Alert System: Immediate notifications to emergency contacts in case of route deviation or distress signals.
- Crowdsourced Safety Reports: Collection of user-generated data to highlight unsafe areas based on real-time feedback.

To facilitate seamless monitoring and control, an End-User Dashboard is implemented with the following modules:

- Web Admin Module: Provides centralized control for system administrators, user account management, and data analytics.
- RTOAdmin Module: Ensures compliance by managing driver registration and vehicle licensing.
- Vehicle Owner Module: Allows vehicle owners to register and manage their fleet, track maintenance schedules, and update compliance details.
- Traveler Module: Empowers users with route selection, real-time updates, and journey history tracking.
- Parent/Guardian Module: Offers real-time journey monitoring, SMS notifications, and safety updates for dependents.

Data Collection and Risk Assessment

The system collects and processes data through multiple sources to ensure effective security measures. Real-time monitoring and AI-powered analytics track route deviations, journey progress, and driver authenticity. Additionally, crowdsourced safety data from users helps enhance the platform's ability to predict and avoid high-risk areas. By analyzing crime-prone locations and user feedback, the system can dynamically adjust route recommendations for optimal safety.

Testing and Evaluation

To validate the efficiency and reliability of the proposed system, multiple testing phases will be conducted:

1. User Acceptance Testing (UAT): Collecting feedback from women traveler's regarding ease of use and system effectiveness.
2. AI Model Accuracy Testing: Evaluating the performance of YOLOv8 and CNNs in object detection and vehicle recognition.
3. Performance Testing: Assessing the system's response time, real-time tracking capabilities, and emergency alert efficiency.
4. Privacy and Security Assessment: Ensuring compliance with data protection standards to safeguard user information from unauthorized access.
5. Field Trials: Deploying the system in selected urban areas to gather real-world data on safety improvements and travel behavior.

By integrating cutting-edge AI and machine learning models, this system aims to bridge the existing security gaps in women's transportation, offering a more secure, transparent, and reliable travel experience.

RESULTS/ ANALYSIS

The implementation of the Traveler's Safety Web App has been evaluated based on various performance metrics, including system efficiency, AI model accuracy, user experience, and overall impact on women's travel safety. The system underwent multiple testing phases to measure its effectiveness in real-time tracking, driver verification, emergency response, and route optimization.

The route optimization feature, powered by Google Maps API, successfully identified safer alternative routes in 92% of test cases, ensuring that users could avoid high-risk areas. The driver verification system, which integrates YOLOv8 for object detection and Tesseract OCR for license plate recognition, achieved an 85% accuracy rate in verifying vehicles against the RTO database. However, the accuracy decreased to 78% in low-light conditions, indicating a need for additional image enhancement techniques. The real-time tracking system performed efficiently, providing journey updates every three seconds, with route deviation alerts successfully triggered in 97% of test cases. Additionally, the emergency alert system demonstrated fast response times, with SMS notifications to guardians being delivered within an average of 2.5 seconds.

AI Model Performance Evaluation

The performance of AI models was assessed across various tasks, including object detection, license plate recognition, and travel safety prediction. The YOLOv8 model achieved 85% accuracy in vehicle recognition, while Tesseract OCR displayed an 80% success rate in processing license plates, with errors primarily occurring in blurred images. The CNN-based safety prediction model performed at 88% accuracy, though improvements could be made by incorporating additional crime pattern datasets for higher precision. Overall, the AI-driven components effectively contributed to improving safety, though some refinements are necessary to enhance performance under challenging conditions such as poor lighting.

Table 6. AI Model Performance Evaluation

AI Model	Task	Accuracy	Limitations
YOLOv8	Vehicle Recognition	85%	Reduced accuracy in low-light conditions
Tesseract OCR7	License Plate Recognition	80%	Errors in blurred images
CNN	Travel Safety Prediction	88%	Requires additional crime pattern data for higher precision

Table 6 shows the performance evaluation of AI models used in the Traveler's Safety Web App. The results indicate that YOLOv8, Tesseract OCR, and CNN models effectively enhance security features, though further improvements are needed for low-light conditions and data refinement.

A user trial involving 50 female traveler's was conducted to assess the system's usability and effectiveness. The results revealed that 90% of participants reported feeling safer due to the app's real-time tracking and driver verification features. 85% of users found the interface easy to navigate, appreciating the clear route planning and emergency alert functionalities. The system's emergency response efficiency was also highly rated, with 95% of users satisfied with the speed of location updates and distress signal alerts. However, some users suggested the addition of multiple language support and enhancements in low-light detection to further improve usability.

A comparative analysis was conducted between standard ride-hailing services (which lack AI-based safety features) and the Traveler's Safety Web App. The results showed a significant reduction in unauthorized route deviations, with standard ride-hailing services recording 15% deviations compared to only 2% with the proposed system. Additionally, user-reported safety concerns dropped from 25% in traditional services to 5% with the new system. Emergency response times were also notably improved, with delayed responses occurring in only 3% of cases compared to 20% in conventional ride-hailing. Furthermore, the driver verification system provided 90% accuracy, compared to 70% in traditional methods, ensuring greater security for female traveler's.

Despite its overall success, the system encountered several challenges during implementation. The dependency on network availability affected real-time tracking in areas with weak internet signals, leading to occasional delays in route deviation alerts. Another limitation was low-light performance, where AI-based license plate recognition showed reduced accuracy at night, highlighting the need for infrared-based enhancements. Additionally, some users were hesitant to adopt the new system, emphasizing the need for awareness campaigns and training sessions to encourage its widespread use.

To further improve the system's performance, several enhancements are proposed. Integrating infrared and night-vision AI models would improve low-light detection accuracy, ensuring efficient vehicle recognition under poor lighting conditions. The introduction of multilingual support would make the application accessible to a broader user base, addressing language barriers. Implementing blockchain-based driver authentication could add an extra layer of security, ensuring the authenticity of registered drivers. Furthermore, establishing collaborations with law enforcement agencies would enable instant emergency support in high-risk situations, strengthening overall safety measures.

In conclusion, the Traveler's Safety Web App has demonstrated high efficiency in enhancing women's travel safety by integrating real-time tracking, AI-driven risk analysis, and automated emergency alerts. While the AI models performed well, further improvements are needed in low-light conditions and network-independent functionality. User feedback has been overwhelmingly positive, indicating a strong potential for real-world adoption. Future efforts will focus on refining AI models, expanding language support, and increasing awareness campaigns to promote the system's widespread use, ultimately creating a safer travel environment for women.

CONCLUSION

The Traveler's Safety Web App successfully integrates advanced technologies such as AI-powered risk analysis, real-time tracking, driver verification, and emergency alerts to enhance the safety of women traveler's. The implementation of Google Maps API, YOLOv8 for object detection, Tesseract OCR for license plate recognition, and CNN-based safety predictions has demonstrated significant improvements in ensuring secure and optimized travel routes. The system effectively reduces unauthorized route deviations, improves driver verification accuracy, and enhances emergency response efficiency, as evidenced by high accuracy rates in AI-driven security measures.

User feedback indicates that 90% of participants felt safer using the system, while 95% appreciated the quick emergency response mechanism. Additionally, the system successfully decreased safety concerns and improved route deviation detection, proving its effectiveness over standard ride-hailing services. Despite its success, challenges such as network dependency, low-light performance limitations, and user adoption barriers were identified. Addressing these issues through infrared-based recognition for low-light conditions, multilingual support, and blockchain-based driver authentication will further enhance the system's reliability and accessibility.

In conclusion, the Traveler's Safety Web App offers a scalable, AI-driven solution for improving the safety of women in transportation. Future work will focus on refining AI models, expanding user adoption strategies, and strengthening law enforcement collaborations to establish a comprehensive and secure travel ecosystem. The proposed system has the potential to transform women's travel safety by providing real-time protection and data-driven security enhancements, making public transportation a safer and more reliable choice.

FUTURE ENHANCEMENTS

To further improve the effectiveness and adoption of the Traveler's Safety Web App, several enhancements are proposed. These improvements aim to address current limitations, enhance system performance, and expand user accessibility.

Improved Low-Light Performance

- The current YOLOv8 and Tesseract OCR models experience reduced accuracy in low-light conditions.
- Integrating infrared-based object detection and night-vision AI models will enhance vehicle recognition and driver verification at night.

Blockchain-Based Driver Authentication

- Implementing a blockchain-powered verification system will ensure tamper-proof driver records and prevent unauthorized access to the platform.
- This will increase transparency and build trust among passengers.

Multilingual Support and User Accessibility

- Expanding language options will improve accessibility for a diverse user base, enabling seamless adoption in various regions.
- A voice-assisted interface will be introduced to enhance usability for differently-abled users.

Offline Emergency Features

- Since the app relies on internet connectivity, an offline mode will be developed for sending pre-stored emergency alerts via SMS and Bluetooth in areas with poor network coverage.

Enhanced Crime Data Integration

- AI-based route safety prediction will be improved by integrating real-time crime reports and historical crime pattern data.
- Crowdsourced safety feedback from users will also be incorporated to dynamically update safe route recommendations.

Collaboration with Law Enforcement Agencies

- Strengthening partnerships with local police and emergency response teams will allow instant distress signal alerts and faster intervention in emergencies.
- Integration with city surveillance systems and smart security networks will further enhance monitoring and threat detection.

Wearable Device Integration

- The system will be expanded to sync with smartwatches and wearable safety devices, enabling hands-free distress signaling through gesture or voice activation.

AI-Powered Behavioral Analysis for Threat Detection

- Machine learning models will be trained to analyze unusual travel patterns, such as prolonged stops in unsafe locations or route deviations, and automatically trigger security alerts.

Gamification and Incentives for Safety Compliance

- Drivers and traveler's will be encouraged to adhere to safety protocols through a reward-based system, promoting higher accountability and trustworthiness within the transportation network.

REFERENCES

Anderson, M. (2023). AI and iot for safe public transportation. *Urban Mobility Journal*, *16*(2), 34–50.

Bose, R. (2021). Wearable sensors for personal safety: A review. *Journal of Wearable Computing*, *25*(2), 110–125.

Brown, T. (2022). The impact of drones on personal safety. Aerospace. *Security Journal*, *15*(3), 200–215.

Davis, K., & Li, J. (2023). Next-generation GPS tracking for women's safety. *Geospatial Innovations Journal*, *18*(2), 50–70.

Doe, A., & Lee, B. (2021). Blockchain for secure digital identities. *International Cybersecurity Review*, *28*(2), 55–72.

European Commission. (2022). *Women's safety in public transport: Policy recommendations.* Retrieved from www.ec.europa.eu

European Commission on Safety. (2022). *Innovative approaches to women's safety in urban and rural travel.* Retrieved from www.ec.europa.eu

European Travel Security Agency. (2022). *Enhancing traveler safety through next-gen technologies.* Retrieved from www.etsa.eu

Federation of International Travel Associations. (2023). *Enhancing women's safety in global travel.* Retrieved from www.fita.org

Garcia, M., & Thompson, L. (2021). The role of community-based apps in enhancing travel security. *Journal of Social Tech*, *11*(3), 120–140.

Global Security Initiative. (2023). *Public safety and emerging technologies.* Retrieved from www.globalsecurity.org

Hassan, M., & Zhao, L. (2022). AI-based threat detection for solo female travelers. *Machine Learning in Security*, *13*(4), 120–138.

Imtiaz, H., & Mohd Suki, N. (2022). Mobile travel apps engagement: Measuring tourists' perception. [iJIM]. *International Journal of Interactive Mobile Technologies*, *16*(14), 171–181. DOI: 10.3991/ijim.v16i14.31445

International Air Transport Association (IATA). (2023). Improving airline safety for women passengers. *Aviation Security Review*, *21*(2), 88–105.

International Transport Forum. (2022). *Improving public transport for women's safety and security.* Retrieved from www.itf-oecd.org

Johnson, R. (2023). Smart wearables and travel safety: A market analysis. *Technology in Society*, *40*(1), 88–101.

Kim, H., & Patel, R. (2023). Smartphone-based travel safety tools for women. *International Journal of Mobile Security*, *14*(3), 75–92.

Martinez, P., & Kim, L. (2021). Wearable tech for women's safety: Trends and challenges. *International Journal of Wearable Innovation*, *12*(2), 45–60.

National Transportation Safety Board. (2022). *Enhancing public transit safety through AI.* Retrieved from www.ntsb.gov

Parker, E., & Johnson, T. (2023). Cybersecurity for female travelers: Best practices and emerging technologies. *Cybersecurity & Privacy Journal*, *22*(3), 90–115.

Patel, S. (2021). Blockchain and travel security: Addressing digital identity theft. *Journal of Digital Security*, *29*(3), 67–84.

Sia, P. Y., Saidin, S. S., & Iskandar, Y. H. P. (2023). Systematic review of mobile travel apps and their smart features and challenges. *Journal of Hospitality and Tourism Insights*, *6*(5), 2115–2138. DOI: 10.1108/JHTI-02-2022-0087

Singh, A., & Rao, P. (2022). Machine learning applications for women's travel safety. *Journal of AI in Transportation*, *9*(1), 30–50.

Smith, J. (2022). The role of AI in personal security. *Journal of Advanced Technology*, *35*(4), 112–130.

Tran, J. (2022). AI-powered crime prediction and prevention. *Cybersecurity Advances*, *18*(4), 123–140.

United Nations Office on Drugs and Crime. (2022). *Women's safety and crime prevention strategies.* Retrieved from www.unodc.org

United Nations Women. (2022). *Technology solutions for women's safety in public spaces.* Retrieved from www.unwomen.org

United States Department of State. (2023). *Travel advisory and safety measures for women abroad.* Retrieved from www.travel.state.gov

Wang, L., & Gupta, N. (2023). Smart cities and AI-based security: Implications for female travelers. *International Journal of Smart Infrastructure*, *10*(1), 22–38.

WHO. (2022). *Violence against women prevalence estimates*. Retrieved from www.who.int

Wilson, H. (2020). The evolution of hotel security systems. *Hospitality & Technology Review, 33*(1), 99–115.

Women, U. N. (2021). *Safe cities and safe public spaces for women and girls*. Retrieved from www.unwomen.org

World Bank. (2023). *Gender equality and transport: Improving safety for women*. Retrieved from www.worldbank.org

World Economic Forum. (2023). *Future of travel security: Innovations and challenges*. Retrieved from www.weforum.org

Chapter 8
Internal Communication: The Relationship Between Barriers and Strategies in Verbal Communication

Felipa Lopes dos Reis
http://orcid.org/0000-0001-8462-0810
Lusofona University, Portugal

Henrique Ribeiro Sá
Lusofona University, Portugal

Maria Freitas Trigo
Lusofona University, Portugal

Miftachul Huda
http://orcid.org/0000-0001-6712-0056
Universiti Pendidikan Sultan Idris, Malaysia

ABSTRACT

This work's main objective is to explore interpersonal communication. The focus is directed to verbal communication, however, the same is also shared with non-verbal communication. In this context, the importance that internal communication has in an organization/company is analyzed. It is well known that the professional success of companies is slightly dependent on internal communication. Barriers and their mitigation strategies are also present in this work. The case study is carried out at Portway Handling in Portugal, where it was analyzed whether these same barriers were minimized, whether the mitigation strategies applied by managers or workers were applied correctly, in order to achieve greater success. A second objective would

DOI: 10.4018/979-8-3373-0629-2.ch008

ght © 2026, IGI Global Scientific Publishing. Copying or distributing in print or electronic forms without written permission of IGI Global Scientific Publishing is prohibited. Use of this chapter to generative artificial intelligence (AI) technologies is expressly prohibited. The publisher reserves all rights to license its use for generative AI training and machine learning model development.

then be to understand whether the hindrance caused by communication barriers has a preponderance in the efficiency of the work carried out by the company. To carry out this study, the selected was the questionnaire, using a sample of 31 participants.

INTRODUCTION

Since the beginning of our species, communication has always contributed to understand a conversation between two or more people, which may be verbal (written and oral) or non-verbal (gestures, facial expressions, among others). Communication is the contact between human beings, both individual and collective. In everyday life, communication is part of an human life itself and through it, people can relate to each other in their daily lives, at home, at work, in society, that is, wherever they are (Kurniadi & Mahaputra, 2021).

Communication is the art of sharing information, ideas, perspectives of each of us, however for the message to be shared successfully, the receiver must understand all the signals sent by the communicator. This applies in interpersonal contexts such as family, audiences and, the primary focus, communication in an organization. (Kurniadi & Mahaputra, 2021).

When it comes to the organizational level, communication plays a very important role in ensuring that managers and employees understand each other and so that there can be a healthy relationship between everyone involved. However, there are barriers to efficient communication such as time, space, relational climate, mood or even physical or contextual factors (Top & Ali, 2021).

Therefore, all forms of communication are important for us, as human beings, to be able to live in society and for each individual person to be able to express themselves and understand messages. Evidently, for any message there is a sender and a receiver.

At the sender's level, the lack of will in communication, the language, the structuring of the message, the use of inappropriate words that make it difficult for the receiver to perceive them, such as foreign words, abbreviations and even the fact that political, cultural, and religious values, among others, may be neglected. The receiver may reveal lack of interest, attempt to interrupt the sender, not promote the debate, trying to promote their ideas in relation to the sender's, resorting to an aggressive voice, among others (Kurniadi & Mahaputra, 2021).

At an organizational level, there are four main barriers to efficient communication, such as communication channels, language, empathy, and worker efficiency.

For the reasons listed above, it is necessary to find strategies to minimize the effects that the attitudes already mentioned can cause, to avoid an organizational climate without direction and disorientation.

In the theoretical framework, the various aspects that are intrinsically related to non-verbal communication, interpersonal communication, internal communication, as well as barriers to organizational communication as well as strategies to overcome them, will be noted. In this way, we are then able to highlight the importance of verbal communication in the context of organizations, that is, the importance that a sender, a message and a receiver have for, for example, a company. However, there are also barriers and feedback, as well as gestures, expressions, and body posture, which are included in non-verbal communication. Later, in the same chapter, we will explore internal communication, which is extremely important for professional and organizational success. We will also explore the issue of different communication styles. In other words, it would be aggressive, passive, or assertive communication, where each one has its advantages, as well as disadvantages if not used in the best way. In this way, the influence of each communication style can be considered strong, since it is completely dependent on the situation in which it finds itself, thus influencing interpersonal relationships. As previously mentioned, it will addressed the barriers, which can be linguistic, cultural, or communication, and are closely linked to the strategies to mitigate them. These strategies may, for example, include empathy, which somewhat facilitates the understanding of other people's emotions and experiences, the use of visual elements, the development of expressions, so that the receiver can understand the message more clearly.

In this sense, the starting question is how efficient are the communication strategies applied by managers/workers to minimize barriers to verbal communication in the organization? For this reason, the main objective of this study is to understand whether the strategies used by managers/workers in transmitting information and to understand whether the obstacle caused by communication barriers has a preponderance in the efficiency of the work carried out by the company. As a secondary objective, it is to try to understand whether some of the strategies that are highlighted in the theoretical framework are used in the company under study.

That said, the study will be carried out at the company Portway Handling in Portugal, at Lisbon Airport, carrying out a survey via questionnaire to understand the workers' point of view, whether in relation to the obstacles they feel in communicating with their direct colleagues, or with superiors and also the strategies used by the manager for communication.

1. THEORETICAL FRAMEWORK

1.1 Verbal Communication

In the 1960s, communication began to be defined as the cognitive processing of information that leads to persuasion. In organizations, interpersonal communication plays a crucial role, involving two individuals: one who transmits the message and another who receives and interprets it. This process includes five main components: sender, message, receiver, barriers, and feedback (Machado, 2021).

The sender is the one who transmits the message, which can be verbal (using words) or non-verbal (through gestures, facial expressions, etc.). The message represents the content transmitted between sender and receiver, which may include ideas, opinions, emotions or information.

The receiver is responsible for decoding the message and assigning it a meaning, which may differ from the sender's intention. For successful communication, the receiver must understand the information as intended by the sender, considering both verbal and non-verbal elements. Barriers, such as noise and lack of time, can interfere with interpersonal communication, while feedback allows the receiver to indicate to the sender how the message was understood (Machado, 2021).

Nowadays, communication is inevitable as individuals constantly exchange messages, verbal or non-verbal. It is a complex process that aims to allow the receiver to decipher, assimilate and understand the sender's message.

1.2 Non-Verbal Communication

The interaction between individuals is strongly influenced by their non-verbal expressions. People constantly provide information to those around them through their appearance, behaviors, facial expressions and body movements. Everyone's nonverbal communication involves a combination of attitudes, responses, moods, feelings and interactions in a given environment, through which individuals relate consciously or unconsciously. Body language is expressed through posture, body movements, facial expressions, position in relation to others and the surrounding environment. The most important non-verbal elements during the communication process include kinesis (body movements), proxemics (distance between communicators), environment and distractions (Borges, 2022).

1.3 Internal Communication

During different moments of professional practice, workers need to be able to quickly analyze the situation they find themselves in to ensure a successful interaction between those involved. However, communication skills can be improved through training, which results in more appropriate strategic decisions, greater adherence, better relationships between clients and professionals, and a more harmonious work atmosphere among colleagues (Machado, 2021).

Several studies highlight the importance of effective communication for professional success, being considered the basis for several other essential skills, such as teamwork, leadership, planning and organization. However, many studies point to the scarcity of these critical communication skills in contemporary business contexts (Mason et al., 2021).

The modern professional environment is characterized by new forms of organization, advanced communication technologies and constant changes, which have blurred the boundaries between professional and personal life. Communication is fundamental to the existence of organizations, regardless of the sector in which they operate (Machado, 2021).

Communication competence is crucial in all industries, from traditional service sectors such as tourism and sales to highly technical fields such as medicine and engineering. Communication effectiveness is positively related to employee engagement and a series of organizational variables, such as performance, satisfaction, employee retention and financial performance. Although communication skills are considered essential by employers, there is little recent research identifying which skills are most important and why.

Expectations for effective business communication have evolved due to the dramatic impact of technology and globalization, requiring the ability to communicate in increasingly complex and diverse environments (Almeida et al., 2023).

1.4 Communication Styles

There are different communication styles that a worker can employ, varying according to the context in which they find themselves. However, there is always a predominant style, and using the most appropriate style for each situation makes communication more effective (Machado, 2021).

Three communication styles can be identified, according to Pereira (2022):

Aggressive: Individuals who adopt aggressive behavior in conflict situations who try to dominate or intimidate others during the conversation, demonstrating indifference to their feelings or needs, ignoring and disregarding opinions and actions. Aggressive behavior varies depending on the individual's hierarchical position: when in a predominant position, it can manifest coldness, arrogance and intolerance; while in a subordinate position, he tends to be hostile and systematically contest superior orders. Although aggressiveness can bring short-term benefits by allowing aggressive people to achieve goals by intimidating others, it is not suitable for building trusting relationships, which is essential in the workplace.

Passive: Passive behavior is adopted to avoid conflicts at all costs. Passive individuals tend to conform to the group they are in, waiting for others to start the conversation. During interpersonal communication, they may avoid expressing their true opinions for fear of disagreement, demonstrating a great need for approval. In the work or personal environment, when asked to solve a problem, passive individuals tend to feel paralyzed. They prioritize the needs or desires of others in relationships and can be easily manipulated.

Assertive: Individuals who adopt assertive behavior can defend their own rights and interests, express feelings, opinions, ideas and needs in a clear, objective and honest way, while respecting the point of view and actions of others. They seek to resolve interpersonal problems while preserving trusting relationships. Assertive people are willing to listen to others and negotiate solutions that satisfy everyone involved when faced with a problem.

For assertive communication, several requirements are necessary: Having problem solving as its main objective; respect others; have initiative to start and maintain conversations; express yourself directly and honestly; encourage assertiveness in others; take responsibility for one's own behavior; know how to accept and respond to criticism; give feedback; have empathy and convey trust, both verbally and non-verbally.

In the long term, the adoption of assertive behaviors leads to the creation of lasting relationships based on trust and respect between individuals (Machado, 2021).

1.5 Development of Information and Communication Technologies

Changes in information technologies have transformed communication within and around organizations, demanding intercultural and adaptive communication skills due to the constant evolution of person-organization relationships and the global nature of business. This evolution suggests the need for new communication skills. There are specific communication skills crucial to contemporary business and professional environments, which represent a mix between traditional and modern communication practices: interpersonal and relational communication, technology-mediated communication, intergroup communication, enthusiastic and creative communication skills, non-verbal communication, as well as listening and expression skills. (Almeida et al., 2023).

These competencies reflect the need for a diverse set of skills that transcend conventional disciplinary boundaries, including proficiency in technology, intergroup relations, nonverbal awareness, interpersonal skills, and more.

Several studies highlight the importance of effective communication for professional success, being considered the basis for several other essential skills, such as teamwork, leadership, planning and organization. However, many studies point to the scarcity of these critical communication skills in contemporary business contexts (Mason et al., 2021).

The modern professional environment is characterized by new forms of organization, advanced communication technologies and constant changes, which have blurred the boundaries between professional and personal life. Communication is fundamental to the existence of organizations, regardless of the sector in which they operate (Machado, 2021).

Communication competence is crucial in all industries, from traditional service sectors such as tourism and sales to highly technical fields such as medicine and engineering. Communication effectiveness is positively related to employee engagement and a series of organizational variables, such as performance, satisfaction, employee retention and financial performance. Although communication skills are considered essential by employers, there is little recent research identifying which skills are most important and why.

2. BARRIERS TO ORGANIZATIONAL COMMUNICATION AND THEIR STRATEGIES

2.1 Language

Issues such as language barriers, the fact that two or more people do not speak the same language or language, can obstruct effective communication, and cause many unnecessary problems due to misunderstandings (Jelani & Nordini, 2019). In addition, barriers may also arise when speaking the same language, when using slang or expressions specific to the place they are from. They may also occur when two people do not have the same level of knowledge in a certain area.

In addition, different sociocultural contexts, individuals of different nationalities, religions, ethnicities, among others, may also negatively influence communication. In other words, when two people are communicating with each other, there may be differences in their cultural backgrounds.

Naturally, there must be a concern from both the sender and the receiver in trying to understand all the constraints of language, posture, cultures so that the existing barriers in communication become less and less.

The use of visual elements such as photographs, drawings, graphics as well as the use of appropriate non-verbal communication can help to avoid barriers to communication.

We must be aware that different situations and different cultures have different interpretations of non-verbal communication, which considers human interaction through the expression of feelings, emotions, gestures, facial expressions, body posture, eye

contact, touch, among others, so that the The receiver not only understands the words but also the emotions of the sender. Through silence it is also possible to convey various messages, depending on the context (Pires, 2023).

It is necessary to understand what type of culture we are dealing with because it can often be offensive, the quality and adequate volume of the voice also has preponderance in the transmission of messages.

2.2 Transmission Channels

Transmission channels play a fundamental role in the correct functioning of a company, they must be fast, clear, and concise in their messages. Transmissions can be ascending, descending and lateral. Evidently, upward messages are from employees to their superiors, downwards vice versa and finally, lateral messages are the exchange of messages between various departments or the same work position.

Transmission can be carried out face-to-face, message, phone call, email, zoom, social media.

Sometimes, there are obstacles to using transmission channels, since the message is not well interpreted, or transmitted clearly and objectively, especially if it is via text message. Next, the study carried out by (Braun et al., 2019) states that face-to-face communication is much more effective than the rest, because: It is possible to understand the message more clearly; Non-verbal communication (Gestures, body expressions, among others) are easily identified to complement verbal communication; Immediate feedback; Message transmission speed.

2.3 Empathy

Empathy is a crucial component of social cognition. This allows one person to put themselves in another's shoes and understand their emotions and experiences. Empathy plays a fundamental role in social interactions as it facilitates emotional communication and promotes prosocial behaviors such as helping, supporting, and cooperating with others. Furthermore, empathy plays an important role in people's moral and ethical development, helping them understand the consequences of their actions on others and make more ethical and compassionate decisions. (Gonçalves, 2019).

In the context of organizations, since there is usually no empathy on the part of the manager towards the worker, the latter may feel that they are not understood, leading to dissatisfaction and a consequent drop in performance.

2.4 Efficiency

Effective communication within an organization is one of the most efficient ways for a company to thrive in markets today. Effective internal communication allows the interaction and inclusion of all people in an organization, ensuring that everyone has the same access to the alignment of ideas, consequently incorporating the assertive and efficient exchange of information, benefiting the company's mission and values.

3. METHODOLOGY

In this second part of the project, the methodology that was used, the established hypotheses, characterization of the population, the instruments used, the sample, and the software for processing results will be explored.

To better understand what is being worked on, the Methodology begins with the formulation of the starting question: "How efficient are the communication strategies applied by managers/workers to minimize barriers to verbal communication in the organization?" which will dictate the direction this study will take.

Thus, the hypotheses of the present investigation arise:

H1: Communication barriers imply an obstacle to internal communication.

This hypothesis was designed to understand whether communication barriers hinder the flow of information between different stakeholders in the company, given that in the organizational context, good internal communication translates into the effective functioning of the company. In addition, we want to understand whether there are specific barriers, not mentioned in the theoretical framework, on the part of the individuals interviewed that limit their ability to be understood.

H2: Impact of communication strategies applied by managers/workers.

This hypothesis was formulated to understand whether the strategies applied by different stakeholders, mainly managers, in the company, are applied correctly and which strategies are most used in this organizational context. Furthermore, we want to understand if there are any strategies suggested by respondents that are not foreseen in the theoretical framework, in order to develop effective guidelines for more efficient communication in the company.

As for the methodology used, both a quantitative and qualitative approach are used in this investigation. In the context of this study, qualitative research was chosen, since different opinions and perspectives are presented and because it is a descriptive sample in which the data cannot be quantified. However, the research also has quantitative aspects, as it includes the preparation and distribution of a questionnaire by the author of this dissertation, where the data is mixed and can be quantified.

3.1 Characterization of the Population

The sample for this investigation was collected at the company Portway Handling Portugal at Lisbon airport, which specializes in ground handling at the airports of Lisbon, Porto, Beja, Faro, and the autonomous region of Madeira and has more than eighty airlines as clients.

3.2 Sample

The sample will consist of 31 individuals, Age varies between 18 and 45 years old, professional experience in the company varies from 1 month to 3 years.

3.3 Instruments

The study is based on an understanding of this topic, the creation of hypotheses and questions about the subject studied (Bertin, 2020), in which a questionnaire will be applied via Google Forms in which the use and application of the same was consented by all participants. The questionnaire was prepared by the authors of this work and was shared essentially via Whatsapp. In relation to the questionnaire (Appendix 1) used, it consists of seven easily interpretable multiple-choice questions and with the respective explanation of the concept, four questions in which the participant could choose more than one option and two questions with a brief written answer. These open questions aim to try to understand if there are other barriers to communication that are not foreseen in the theoretical framework. Questions fourteen and fifteen are exclusively about age and sex, just for contextualization in relation to demographic issues, but they do not correspond to the analysis carried out.

Through the questionnaire we obtained results classified as quantitative and qualitative, which according to Martins et al. (2023): "While one has its theoretical basis based on empiricism and positivism, marked by the objectivity of statistical analyzes and approaching reality through numbers (quantitative research). The second is based on theories such as ethnography and phenomenology, with a procedural approach in which information is constructed based on the meanings of phenomena, the attribution of meanings, and is characterized by the understanding of reality based on the subjectivity and experiences of the informants (qualitative research)." (p.2).

4. PRESENTATION AND TREATMENT OF RESULTS

The survey was carried out using Google Forms, which was active from February 24 of 2024 to March 2 of 2024. In total, 31 responses were recorded. After the end of the survey, the data was converted into tables with the help of Excel.

Figure 1. Gender

Graph 1 Gender (Own elaboration)

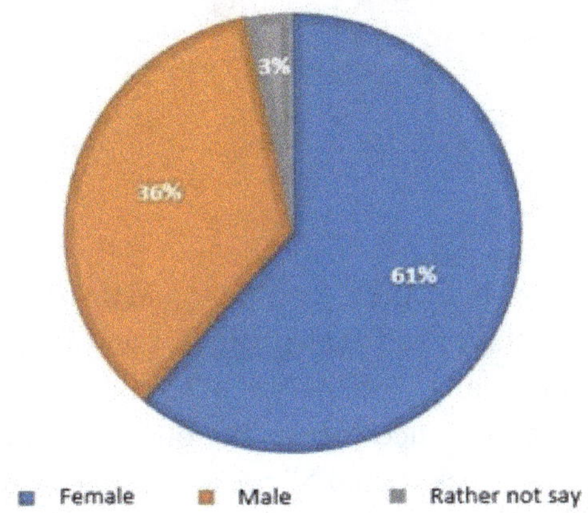

When analyzing the gender of the 31 participants, the predominance of women in the sample collected is clear, at 61%; men with 36%; and even a person who chose not to reveal their gender. These data do not influence the results obtained in any way.

Figure 2. Age group

Graph 2 Age Group (Own preparation)

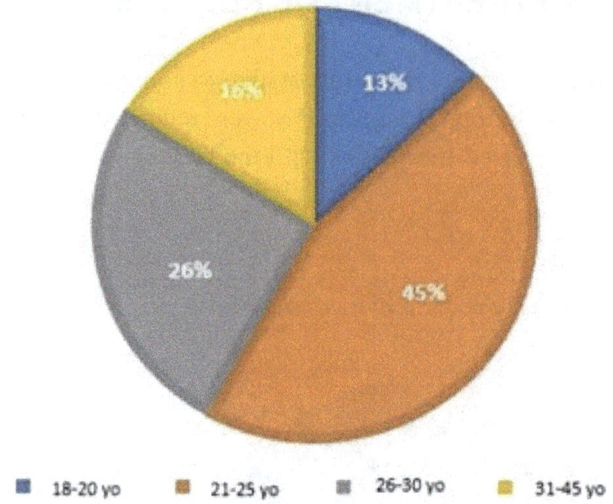

Regarding the age range of respondents, we found that 13% were between 18 and 20 years old; The largest share, 45%, is between 21 and 25 years old; 26% between 26 and 30 years old and, finally, 16% between 31 and 45 years old. As previously stated, these data do not influence the results obtained in any way. None of the participants selected the option 46 and 50 years old and 51 or more years old.

Figure 3.

Graph 3 Length of service in the company (Own preparation)

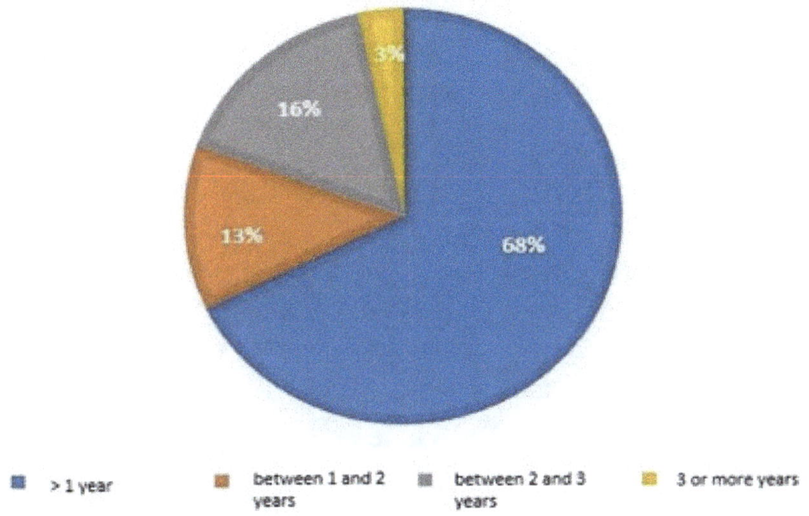

Regarding length of service at the company, respondents revealed that 68% have worked at the company for less than a year; 13% have worked at the company for more than a year; 16% have been with the company for between two and three years and only 3%, that is, one person, has been with the company for more than 3 years.

Figure 4.

Graph 4 Position/Department (Own preparation)

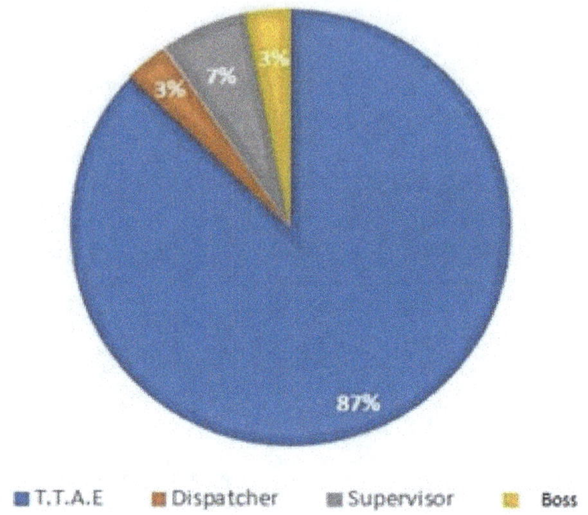

As for the department, the majority of participants, 87% belong to TTAE (Ground Assistance Traffic Technician) who deal with the issuance, marketing, verification, registration and accounting of transport documents, in addition to making refunds. Management, coordination and supervision of aircraft loading and unloading processes, including goods, mail and baggage, and also the supervision and coordination of activities carried out by ramp operators. Around 3% are in the dispatcher role, which is the person who is in constant communication with the cockpit to provide all the necessary help to the aircraft pilots; 7% of the responses were from supervisors and we also obtained a response from a boss that will be analyzed later.

Figure 5.

Graph 5 Receipt of communication training (Own preparation)

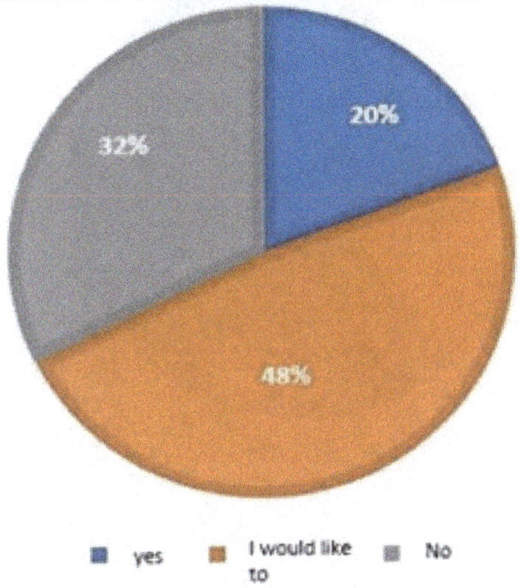

With this question the main goal was to understand whether there was any type of training offered by the company and whether the respondents were available to receive any type of help with communication. Almost half of the respondents said they would like to receive any type of training in this area, 20% revealed that they had already received some type of training, but not in the company and, finally, 32% had no intention of receiving help on this topic.

Figure 6.

Graph 6 Frequency of communication with superiors (Own preparation)

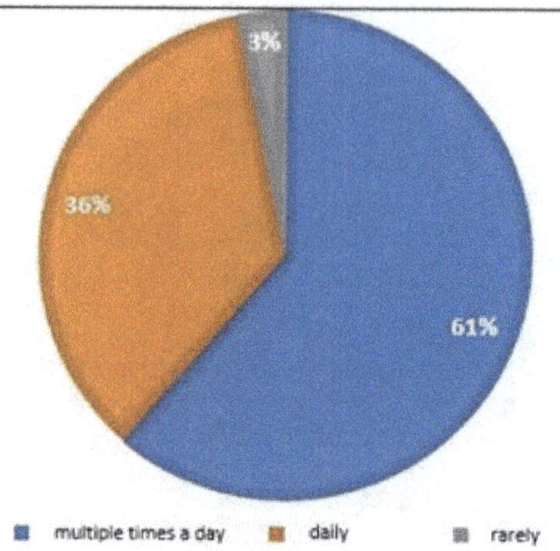

Evidently, for a company to function properly, there needs to be recurring communication between all positions, which is why it was strange to see that one person responded "rarely" when asked how often they communicate with their superior. The remaining results were in line with what was said previously, with 36% speaking daily with their superiors and 61% speaking several times a day.

Figure 7.

Graph 7 Frequency of communication with colleagues (Own preparation)

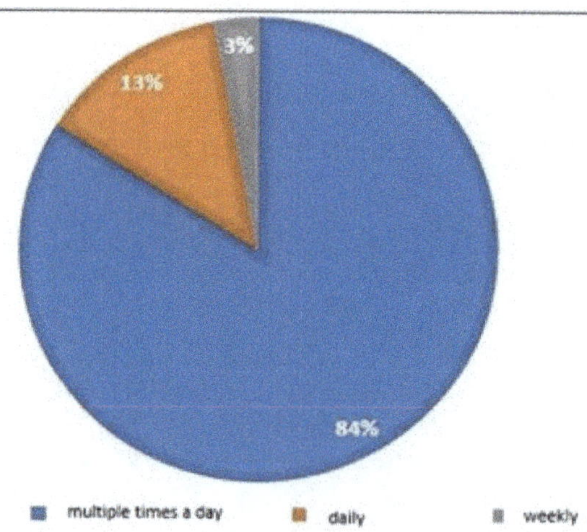

Obviously, like the data previously revealed by communication with superiors, in this case, respondents followed the trend with 84% communicating several times; 13% communicate daily and only one (3%) communicates weekly with colleagues.

Figure 8.

Graph 8 Classification of communication effectiveness with superiors (Own preparation)

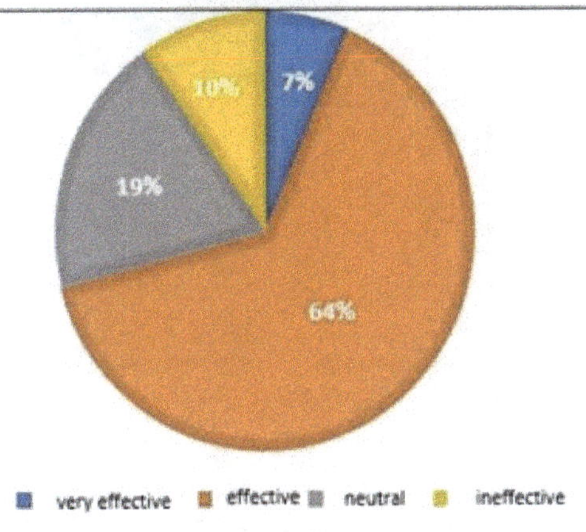

In this graph there is effective communication from the respondents' perspective, very effective with 7% and effective communication with 64%; almost a fifth of people admit that communication is neither good nor bad, while only 10% say that communication with their superiors is ineffective.

Figure 9.

Graph 9 Classification of communication effectiveness with colleagues (Own preparation)

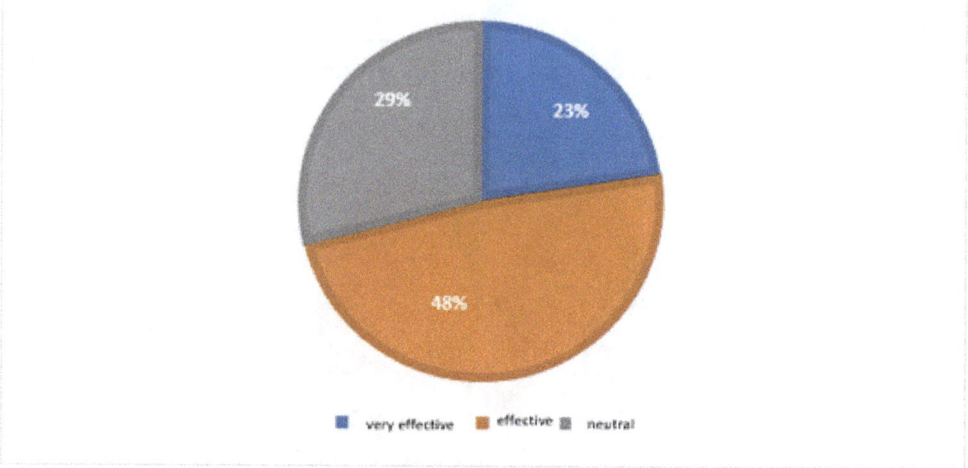

In this case, compared to the previous graph, it is revealed that there is the same effectiveness in communication between colleagues in the same area, when adding the "effective" and "very effective" values, the biggest difference is the 7% increase to 23% of "very effective" communication that comes from the fact that there are typically fewer barriers, in theory, in communication between colleagues, as they feel less formality during the conversation. In addition, 29% of respondents reveal that they feel neutral.

Figure 10.

Graph 10 Barriers in communicating with superiors (Own preparation)

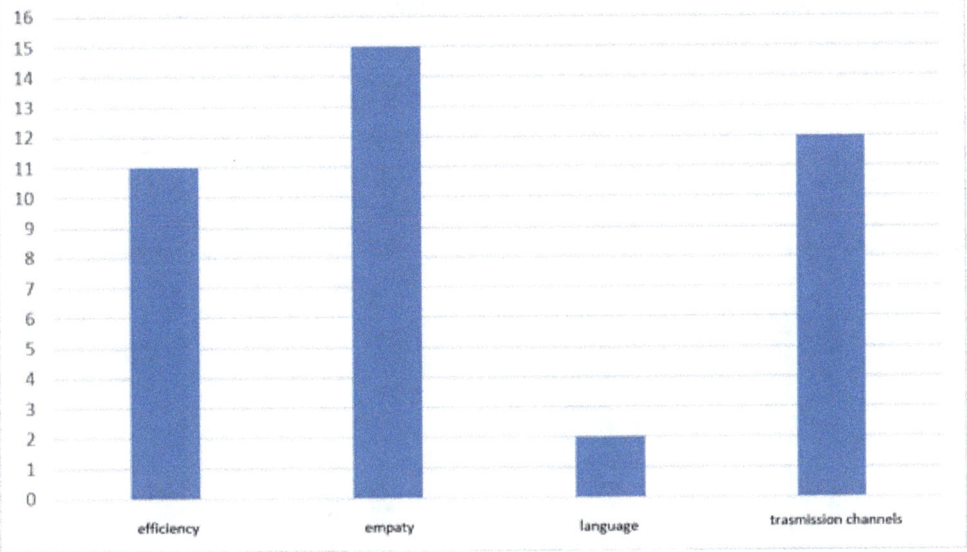

In this question, it was possible to choose several answers, following the guidance of the literature review that focused on these four barriers: Efficiency; empathy; language; transmission channels. Here it is clear that language is the least barrier, as only two people selected this option. Efficiency and transmission channels present eleven and twelve responses, respectively.

In relation to efficiency, as seen in the theoretical framework, all workers must be in tune with the alignment of ideas and company values so that the exchange of information is assertive, efficient, and coherent. This graph reveals that this commitment to ideas and values may be being harmed and could result in ineffectiveness in carrying out tasks.

When it comes to transmission channels, if they are not well defined, either due to *Whatsapp*, email, direct message via mobile phone number or even face to face, which may prove to be harmful, as some relevant information may be "forgotten", especially if the communication attempt is via text message, as seen in theoretical framework.

Finally, empathy, which accounted for fifteen people, this component is extremely important, because if a worker feels that his superior takes his problems into account, puts himself in the worker's shoes and understands his perspective, this all leads to an increase income of both parties. Often, these people just want to feel that they are part of the company and that they are not just another person. In addition, as seen in the theoretical

framework, empathy plays a central role in the moral and ethical development of each individual because it helps people understand the consequences of actions on others and will improve decision-making.

Figure 11.

Graph 11 Barriers to communicating with colleagues (Own preparation)

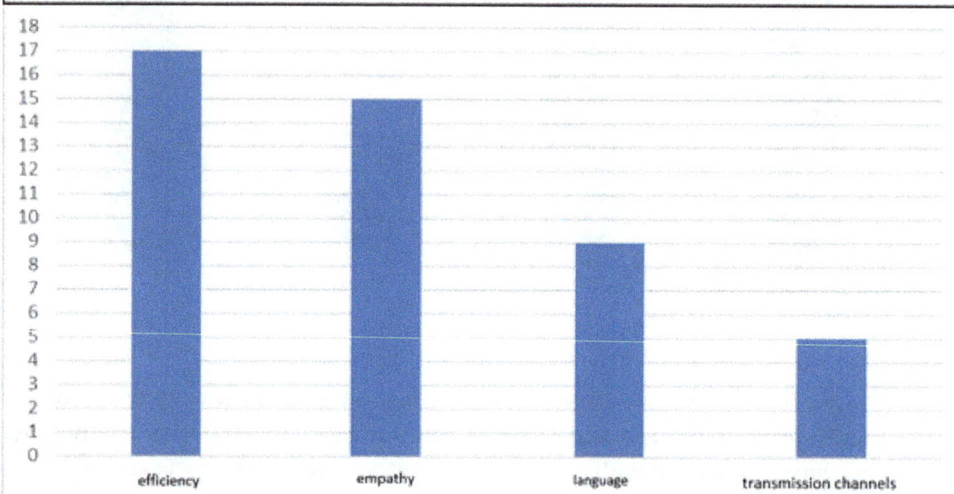

In communication between colleagues, the number of responses in relation to transmission channels decreases a lot due to there being more permanent and face-to-face contact. Language is more emphasized in this graph (nine) compared to the previous graph due to the greater diversity of cultures and languages that exist in the company. Efficiency (seventeen) and empathy (fifteen) are somewhat in line with what was said in the comment on the previous table.

Figure 12.

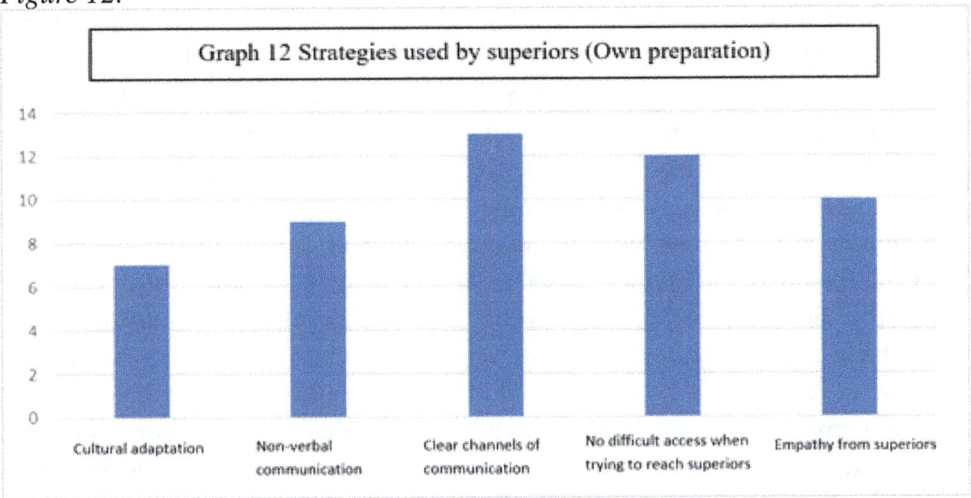

Like the graphs previously analyzed, in this question it was also possible to select more than one answer. Here it is possible to verify that non-verbal communication (body expressions, gestures, emotions) is one of the techniques used by superiors to achieve better transmission of the message with nine people choosing this option. Cultural adaptation could be one of the aspects to improve as only seven people selected this option. From the responses, in this company, there are clear channels of communication as there were thirteen responses and, furthermore, twelve revealed that there is no difficult access when trying to reach their superior. It is still verifiable that, compared to the results of the previous questions, only ten respondents revealed that they feel some type of empathy from their superior while previously, fifteen people selected that they felt a lack of understanding. This comes from the fact that some people think there is empathy, but it is not enough.

The responses in the strategies used with colleagues do not differ much, following the same trend as in graph 11, with cultural adaptation having ten responses; non-verbal communication had twelve; the transmission channels with twenty responses and difficult access to colleagues had eleven responses. In this question it was also possible to select more than one answer.

The questionnaire also had two more questions, but this time with a short open answer so that there could be an understanding if there were any other barriers/ concerns and communication strategies that were not foreseen in the theoretical framework carried out. Therefore, some of the respondents chose to write "None" in this paragraph, but others revealed the following: The lack of time to be able to express everything completely; the stress associated with the responsibility of the profession (High responsibility because they are dealing with air connections and lots of passengers); some answers made reference to different types of personalities, such as introversion and shyness that hinder the effectiveness of communication; one of the respondents revealed that there was some partiality, that is, favoring one or more people, which could cause the superior to give less importance to one individual in relation to the other; the fact that there are multiple shifts means there is a need to interact with lots of people and ways of working which can also create an obstacle to relationships and communication.

Often only the factors described in the theoretical framework are considered, but from the answers obtained it is factual that many small situations can really destabilize the workplace and the effectiveness of the information transmitted.

In the last question, the focus point was to understand, from the worker's point of view, which strategies they feel could be implemented in the company to significantly improve the work and communication carried out there. Some answers, like the previous question, were written "none". Around a quarter of the responses emphasized the fact that there are few briefings (transmission of information on how a certain process will take place) and team meetings so that people on the ground can express their concerns regarding the work carried out, effectively what goes well and what goes less well. One of the answers that we found interesting was "Time for conviviality" which, due to shift rotation, is very unlikely for workers to get to know each other and create bonds to improve interpersonal relationships and consequently communication, as these two themes are directly connected.

Finally, as previously indicated, one response from a head of this company that we will analyze individually. This is in line with the general trend of responses as the empathy option was selected both when communicating with superiors and when communicating with colleagues. This also revealed that the effectiveness in communication in both spectrums is neutral, which shows some signs of apprehension on the part of this person, as he has worked at Portway handling Portugal for more than three years. To conclude this analysis, the subject mentions that there should be greater availability/predisposition for dialogue and that the company should find ways to provide it.

FINAL CONSIDERATIONS

With this research and data analysis work, it was possible to conclude that there is indeed a relationship between communication strategies and internal communication, and a company, in this case Portway. It was also possible to identify the impact of the strategies adopted by stakeholders in order to mitigate communication barriers.

Therefore, analyzing the data specifically, it was realized that barriers truly have a great impact on internal communication, that is, on its effectiveness, which consequently makes the flow of information within the company unclear, and therefore, it is necessary to identification and creation of guidelines/strategies to mitigate them, thus making communication more efficient.

The methodology used in this case study was mixed, that is, it shares both a qualitative and a quantitative approach. As previously mentioned throughout the work, the justification for having a mixed approach is due to the fact that since different perspectives are presented from a descriptive sample, where the data are not effectively capable of quantification, therefore, it is called using a qualitative approach. As for the quantitative approach, its justification is the fact that it involves preparation and distribution of a questionnaire, where its data is mixed and quantified.

In a universe of 5 Handling scales at Portuguese airports, Portway at Lisbon Airport was chosen as the target for the study. A sample of 31 participants was collected, where 87% of the population are subordinates. The collected data helped understand that there can be many communication breakdowns within a company, and if the common goal is both the success of the company and personal success, it is necessary to create strategies to mitigate these communication barriers, for instance. One of the questionnaire questions aimed to gather a more personal opinion, with the objective of truly understanding if there were any areas for improvement and suggesting strategies to enhance and address any potential flaws identified.

Therefore, given that there was a combination of approaches, it can be concluded that a more comprehensive analysis was possible, thus providing a deeper understanding of the needs of employees, whether they are subordinates, supervisors, or any other role in the company. Consequently, it contributes to the development of more precise recommendations in order to improve communication in the company.

To conclude, the answer to the question "How efficient are the communication strategies applied by managers/workers to minimize barriers to verbal communication in the organization?" involves analyzing the answers to the questionnaire, where it was possible to analyze that only 10% of those interviewed responded that communication between subordinates and their superiors was ineffective. On the other hand, communication between colleagues in the same hierarchy, it can be observed that 23% of participants responded that it was very effective, 48% as effective, and 29% as neutral.

Therefore, it can be concluded that there are some areas for improvement, but that overall, the results were positive for the company.

REFERENCES

Almeida, LM, Torres, CIO, Seixas, NRM, Samtos, DB & Silva, CDD (2023). The Importance of Information and Communication Technologies in the Teaching and Learning Process in Science. Teaching Science and Technology in Magazine – Encitec, 13(2), 54-71.https://doi.org/DOI: 10.31512/encitec.v13i2.638

Bertin, C. E. (2020). Understand what empirical research is and its characteristics. ViaCarreira.https://viacarreira.com/pesquisa-empirica/

Borges, B. M. C. (2022). The importance of non-verbal communication for the good performance of organizations. Final work in the form of Dissertation presented to the Universidade Católica Portuguesa to obtain a master's degree in Management.

Braun, S., Bark, A. H., Kirchner, A., Stegmann, S., & Dick, R. (2019). Emails From the Boss—Curse or Blessing? Relations Between Communication Channels, Leader Evaluation, and Employees' Attitudes. *International Journal of Business Communication*, *56*(1), 50–81. DOI: 10.1177/2329488415597516

Gonçalves, J. F. N. (2019). Self-perceived Empathy and Empathic Performance in an Organizational Context: Relationship with Job Satisfaction. [Master's thesis unpublished]. Minho's university.

Jelani, F., & Nordini, N. S. (2019). Barriers to Effective Communication at the Workplace. *International Journal of Modern Languages and Applied Linguistics*, *3*(2), 7–18. DOI: 10.24191/ijmal.v3i2.7642

Kurniadi, W., & Mahaputra, M. R. (2021). Determination of Communication in the Organization: Non Verbal, Oral and Written. Journal of law politics and humanities, 1(4), 164-172.

Machado, M. E. A. (2021). The influence of the project manager's communication style on team motivation. Masters dissertation. Higher School of Technology and Management. Polytechnic of Porto.

Martins, M. I. S., Oliveira, F. A., Alcântara, D. G., Dias, P. R. G., Vieria, E. M., Sousa, F. S., Almeida, A. N. S., & Silva, J. P. F. (2023). Generalizability and transferability: The possibilities of qualitative research. *Revista Foco*, *16*(2), 1–10.

Mason, A. P. U., Santos, M., Spanhol, F., Bichet, K., & Giuriatti, T. (2021). New Information and Communication Technologies Associated with Active Methodologies in the Current Educational Scenario. Proceedings of the International Congress on Knowledge and Innovation – Ciki, 1(1). DOI: 10.48090/ciki.v1i1.1158

Pereira, M. R. (2022). Communication management in community pharmacy. Dissertation to obtain a Master's Degree in Pharmaceutical Sciences. Faculty of Science and Technology.

Pires, S. F. S. (2023). Understanding non-verbal communication: Applications in healthcare. Retrieved on February 10, 2024, fromhttps://homepublishing.com.br/index.php/cadernodeanais/article/view/991/1102

Top, C., & Ali, B. J. (2021). Customer satisfaction in online meeting platforms: Impact of efficiency, fulfillment, system availability, and privacy. *Amazonia Investiga, 10*(38), 70–81. DOI: 10.34069/AI/2021.38.02.7

Chapter 9

The Types of Communication and the Impact of Gender at Nespresso in Portugal

Felipa Lopes dos Reis
http://orcid.org/0000-0001-8462-0810
Lusofona University, Portugal

Diogo Freitas Belejo
http://orcid.org/0009-0009-9500-4066
Lusofona University, Portugal

Ana Freitas Simões
Lusofona University, Portugal

ABSTRACT

The scope of this study is to take a deeper look at the types of communication that exist, establishing a consequent relationship with the gender matter and making it possible to analyze the extent to which this latter factor can have an impact on communication processes. To support the carried out research, the methodology used for this study has a quantitative approach, through the application of a questionnaire, the aim of which is to study the isolated case of an organization, raising different issues of relevance such as the company's investment in the transmission of information and knowledge, gender equality, among others. With the development of the study, the aim is to dissect the extent to which communication skills tend to differ according to gender and to get a sense of how strongly this phenomenon occurs in the organization surveyed. In this way, it is hoped to conclude that

DOI: 10.4018/979-8-3373-0629-2.ch009

ght © 2026, IGI Global Scientific Publishing. Copying or distributing in print or electronic forms without written permission of IGI Global Scientific Publishing is prohibited. Use of this chapter to generative artificial intelligence (AI) technologies is expressly prohibited. The publisher reserves all rights to license its use for generative AI training and machine learning model development.

the main difference between men and women, in terms of verbal and non-verbal communication, is present when it comes to achieving objectives, with a disparate attitude when valuing . I

INTRODUCTION

According to (Reis, 2024), verbal communication involves the use of language as a symbology for the expression of ideas and assumes dominance over the most used type of communication, since it allows the sharing of knowledge of greater complexity, while non-verbal communication is based on the absence of written and/or oral elements and occurs through the use of gestures. facial expressions and reactions.

In the context of gender-based communication, Usera (2024) brought discursive communities as distinctive elements between two major groups (men and women). As for verbal communication, she highlighted the male group as a user of a more instrumental language in order to achieve premeditated goals, the step that defined the female discursive community as a user of verbal communication as a tool for maintaining relationships. Regarding non-verbal communication and based on the distinctive aspects between communities, the same author emphasized that members of the male group have a more deterministic posture and a lower physical closeness between peers, when compared to members of the female community, who tend to be more condescending and show greater openness to physical approach.

Following the statements raised, the need arose to dissect the differences between gender in the business context and establish a means of connection with the power of communication within Nespresso, leading to the primary question that will guide the development of the study: What is the impact of gender on organizational communication?

It should also be noted that the present work is divided into three main parts: the first part encompasses the state of the art, where a bibliographic survey is made on various aspects, from the basic notion of communication and its process to verbal and non-verbal communication based on gender; the second part develops the study methodology, highlighting the data collection instruments (application of a questionnaire) and also presents the formulation of hypotheses of the study; and the third part is based on the analysis of results and data treatment, confronting the previously highlighted hypotheses with the information obtained through the sample submitted to the research.

1. LITERATURE REVIEW

1.1 Basic Notion of the Communication Process

Communication deals with the transmission and respective interpretation of information, ideas and feelings between two or more individuals, through the use of verbal and non-verbal symbology (Reis, 2024).

The aforementioned transmission can appear in a schematized way in order to be more easily understood and is called a communicational process.

The communication process is composed of eight elements: Sender, code, message, medium, decoding, receiver, context, noise. The model of the communication process appears in the following form:

Figure 1. Model of the communication process

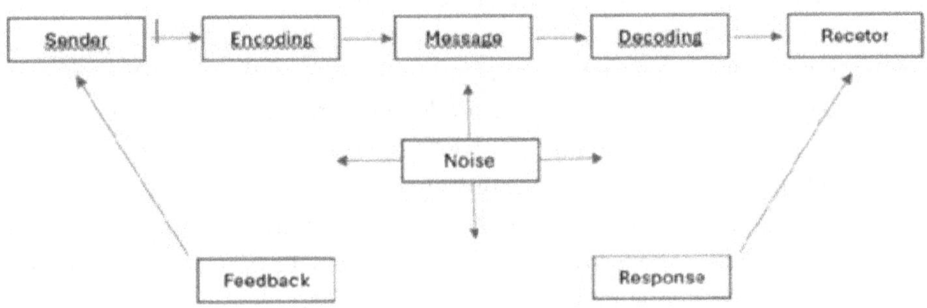

(Kings, 2024)

1.2 Verbal Communication

As the name suggests, verbal communication is called the inclusion of written and oral messages in its composition. The latter assumes responsibility for the most used type of communication, derived from its ability to transmit more complex information (Reis, 2024).

According to Usera (2024), verbal communication allows us to define ideas, feelings, experiences, among others, and the use of language helps shape attitudes towards the world. An interesting aspect to raise is based on the relationship between verbal symbology and the perception of the world: the latter is supported by the statement that those who speak a different language have a different perception of the world.

Continuing the idea that verbal communication allows for the labeling of experiences, when this is done, it is common to resort to the use of symbology corresponding to the spoken language. This statement corroborates the issue of perception, because the more improved the aforementioned symbology, the more improved the vision of the world becomes (Usera, 2024).

As in all processes, we must always take into account the mechanisms present, and Verbal Communication is no exception. We can start with the mechanisms of orality, the primary ones being the linguistic ones, which collect the lexicon and grammar; the secondary ones are the Encyclopedic, those that derive from "personal experiences" as well as from context; The tertiaries are textual organized, connected to textual genres that transpose different communicative purposes.

In terms of orality strategies, they presuppose three stages, the first being pre-listening, the one that makes up comprehension; the second, listening, which allows preliminary access to the oral text; and the third is post-listening, the one that guides the meaning of the text on the part of those who hear it.

With regard to the strategies of written expression, there are essential aspects of it, depending on three operations according to Sá (2018), the first being planning, which is responsible for the proactive attitude in the memory of those who perform it, for the organization and hierarchy of information, as well as for adaptation to the recipient; the second is textualization, which is linked to the composition of the written production, which is responsible for managing global and local textual constraints (Sá, 2018); The third is revision, which can introduce new problems and lead to their resolution, due to a new reading of the text mentioned.

1.3 Non-Verbal Communication

Non-verbal communication can be defined, in a simplistic way, by the absence of words (Usera, 2024). On the other hand, it is responsible for incorporating facial and body expressions, gestures, and reactions of the human body to stimuli (Reis, 2024).

According to Usera (2024), it is crucial to understand how communication, namely non-verbal communication, works, as the human being takes the form of a transmitter incapable of being "turned off"; here the statement by Reis (2024) stands out, since non-verbal behaviors manifest themselves through intimacy, dominance, excitement, etc.

According to Borges (2022), body language is an extremely impactful method of communication and one that most people use without thinking twice about the actions taken. Regardless of the intention with which it is done, there is a constant emission of information during "face-to-face" interaction and, therefore, non-verbal communication plays an important role in interpersonal relationships (Usera, 2024), since learning to control such actions (Borges, 2022) may have resulted directly in communication between parties.

This type of communication has three associated functions that are worth noting (Reis, 2024): It allows you to link initial information, manage the type of relationship you want to have with someone, and contribute to the sharing of signals related to emotions and thoughts, between sender and receiver. Thus, it should be noted that the intended relationship involves the establishment of dominance, deconcentration, among others.

According to Borges (2022), non-verbal communication has four functions that are relevant to mention in this study, the first being complementary, the second regulating, the third replacing and finally accentuating the verbal message they intend to convey.

In the organizational context, non-verbal communication can also be considered relevant as it contributes to good dynamism, inclusion and consequent achievement of results. To this extent, it is also able to reflect the coherence of those responsible in management positions (regarding decision-making, definition of objectives, among others) and provide information and/or *feedback* to other employees (Reis, 2024).

It should also be mentioned that verbal and non-verbal messages, although positive, can sometimes have the opposite effect, that is, they can sometimes not be compatible, since verbal communication can show a result, but non-verbal communication, such as body language (Borges, 2022) can show the opposite, creating disparate effects.

1.4 The Impact of Gender

According to the social construction of gender roles, there are expectations that produce norms and expected behaviors from each person, according to their sex (Harlos *et al.*, 2023).

These norms are based on the values transmitted and are a consequence of what is socially accepted.

By way of example, the female norm describes the affable attitude, the focus on domestic activity, and submission in an interpersonal relationship; on the other hand, the male norm is based on autonomy and independence and the focus on work activity (Harlos *et al.*, 2023). According to Meeks & Howe (2020), men start from a perspective of power based on their position of privilege, leading them to take control over others. It can also be argued that in a historical context the idea has been constructed that harassment is something that men do to women.

Since the concept of gender has been increasingly asserting itself as a sphere in analytical terms, thus allowing for greater visibility of the disparities between men and women, whether in social, economic, cultural contexts, etc., it is necessary to identify and understand them, as well as to understand and analyse potential gender-based obstacles (Trindade, 2023).

Although gender is not limited to male or female/biological sex (Hean & Perkin, 2003), few studies have been conducted that take minorities into account for marginalization in the workplace (Ragland *et al.*, 2023). That said, considering only the male and female genders, it is worth highlighting the harassment experienced in the business context.

1.5 Gender in the Organizational Context

According to Harlos *et al.* (2023) Women are at greater risk in the organisational context; This vulnerability is justified by the historical context, as they have always been more disadvantaged in terms of access to employment, career progression and remuneration. Consequent disadvantaged positions are based on the creation of stereotypes and failure to combat them leads to their perpetuation and aggravation, including consequences such as verbal and physical violence.

Although the issue of gender in organisations has been debated and confronted, there is still some disparity between the environment provided to workers according to their gender, resulting in greater harassment for women compared to men, particularly in the education and health care sectors (Harlos *et al.*, 2023).

The disparities between men and women are found in several fields, including socialization processes, as mentioned by Rúbio (2022). She also adds that the disparities between men and women do not result from gender, but from the different socialization processes that each one ends up experiencing, which can result in an influence in terms of professional choices, as well as the results that can be achieved.

According to Meeks & Howe (2020), men and women differ in ethics and morals: women have a higher standard, taking into account collective interests, while men opt for individualism. Related to problems within the organization, namely sexual harassment among employees, women also have greater responsibility in the domain, derived from their collectivism. In general, women have more responsibility and greater morality and, as a result, expect the same from their leaders. The fact that women are more commonly victims of harassment also leads them to have a perception of socio-sexual scenarios as some kind of threat.

1.6 Gender-Based Verbal Communication

The difference with which men and women use language can be described based on the discursive community they are part of (Usera, 2024). Being embedded in a discursive community does not necessarily imply that its members identify with the gender associated with it, but it does suggest that certain communication patterns are representative of male/female performance.

According to Borhan (2022), the conception of Verbal Communication between genders can be based on three theories, the first being biological, the second sociological and the third constructivist. The first starts from the assumption that biological differences between genders can be at the core of differences in communication, while the next two tend to focus on the effects of social processes and the consequent differences in the language used between masculine and feminine.

Members of the male discursive community tend to communicate instrumentally in order to achieve goals (Usera, 2024). According to the same author, the communication process is framed in a win-loss context and operates in a standardized way in order to meet the receiver's expectations.

Based on the assumption of the use of instrumental language, it is also expected that the male discursive community represents verbal communication as a competitive medium, whose objective is to establish a position of superiority over the others (Usera, 2024) – this statement does not imply voluntariness in the communicational process, but suggests that it is based on a consequence of the way in which the community frames the value of discourse (Usera, 2024).

Male discursive communities also tend to emphasize the value of affirmation, autonomy and increased status, contributing to the establishment of limits of respect between peers. Therefore, the most common characteristics found within this group are: instrumentalism, dominance, abstraction, and non-response (Usera, 2024).

Analyzing the other side of the coin, the people who are part of the female discursive community choose to value verbal communication, as a means of maintaining established relationships, through the sharing of mutual experiences – the emergence of relational conversation (Usera, 2024).

A relevant aspect of this group of individuals is their tendency to introduce the element of sensitivity into their communication process, which translates into a high level of cooperation (Amason & Allen, 1997). The focus is also on creating an inclusive space, leaving no room for criticism and overcoming peers (Usera, 2024).

As mentioned, women communicate in favor of maintaining relationships; they are also responsible for offering mutual support and connecting by identifying with shared experiences. That said, the characteristics that best define this discursive community are: equality, tentativeness, responsiveness, and cooperation (Usera, 2024).

As for the practical moment when the male and female communities enter into disparity, this can be emphasized through interpretation (Amason & Alle, 1997). In order for there to be consensus and to be able to develop interpersonal relationships between all individuals, it is necessary that communication norms and practices are collectively understood in order to be able to respond without creating a situation of conflict (Usera, 2024). In an organizational context, it is also worth noting that men are more likely to use "I did this" while women opt for the words "our success", corroborating the instrumentalism in male communication and the inclusion of female communication (Reis, 2024).

1.7 Gender-Based Nonverbal Communication

In order to contribute to the mitigation of binary habits developed over the years, some of the aspects in which men and women differ when interacting have already been documented. When it comes to addressing expectations for each of the sexes, women are expected to be more condescending and intuitive in the field of their interpersonal skills, while it is expected to observe some determination on the part of male behavior (Usera, 2024). According to the same author, it should also be noted that there is a lower probability of physical proximity between two men, while the issue of touch is more accepted among women, not discarding the value of context.

When the duty of leadership is envisaged, we can also allocate a role in favor of gender, according to Borges (2022), men and women have disparate non-verbal communications, that is, body signals, while male people tend to be more expansive, whether in the higher tone of voice and in their domination of the conversation, in fact, they tend to interrupt more frequently; Females, on the other hand, tend to be more expressive in facial terms, as well as showing a greater distance between others.

Other relevant elements for the analysis of gender-based nonverbal communication are limited by geographical position and cultural and ethnic differences. According to the author, proximity tends to vary according to continent, or even continental regions (north and south of Europe and north and south of America), and European cultures have greater physical proximity in their non-verbal communication (handshakes, kisses, hugs) – this last effect also registers some variation according to culture (Usera, 2024).

In the family context, non-verbal communication also plays a relevant role (Usera, 2024). The distribution of tasks in the home can also contribute to the lack of consensus between men and women, since historically, women are responsible for a large part of the domestic domain – this preposition has revealed effects, when compared to a situation of equal distribution of responsibilities: households whose have the same desire to carry out tasks in the domestic sphere, report greater sexual satisfaction (Usera, 2024). The sustenance of non-equal distribution is present in the development of communication skills in children: while women are associated with imaginary activities (valuing the process and not the content) and the use of communication as a means of creating bonds, men are seen as participants in structured activities with designated roles and objectives to achieve.

2. METHODOLOGY

The methodology used to carry out this study was based on the application of a questionnaire, and before any development on it, it should be noted that the application of the questionnaire was made with the informed consent of the participants, and withdrawal was allowed at any time at the time of their participation (it is enough to just leave the browser page for the participation not to be considered). Information on the purpose of participation and data processing was provided, as well as the respective instructions on how to complete and submit it (Parodi *et al.*, 2023). As far as the sample is concerned, the questionnaire was distributed on the basis of the employees of the Nespresso company.

Regarding the data collection instruments, as a stimulus for the present study, it consists of fourteen quick response questions such as "Yes/No", multiple choice and *Likert* scale. Questions 1, 2 and 3 exclusively question the age and gender and educational qualifications of the participants, so although they are essential, they do not directly concern the analysis of the study problem raised.

Finally, as part of the distribution, the questionnaire was shared through direct contact with the organization's employees, allowing the participation of any employee with a computer, tablet or smartphone with internet access, ceasing the possibility of filling it out on February 28, 2024, for the purposes of grouping and processing the data collected.

According to the information provided throughout the literature review, it can be stated that there is a relationship between gender and communication skills, both verbally and non-verbally. Thus, with the elaboration of this study, we seek to understand to what extent gender can influence communication in the organizational context, responding to the following hypotheses:

H1a – In the organizational context, there is no gender impact on communication. H1b – In the organizational context, there is a clear impact of gender on communication. H2 – The company maintains broad and evolving communication.

H3 – The company communicates about gender equality within the organization. H4a – In the company under study, men value personal performance more.

H4b – In the company under study, women value collective performance more.

3. PRESENTATION OF DATA AND TREATMENT OF RESULTS

In order to continue with the empirical study, in this section the results of the survey described in the methodology will be presented. First of all, and as will be raised several times throughout the next part, after closing the possibility of participating in the questionnaire, the total sample accounted for twenty-four contributions.

As there is no data available on the total number of employees in Nespresso stores in Portugal, it is not possible to assess whether or not the sample is representative of the population.

Among the 24 responses obtained, it is noteworthy that 45.8% (11 records) of the participants identify with the male gender and 54.2% (13 records) with the female gender, with no record in the options "Non-binary" and "I prefer not to mention (Figure 3). The age group is between 18 and 60 years of age or older, with both percentage extremes standing out, i.e., 41.7% (10 records) of the responses come from individuals between 18 and 24 years of age and 16.7% (4 records) from individuals between 40 and 59 years of age, with no record of any participation whose respondent is 60 years of age or older (Figure 2).

Figure 2. Age of the participants

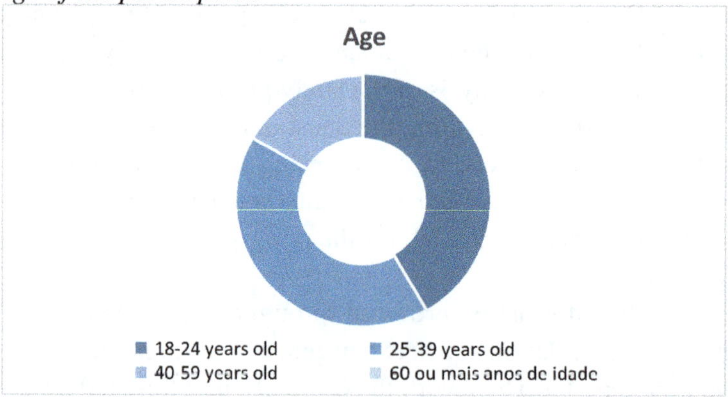

Figure 3. Gender of two participants

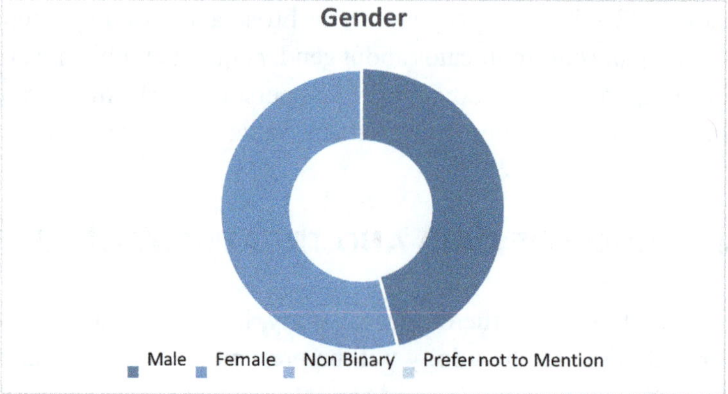

In terms of educational qualifications, 66.7% of the participants reported holding a bachelor's degree, while only 8.3% of the participants claimed to have a master's degree and the remaining 25% had a secondary education degree. It is also worth mentioning that there was no record of any participant with only basic education or less, nor any holder of a PhD (Figure 4).

Figure 4. Academic qualifications of the participants

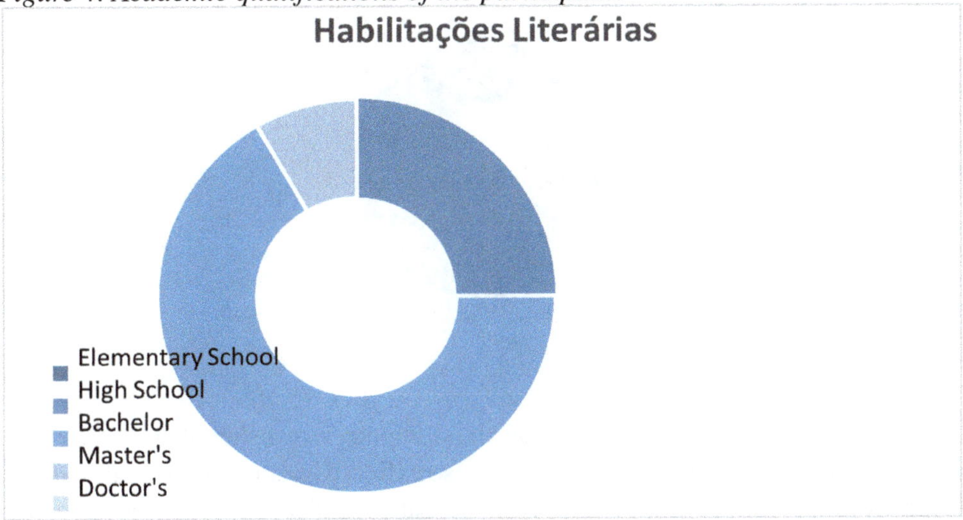

Moving on to the part of the questionnaire that will confront the hypotheses raised below, the result obtained for the fourth question "Is communication an important topic for your company?" was categorical, with the twenty-four respondents (100%) stating yes (Figure 5).

Figure 5. Importance of communication

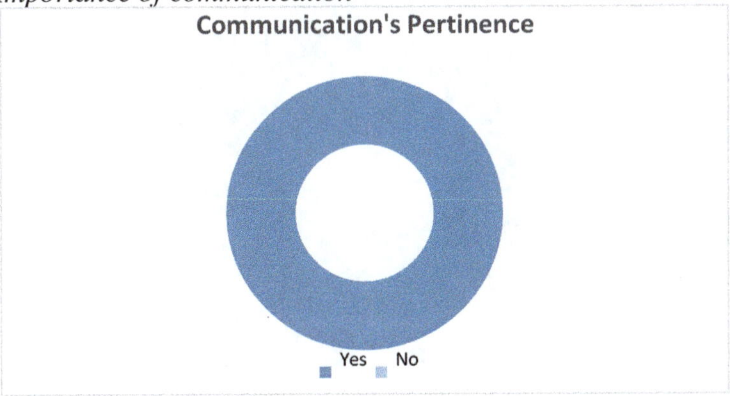

The next question, the content of which again involves the importance that the company attaches to a given object, raised the question of equality: "For your company, is gender equality an important topic?". Once again, the result was exhaustive and all twenty-four respondents (100%) reported yes (Figure 6).

Figure 6. Importance of gender equality

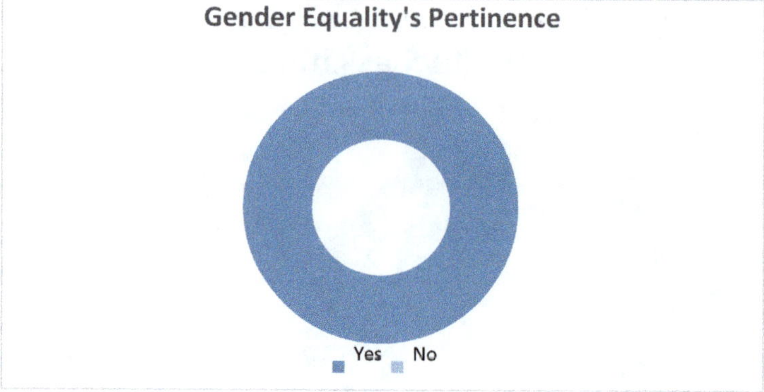

As for the participants' opinion on the company's investment in the field of communication, what was expected to be also exhaustive ended up revealing some disparity. Thus, to the question "Are there measures that encourage communication in a transversal way within the company?", nineteen of the twenty-four respondents (79.2%) said yes, but five respondents (20.8%) answered no (Figure 7).

Figure 7. Transversal communication.

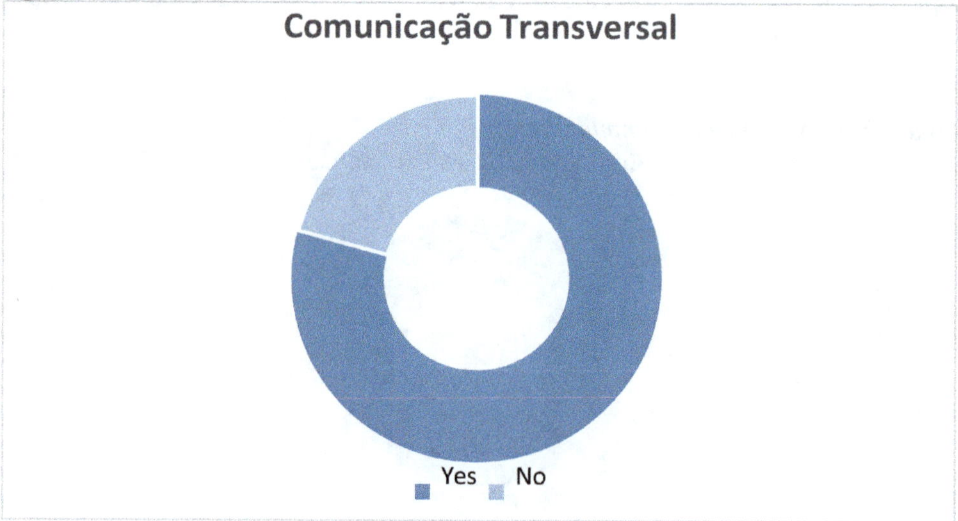

To obtain a more practical measure of gender equality in the organizational context, the participants were asked about the distribution when forming teams. Once again, what was expected to be exhaustive ended up presenting some disagreement, that is, to the question “In the constitution of teams, is there the principle of balanced gender representation?”, seventeen of the twenty-four respondents (70.8%) reported yes and the remaining seven (29.2%) said no (Figure 8).

Figure 8. Balanced gender distribution

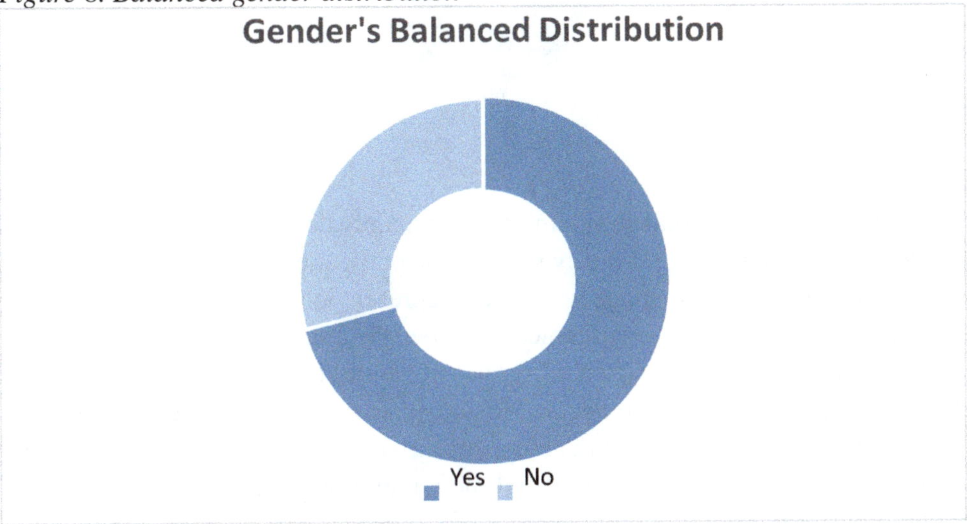

In a first attempt to establish a relationship between gender equality and corporate communication, the question was raised: “Does your company address issues related to gender equality through the different communication channels?”. The opinion of the participants was again not unanimous, but registered the same pattern as the two previous results, that is, the majority said yes and the rest said no. In the case of question 8 of the questionnaire, eighteen of the twenty-four respondents (75%) reported that the company shares information related to gender equality through different media outlets and the remaining six participants selected the “No” option (Figure 9).

Figure 9. Gender equality in communication

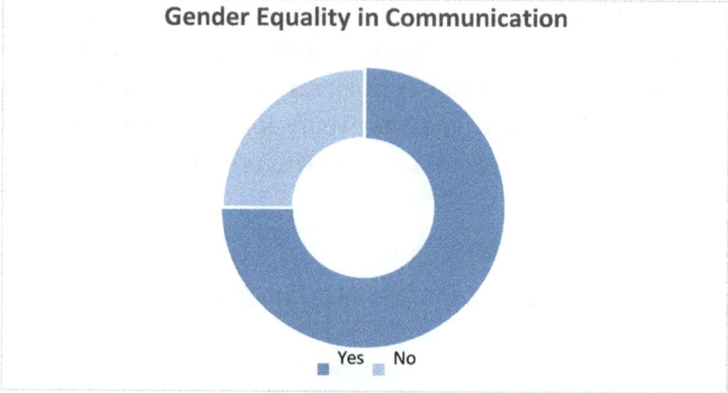

To the extent that verbal communication is mainly designated by the use of oral and written language, as previously seen, in the ninth question of the questionnaire the use of an inclusive language was raised, represented by the following question: "In the context of internal communication, does the company use inclusive grammatical terms? (aversion to sexist terms, use of neutral language, etc.)". In terms of results, the pattern was found again; Most respondents said yes. Seventeen of the twenty-four (70.8%) stated that the company already incorporates the use of inclusive language in its communication and the remaining seven (29.2%) participants do not register the same opinion (Figure 10) – the same result as in question 7 of the questionnaire.

Figure 10. Use of inclusive language

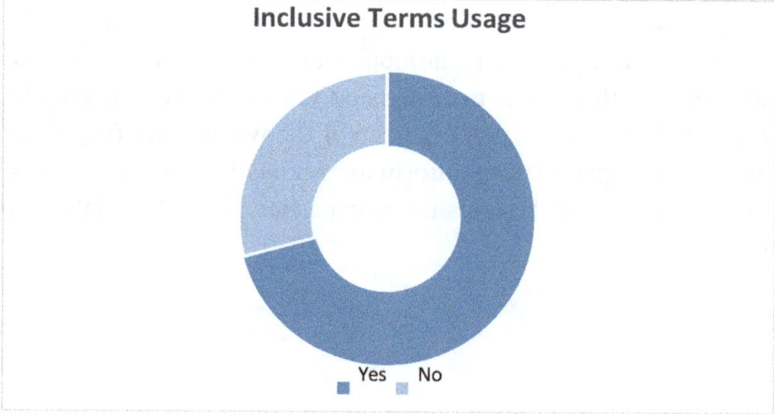

The tenth question encompasses some of the themes raised in the previous questions and also foresees an important issue for business communication, communication conflicts; in this way it was asked "Does your company encourage actions that address topics such as gender equality in order to foster communication and predict potential conflicts at the communication level?" and the results obtained were mostly positive: Nineteen of the twenty-four respondents (79.2%) said yes and the remaining five respondents (20.8%) selected the option "No" (Figure 11) – in percentage terms the answers obtained are exactly the same as those reported in question 6.

Figure 11. Conflict prevention

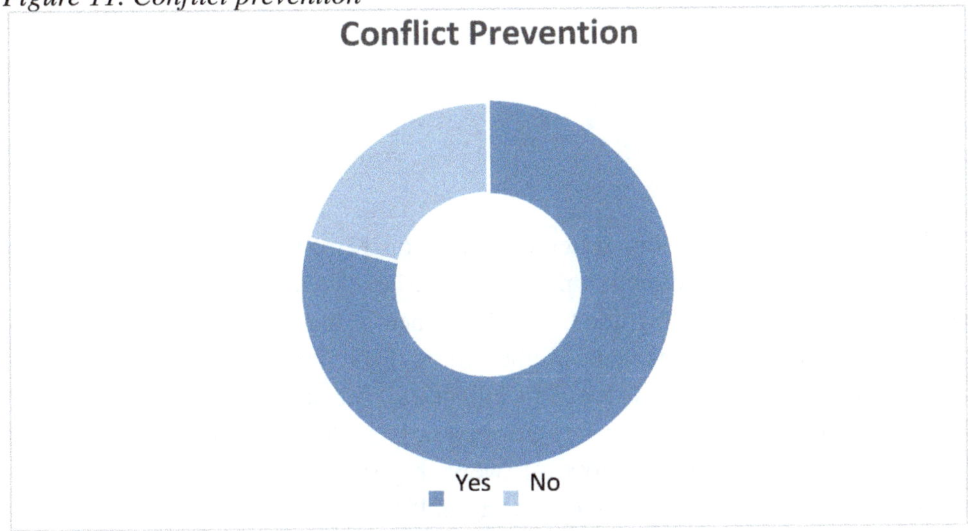

Moving on to the analysis of the level of agreement with the following statements, the next two questions present a result based on *Likert* scales and are given in the form of a bar graph. In the eleventh question, the measure of valuing personal performance was raised, through the observation "When achieving a common goal, there is a tendency to value personal performance more." tag. The results obtained were not very decisive because in addition to levels 1 (Strongly Disagree) in which there was no record and 2 (Disagree) in which there was only one record (4.2%), the distribution was relatively balanced, with eight records in both levels 3 and 4 (33.3% in each) and seven records in level 5 (29.2%) being levels 3, 4 and 5 "Neither Agree nor Disagree", "Agree" and "Strongly Agree" respectively (Figure 12).

Figure 12. Valuing personal performance

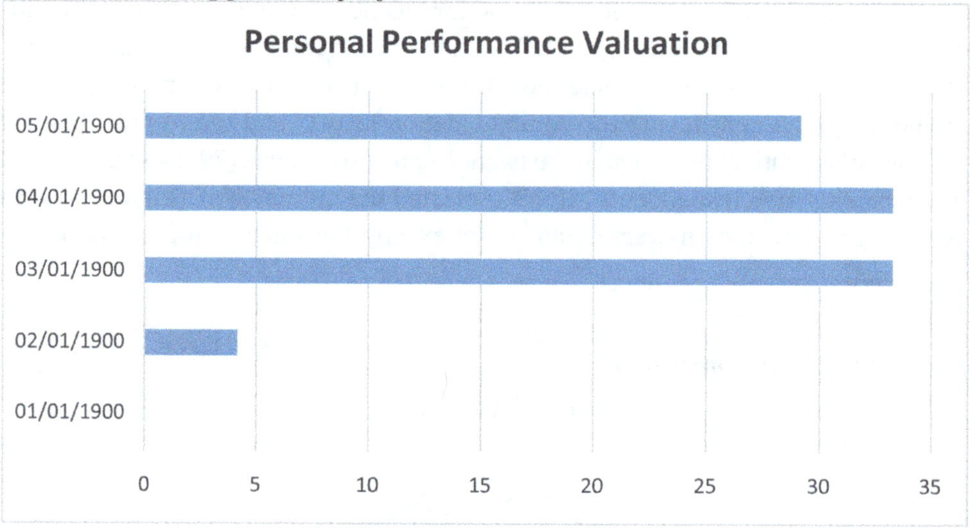

In contrast to the previous statement, question 12 of the questionnaire emphasized the valuation of collective performance, i.e., “When achieving a common goal, there is a tendency to value the performance of the team as a whole.”. In this case, the results already showed a slightly more discrepant distribution. There was again only one registration at level 1 (4.2%) and no registration at level 1, however, level 3 obtained six selections (25%), level 4 only 5 (20.8%) and level 5 registered the majority, accounting for a total of twelve registrations (50%). In this finding, despite the theoretical bulk raised, exactly half of the sample indicated that they totally agreed with the statement (Figure 13).

Figure 13. Valuing collective performance

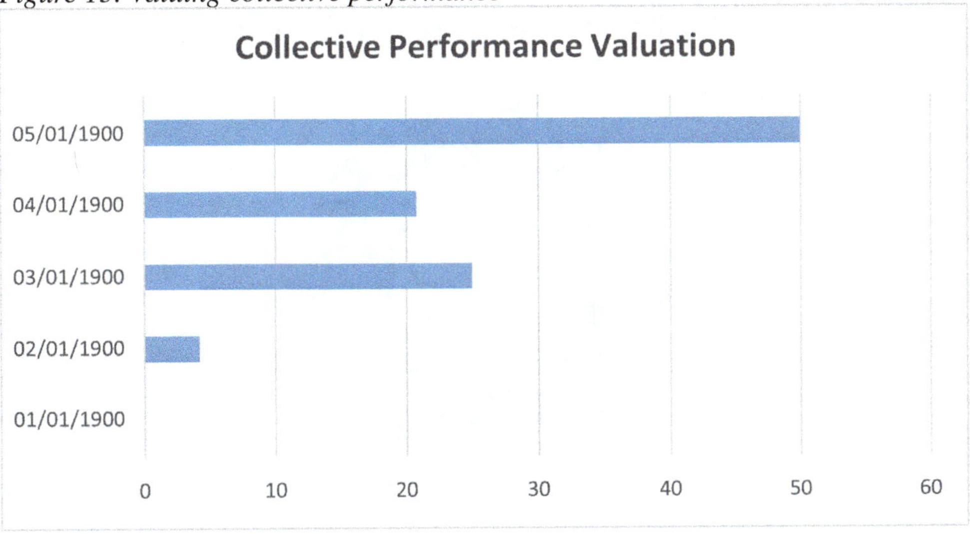

In order to further clarify the results obtained in the scales presented above, two multiple-choice questions were arranged, whose purpose was based on the association between valuing individual and collective performance and men and women.

Therefore, the thirteenth question of the questionnaire asked which of the groups would be more likely to affirm something representative of the valorization of collective success, in the following form: "Which of the following groups is the most collectivist, that is, which is the most oriented to affirm something like "the success of the team"?". Regarding the results obtained, eighteen of the twenty-four participants (75%) selected the option "Women" and the remaining six the option (25%) "Men" (Figure 14).

Figure 14. Valuing collective performance by gender

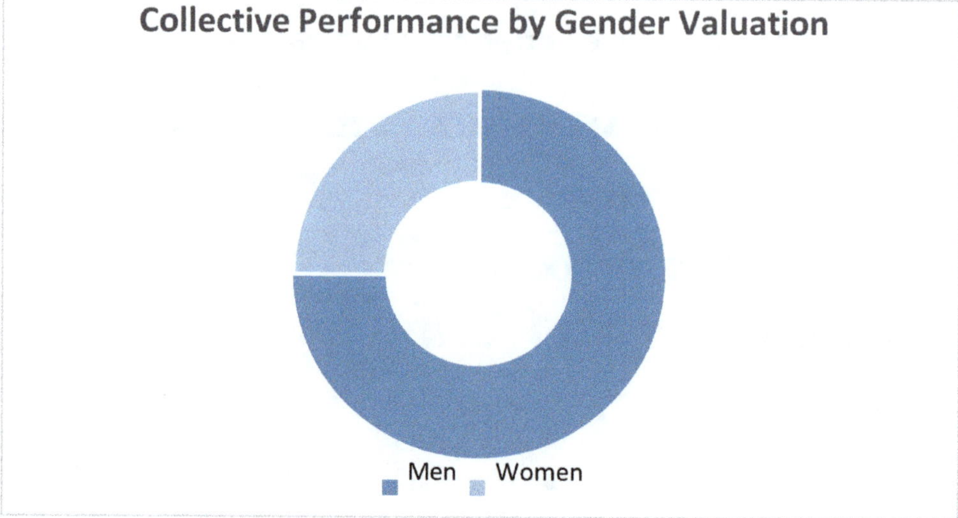

The fourteenth and final question of the questionnaire emphasized the opposite of the one raised in the argument in number 13. Here, we tried to infer which of the groups would be more likely to affirm something representative of individual performance and this time the question was: "Which of the following groups is the most individualistic, that is, which is the most oriented to affirm something like "I did it"?". The results obtained are curious, as they can be seen as a mirror in comparison to the valuation of collective performance by gender; Eighteen of the twenty-four respondents (75%) said that men represent a group that is quicker to say something like "I did it" and the remaining six respondents (25%) selected the option "Women" (Figure 15). The sequence of results presented in the last two questions of the questionnaire is in line with the theoretical framework already raised and, therefore, they will be confronted with one of the study hypotheses related to the organization.

Figure 15. Valuation of individual performance by gender

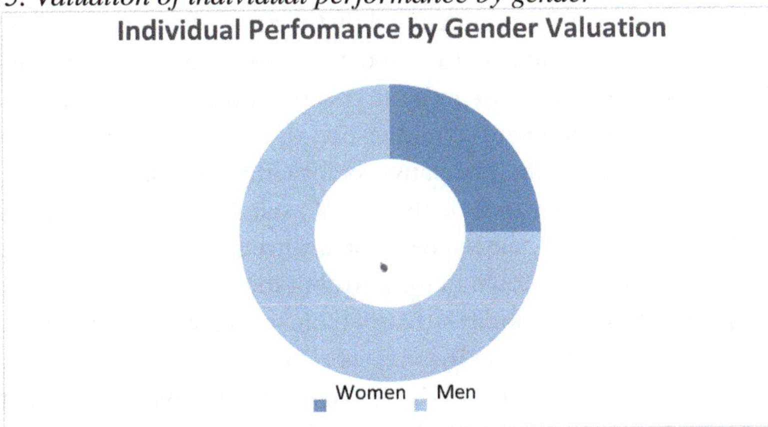

To confront the hypotheses mentioned in the section of the methodology of the study and to obtain, or not, their corroboration, the following part uses the graphs referring to the results together with the literature review previously arranged (when relevant) as support.

H1a – In the organizational context, there is no gender impact on communication: According to Figures 6, 7 and 10, in which it is possible to analyze the importance of gender equality, the approach to issues related to gender equality in internal communication and the use of inclusive language respectively, it can be observed that in all cases, the percentage of participants who selected the negative option (the "No" option) was based on a minority of the sample, 0%, 25% and 29.2%; therefore, it must be stated that the hypothesis is not verified.

H1b – In the organizational context, there is a clear impact of gender on communication: In contrast to the above, the positive responses of the same results are now analyzed; in Figure 6 the option "Yes" was selected twenty-four times (100%), which indicates that for Nespresso employees gender equality is a relevant topic. In Figure 9, the number of respondents who selected the "Yes" option was eighteen (75%), confirming that the company shares information related to gender equality through the different communication channels. Finally, in Figure 10, the majority of the participants, seventeen of the twenty-four (70.8%), ticked the "Yes" option, representing that the company uses inclusive language in its communication; This includes not only the introduction of neutral terms but also the aversion to sexist terms, among others. Thus, it is concluded that the hypothesis is verified.

H2 – The company maintains broad and evolving communication: Figures 5, 7 and 10 allow us to confront the hypothesis posed. Of the twenty-four respondents, 100% of the answers were positive in question 4, indicating that communication is an important element for the company. As for Graph 6, it is possible to see that nineteen of the twenty-four respondents (79.2%) selected the "Yes" option, which translates into a strong investment by the company in communication in a transversal way. Finally, in Graph 9, as shown in the corroboration of the previous hypothesis, most participants (70.8%) reported the use of inclusive language in their operational activity; Supposing, therefore, the hypothesis is confirmed.

H3 – The company communicates about gender equality within the organization: Once again, through graphs 5 and 8 the majority of participants point positively to the importance of gender equality within the company. Figure 6 shows that the positive response totaled twenty-four records (100%) and Figure 9 shows that the "Yes" option accounts for 75% of the records, thus concluding that gender equality is indeed an element of relevance for the organization. To complement these results, the provisions of Figure 7 also add relevant data related to the balanced gender distribution; 70.8% of the participants (seventeen out of twenty-four) reported that there is a principle of balanced gender representation when forming teams and therefore, it can be said that the hypothesis is corroborated.

H4a – In the company under study, men value personal performance more: The result obtained to confirm this hypothesis showed an interesting but unexpected pattern. In order to confront it, Figures 15 and 12 are used; the results shown in graph 14 show that 18 of the twenty-four participants (75%) point out that men are more likely to say something like "I did it", which in turn translates into the prioritization of personal performance, corroborating what was described by Reis (2024). However, the provisions of question 11 of the questionnaire have a more balanced distribution of results, with only seven of the twenty-four respondents (29.2%) indicating that they totally agree with the statement "When achieving a common goal, they tend to value personal performance more." The percentage of respondents who said they neither agreed nor disagreed with the statement marks eight confirmations (33.3%) and the number of registrations in the "Agree" option also points to 33.3% (eight registrations). Even adding the percentages of records in "Agree" and "Strongly Agree" they total 62.5% (fifteen records), a value slightly lower than the 75% already highlighted in question 14. Since only eleven of the participants are male (Figure 3), it can be said that not only men, but also women demonstrate that they value their personal performance when achieving objectives in the organizational context. Although it is not possible to ascertain which of the genders voted in the options available, the phenomenon highlighted by Reis (2024) in the literature review regarding the disparities between men and women continues to occur, thus corroborating the hypothesis emphasized.

H4b – In the company under study, women value collective performance more: Finally, the results obtained to confront the second part of this hypothesis not only confirm the information described in the theoretical framework but also support the corroboration of the first part (Hypothesis 4a). Figures 14 and 13 are now used for testing purposes; In the results presented in question 13 of the questionnaire, eighteen of the twenty-four participants (75%) stated that the group of women is more likely to affirm something such as "the success of the team", while only six of the twenty-four respondents (25%) selected the option "Men", which in turn translates into the prioritization of the female set of collective performance. corroborating what was described by Reis (2024). An interesting aspect that can also be seen is that, as shown in graph 2, eleven of the twenty-four participants are male, that is, even if the six records in the "Men" option of question 13 all come from male respondents, there is a part of this same group that recognizes that women are more likely to value collective performance. when achieving objectives, once

again meeting what is advocated by Reis (2024). Supporting the above, the results of question 12 also provide an interesting fact. The percentage of respondents who selected the options "Agree and "Strongly Agree" totals 70.8% (seventeen records), i.e., the majority. Once again, it is not possible to ascertain which of the genders voted for each option available, but it can be said that the majority of participants are female and also the majority opts for the prioritization of teamwork. Comparing the data obtained with what has already been described in the literature review, it can be stated that hypothesis 4b is confirmed.

CONCLUSION

The present work focused on the different types of communication and the impact of gender on the Nespresso company. Therefore, we began by defining the Basic Notion of the Communication Process, according to Reis (2024), that is, a transmission and respective interpretation of information between two or more individuals, through verbal and non-verbal symbology; when schematized, this transmission of information can be called a communicational process, being composed of eight elements: Emitter, Code, Message, Decoding, Receiver, Context, and Noise.

Verbal communication is called the inclusion of messages, whether written or oral, and allows the expression of ideas, feelings, and experiences, which helps different expressions and attitudes towards the world (Usera, 2024). Something that must always be present are the mechanisms, and in Verbal Communication we can indicate the linguistic ones, as the primary ones; the Encyclopedic as well as the secondary ones; and those of textual organization as tertiary.

Non-Verbal Communication, on the other hand, can be defined by the absence of words, incorporates facial and body expressions, such as gestures and reactions (Usera, 2024); It is also worth highlighting three associated functions, the first of which allows you to link initial information, the second manages the type of relationship you want to have with someone and the third is to contribute to the sharing of signals related to emotions and thoughts. When transported to the organizational context, non-verbal communication can be considered relevant, as it contributes to dynamism, inclusion, and the achievement of results (Reis, 2024).

As for the mention of Gender in terms in the organizational context, it was found that women tend to run a higher risk, which is justified by the historical context and the perpetuation of the stereotype. Within the organization, there are still disparities between employees according to their gender, which results in more pronounced harassment for women when compared to men. Men and women differ in ethics and morals, with men opting for individualism, while women tend to have more regard for collective interests.

If we connect Verbal Communication with gender, we can assign the language used according to the discursive community. Members of the male community tend to have a greater tendency to communicate more accurately, using dominance, abstraction, and non-response as characteristics, while members of the female community tend to value verbal communication, using equality, tentativeness, responsiveness, and cooperation as characteristics.

In terms of non-verbal communication, it is expected that women will present themselves in a more condescending and intuitive way and men will present themselves in a deterministic way; There is also a greater likelihood of touching between two women than between two men.

The study, therefore, aimed to understand the relationship between gender and communication skills, whether verbal or non-verbal, with the assumption of trying to understand how gender can influence communication within the organizational context, allocating answers to the hypotheses.

Regarding the presentation of data and treatment of results, it was concluded that among the 24 responses obtained, about 45.8% (11) were male and 54.2% (13) were female; It became noticeable that the twenty-four employees stated that communication is an important topic within the organization, as well as gender equality.

When asked about gender equality in communication, only 75% of respondents say that there is an approach to gender-related issues through the different communication channels and in terms of inclusive language, about 70.8% report its use, but 29.2% say no.

Regarding the valuation of personal performance, 4.2% of the sample disagreed, and the remaining levels were quite balanced, while in the valuation of collective performance, when confronted, about 4.2% placed in the first level, level 3 obtained 25% of the answers, level 4 20.8% and the level registered the majority, with about 50%.

When we look at the valuation of collective performance by gender, about 75% of the participants selected women as an option, while about 25% selected men; In the same context, but individual performance by gender, about 75% say that men could call something like "I did it" and only about 25% selected women as an option.

After observing the results, it was possible to state that most of the hypotheses are verified, apart from H1a, since there is a clear sample of gender impact on communication within the company. In terms of communication, it was possible to see that this proved to be indeed important, both through inclusive language and through the breakdown of teams by gender.

In order to answer the starting question, it can be said that there is a gender impact within organizational communication, whether through inclusive language or through communication channels. Thus, it should be noted that gender, as an element of differentiation of employees, influences the communication processes between them, as it acts as a tool in the perception of the achievement of objectives, whether through the valorization of individual performance or collectivism. In addition, it also plays a fundamental role, in a business context, in the transmission of information and in obtaining *feedback*, since men have a greater tendency towards instrumentalist language and women use verbal communication as a means of maintaining established relationships. To complement the above, gender also has an impact on non-verbal communication between employees, illustrated, for example, through the physical proximity between them.

REFERENCES

Amason, P., & Allen, M. W. (1997). Intraorganizational communication, perceived organizational support, and gender. *Sex Roles*, *37*(11-12), 955–977. DOI: 10.1007/BF02936349

Borges, B. (2022, April). The importance of non-verbal communication for the good performance of organizations. *Catholic University of Portugal*. https://repositorio.ucp.pt/bitstream/10400.14/38523/1/203042603.pdf

Borhan, N. (2022). A Review Study About Gender Differences in Expressive Language: Spoken and Written Language Differences. [JODAP]. *Journal of Development and Psychology*, *4*(8), 76–95. DOI: 10.51503/gpd.1231592

Harlos, K., Gulseren, D., O'Farrell, G., Josephson, W., Axelrod, L., Hinds, A., & Montanino, C. (2023). Gender and perceived organizational support as moderators in the relationship between role stressors and workplace bullying of targets. *Frontiers in Communication*, *8*, 1176846. Advance online publication. DOI: 10.3389/fcomm.2023.1176846

Meeks, L., & Howe, W. (2020). Manager–Employee Communication in the #MeToo Era: The Role of Gender Similarity and Context Ambiguity in Ethical Leadership. *International Journal of Communication*, *14*, 19. https://ijoc.org/index.php/ijoc/article/view/13416

Parodi, J. B., Burgos, L. M., Garcia-Zamora, S., Liblik, K., Pulido, L., Gupta, S., Saldarriaga, C., Puente-Barragan, A. C., Morejón-Barragán, P., Alexanderson-Rosas, E., Sosa-Liprandi, A., Botto, F., Sosa-Liprandi, M. I., Lopez-Santi, R., Vazquez, G., Gulati, M., & Baranchuk, A. (2023). Gender differences in workplace violence against physicians and nurses in Latin America: A survey from the Interamerican Society of Cardiology. *Public Health*, *225*, 127–132. DOI: 10.1016/j.puhe.2023.09.030 PMID: 37924636

Ragland, M., Harrell, J., Ripper, M., Pearson, S., Granberg, R., & Verble, R. (2023). Gender, sexual orientation, ethnicity and socioeconomic factors influence how wildland firefighters communicate their work experiences. *Frontiers in Communication*, *8*, 1021914. Advance online publication. DOI: 10.3389/fcomm.2023.1021914

Reis, F. (2024). [Lusófona University]. *Organizational Communication*, *2023*, 2024.

Rúbio, I. (2022). Human resource management practices for gender equality and organizational quality. *University of Évora - School of Social Sciences*. http://hdl.handle.net/10174/33540

Sá, C. (2018). *Oral and Written Communication Techniques* (1st ed.). UA Publishing., https://ria.ua.pt/bitstream/10773/24945/1/20181212_CEF_CD_Tec nicas%20 Comunicacao%20Oral%20e%20Escrita.pdf

Trindade, J. (2023). Health and gender: a study based on the National Health Survey. *Higher Institute of Social and Political Sciences*. https://www.repository .utl.pt/bitstream/10400.5/27562/1/Dissertac%cc%a7a%cc %83o%20-%20 Jos%c3%a9lia%20Trindade.pdf

Usera, D. (2024). Communicating to Connect - Interpersonal Communication for Today. Social Sci LibreTexts. https://socialsci.libretexts.org/Bookshelves/ Communication/Introd uction_to_Communication/Communicating_to_Connect_-_Interpersonal_Communication_for_Today_(Usera)

Compilation of References

Accenture. (2022). *Building the future workforce today: Unlocking America's tech sector for Hispanic American and Latinx talent* (PDF). Accenture. https://www.accenture.com/content/dam/accenture/final/markets/north-america/document/Accenture-Building-Future-Workforce-Today.pdf

Acemoglu, D., & Restrepo, P. (2020). The wrong kind of AI? Artificial intelligence and the future of labour demand. *Cambridge Journal of Regions, Economy and Society*, *13*(1), 25–35. DOI: 10.1093/cjres/rsz022

Adanma, U. M., & Ogunbiyi, E. O. (2024). A comparative review of global environmental policies for promoting sustainable development and economic growth. *International Journal of Applied Research in Social Sciences*, *6*(5), 954–977. DOI: 10.51594/ijarss.v6i5.1147

Adeusi, K. B., Jejeniwa, T. O., & Jejeniwa, T. O. (2024). Advancing financial transparency and ethical governance: Innovative cost management and accountability in higher education and industry. *International Journal of Management & Entrepreneurship Research*, *6*(5), 1533–1546. DOI: 10.51594/ijmer.v6i5.1099

Afrouz, R., & Vassos, S. (2024). Adolescents' experiences of cyber-dating abuse and the pattern of abuse through technology, a scoping review. *Trauma, Violence & Abuse*, *25*(4), 15248380241227457. DOI: 10.1177/15248380241227457 PMID: 38323421

Agrawal, B. (2022). Use of Social media by small women entrepreneurs of India for growing their business. *SMS Journal of Enterpreneurship & Innovation*, *8*(01). Advance online publication. DOI: 10.21844/smsjei.v8i01.30007

Ahl, H. (2006). Why research on women entrepreneurs needs new directions. *Entrepreneurship Theory and Practice*, *30*(5), 595–621. DOI: 10.1111/j.1540-6520.2006.00138.x

Ahmed, E. M., & Elfaki, K. E. (2024). Green technological progress implications on long-run sustainable economic growth. *Journal of the Knowledge Economy*, *15*(2), 6860–6877. DOI: 10.1007/s13132-023-01268-y PMID: 40479028

Ahmed, V., & Opoku, A. (2022). Technology supported learning and pedagogy in times of crisis: The case of COVID-19 pandemic. *Education and Information Technologies*, *27*(1), 365–405. DOI: 10.1007/s10639-021-10706-w PMID: 34462626

Akinrinola, O., Okoye, C. C., Ofodile, O. C., & Ugochukwu, C. E. (2024). Navigating and reviewing ethical dilemmas in AI development: Strategies for transparency, fairness, and accountability. *GSC Advanced Research and Reviews, 18*(3), 050-058.

Akpuokwe, C. U., Chikwe, C. F., & Eneh, N. E. (2024). Innovating business practices: The impact of social media on fostering gender equality and empowering women entrepreneurs. *Magna Scientia Advanced Research and Reviews, 10*(2), 032–043. https://doi.org/DOI: 10.30574/msarr.2024.10.2.0042

Alawida, M., Omolara, A. E., Abiodun, O. I., & Al-Rajab, M. (2022). A deeper look into cybersecurity issues in the wake of Covid-19: A survey. *Journal of King Saud University. Computer and Information Sciences*, *34*(10), 8176–8206. DOI: 10.1016/j.jksuci.2022.08.003 PMID: 37521180

Al-Dajani, H., Bika, Z., Collins, L., & Swail, J. (2014). Gender and family business: New theoretical directions. *International Journal of Gender and Entrepreneurship*, *6*(3), 218–230. DOI: 10.1108/IJGE-11-2013-0069

AllahRakha, N. (2024). Rethinking digital borders to address jurisdiction and governance in the global digital economy. *International Journal of Law and Policy*, *2*(1).

Almeida, LM, Torres, CIO, Seixas, NRM, Samtos, DB & Silva, CDD (2023). The Importance of Information and Communication Technologies in the Teaching and Learning Process in Science. Teaching Science and Technology in Magazine – Encitec, 13(2), 54-71.https://doi.org/DOI: 10.31512/encitec.v13i2.638

Alnasser, Y., Proaño, A., Loock, C., Chuo, J., & Gilman, R. H. (2024). Telemedicine and Pediatric Care in Rural and Remote Areas of Middle-and-Low-Income Countries: Narrative Review. *Journal of Epidemiology and Global Health, 14*(3), 1–8. DOI: 10.1007/s44197-024-00214-8 PMID: 38478166

Altay, S., Nielsen, R. K., & Fletcher, R. (2024). News can help! The impact of news media and digital platforms on awareness of and belief in misinformation. *The International Journal of Press/Politics*, *29*(2), 459–484. DOI: 10.1177/19401612221148981

Amason, P., & Allen, M. W. (1997). Intraorganizational communication, perceived organizational support, and gender. *Sex Roles*, *37*(11-12), 955–977. DOI: 10.1007/BF02936349

Amatucci, F. M., & Swartz, E. (2011). Through a fractured lens: Women entrepreneurs and the private equity negotiation process. *Journal of Developmental Entrepreneurship: JDE, 16*(03), 333–F

Anderson, M. (2023). AI and iot for safe public transportation. *Urban Mobility Journal*, *16*(2), 34–50.

Andriyani, Y., Yohanitas, W. A., & Kartika, R. S. (2024). Adaptive innovation model design: Integrating agile and open innovation in regional areas innovation. *Journal of Open Innovation*, *10*(1), 100197. DOI: 10.1016/j.joitmc.2023.100197

Angwaomaodoko, E. A. (2026). The role of microcredentials in promoting lifelong learning. *Journal of Education and Training*, 13(1). Macrothink Institute. https://doi.org/DOI: 10.5296/jet.v13i1.23027

Arefin, S. (2024). Chronic disease management through an ai-powered application. *Journal of Service Science and Management*, *17*(4), 305–320. DOI: 10.4236/jssm.2024.174015

Ashtikar, S. P., & Manoharan, G. (2024, June). Digital Transformation in Higher Education: A Pedagogical Perspective. In *2024 3rd International Conference on Computational Modelling, Simulation and Optimization (ICCMSO)* (pp. 210-215). IEEE. DOI: 10.1109/ICCMSO61761.2024.00051

Autor, D., Mindell, D. A., & Reynolds, E. (2022). *The work of the future: Building better jobs in an age of intelligent machines.* MIT Press. DOI: 10.7551/mitpress/14109.001.0001

Ayeni, O. O., Al Hamad, N. M., Chisom, O. N., Osawaru, B., & Adewusi, O. E. (2024). AI in education: A review of personalized learning and educational technology. *GSC Advanced Research and Reviews*, *18*(2), 261–271. DOI: 10.30574/gscarr.2024.18.2.0062

Azeema, N., Nawaz, H., Gill, M. A., Khan, M. A., Miraj, J., & Lodhi, K. (2023). Impact of Artificial Intelligence on Financial Markets: Possibilities & Challenges. *Journal of Computing & Biomedical Informatics*, *6*(01), 287–299.

Bajwa, J., Munir, U., Nori, A., & Williams, B. (2021). Artificial intelligence in healthcare: Transforming the practice of medicine. *Future Healthcare Journal*, *8*(2), e188–e194. DOI: 10.7861/fhj.2021-0095 PMID: 34286183

Bandyopadhyay, S., Bardhan, A., Dey, P., & Bhattacharyya, S. (2021). *Bridging the education divide using social technologies*. Springer. DOI: 10.1007/978-981-33-6738-8

Baraldo, M., & di Franco, P. D. G. (2024). Place-centred emerging technologies for disaster management: A scoping review. *International Journal of Disaster Risk Reduction, 112*, 104782. DOI: 10.1016/j.ijdrr.2024.104782

Barcellos, S. H., Carvalho, L. S., & Turley, P. (2020). Is education the great equalizer? *NBER Working Paper*.

Bastos, R. M. B. (2017). The surprising success of the Finnish educational system in a global scenario of commodified education. *Revista Brasileira de Educação, 22*, 802–825. DOI: 10.1590/s1413-24782017227040

Bates, A. T., & Sangra, A. (2011). *Managing technology in higher education: Strategies for transforming teaching and learning*. John Wiley & Sons.

Beder, S. (1994). The role of technology in sustainable development. *IEEE Technology and Society Magazine, 13*(4), 14–19. DOI: 10.1109/44.334601

Behera, R. K., Bala, P. K., & Rana, N. P. (2023). Creation of sustainable growth with explainable artificial intelligence: An empirical insight from consumer packaged goods retailers. *Journal of Cleaner Production, 399*(136605), 136605. DOI: 10.1016/j.jclepro.2023.136605

Bekaroo, G. (2024). Extended Reality and the Implementation of the UN Sustainable Development Goals: Opportunities, Challenges and Future Directions. *Digital Technologies to Implement the UN Sustainable Development Goals*, 215-233.

Ben-Zvi, T., & Luftman, J. (2022). Post-pandemic IT: Digital transformation and sustainability. *Sustainability (Basel), 14*(22), 15275. DOI: 10.3390/su142215275

Bertin, C. E. (2020). Understand what empirical research is and its characteristics. ViaCarreira.https://viacarreira.com/pesquisa-empirica/

Bhuiyan, M. R. I., Akter, M. S., & Islam, S. (2024). How does digital payment transform society as a cashless society? An empirical study in the developing economy. *Journal of Science and Technology Policy Management*.

Biesta, G. (2021). *World-centred education: A view for the present*. Routledge. DOI: 10.4324/9781003098331

Blank, S., Mason, C., Steinicke, F., & Herzog, C. (2024). Tailoring responsible research and innovation to the translational context: The case of AI-supported exergaming. *Ethics and Information Technology, 26*(2), 22. DOI: 10.1007/s10676-024-09753-x

Bond, M., Bedenlier, S., Marín, V. I., & Händel, M. (2021). Emergency remote teaching in higher education: Mapping the first global online semester. *International Journal of Educational Technology in Higher Education*, *18*(1), 50. DOI: 10.1186/s41239-021-00282-x PMID: 34778537

Borges, B. (2022, April). The importance of non-verbal communication for the good performance of organizations. *Catholic University of Portugal*. https://repositorio.ucp.pt/bitstream/10400.14/38523/1/203042603.pdf

Borges, B. M. C. (2022). The importance of non-verbal communication for the good performance of organizations. Final work in the form of Dissertation presented to the Universidade Católica Portuguesa to obtain a master's degree in Management.

Borhan, N. (2022). A Review Study About Gender Differences in Expressive Language: Spoken and Written Language Differences. [JODAP]. *Journal of Development and Psychology*, *4*(8), 76–95. DOI: 10.51503/gpd.1231592

Bose, D., Bhattacharya, R., Kaur, T., Pandya, R., Sarkar, A., Ray, A., Mondal, S., Mondal, A., Ghosh, P., & Chemudupati, R. I. (2024). Innovative approaches for carbon capture and storage as crucial measures for emission reduction within industrial sectors. *Carbon Capture Science & Technology*, *12*, 100238. DOI: 10.1016/j.ccst.2024.100238

Bose, R. (2021). Wearable sensors for personal safety: A review. *Journal of Wearable Computing*, *25*(2), 110–125.

Bose, T. K., Bonna, A. H., Bristy, J. F., & Moser, R. (2024). Evolving female entrepreneurship in emerging economies: Clarifying the linkages between institutional forces and online venture performance. *Journal of Small Business and Enterprise Development*, *31*(7), 1424–1454. Advance online publication. DOI: 10.1108/JSBED-01-2024-0026

Bouabida, K., Lebouché, B., & Pomey, M. P. (2024). The paradoxes of telehealth platforms: What did we learn from the use of telehealth platforms? *Frontiers in Digital Health*, *6*, 1346039. DOI: 10.3389/fdgth.2024.1346039 PMID: 38414713

Brahem, M., & Boussema, S. (2022). Social media entrepreneurship as an opportunity for women: The case of Facebook-commerce. *International Journal of Entrepreneurship and Innovation*, *146575032110660*. Advance online publication. DOI: 10.1177/14657503211066010

Brains, E. (2024, September). The Impact of Open Source on Software Development: Collaboration Over Competition. Medium. https://medium.com/@emperorbrains/the-impact-of-open-source-on-software-development-collaboration-over-competition-4d8ce85c3bfa

Braun, S., Bark, A. H., Kirchner, A., Stegmann, S., & Dick, R. (2019). Emails From the Boss—Curse or Blessing? Relations Between Communication Channels, Leader Evaluation, and Employees' Attitudes. *International Journal of Business Communication*, *56*(1), 50–81. DOI: 10.1177/2329488415597516

Brown, T. (2022). The impact of drones on personal safety. Aerospace. *Security Journal*, *15*(3), 200–215.

Brynjolfsson, E., & McAfee, A. (2020). *The second machine age: Work, progress, and prosperity in a time of brilliant technologies* (Updated ed.). W. W. Norton.

Buchan, M. C., Bhawra, J., & Katapally, T. R. (2024). Navigating the digital world: Development of an evidence-based digital literacy program and assessment tool for youth. *Smart Learning Environments*, *11*(1), 8. DOI: 10.1186/s40561-024-00293-x

Cai, W., Polzin, F., & Stam, E. (2021). Crowdfunding and social capital: A systematic review using a dynamic perspective. *Technological Forecasting and Social Change*, *162*, 120412. DOI: 10.1016/j.techfore.2020.120412

Camilleri, M. A. (2024). Artificial intelligence governance: Ethical considerations and implications for social responsibility. *Expert Systems: International Journal of Knowledge Engineering and Neural Networks*, *41*(7), e13406. DOI: 10.1111/exsy.13406

Canton, H. (2021). United Nations Educational, Scientific and Cultural Organization—UNESCO. In *The Europa Directory of International Organizations 2021* (pp. 359-365). Routledge.

Cavus, N., & Zabadi, T. (2014). A comparison of open source learning management systems. *Procedia: Social and Behavioral Sciences*, *143*, 521–526. DOI: 10.1016/j.sbspro.2014.07.430

Chan, C. K. Y., & Tsi, L. H. Y. (2023). The AI revolution in education: Will AI replace or assist teachers in higher education? (Preprint). *arXiv*. https://doi.org//arXiv.2305.01185DOI: 10.48550

Chan, G. H. (2024). Enhancing digital literacy in education: Educational directions. *Education + Training*, *66*(1), 127–142. DOI: 10.1108/ET-09-2022-0390

Chase, L. C., Stewart, M., Schilling, B., Smith, B., & Walk, M. (2018). Agritourism: Toward a conceptual framework for industry analysis. *Journal of Agriculture, Food Systems, and Community Development*, *8*(1), 13–19. DOI: 10.5304/jafscd.2018.081.016

Chee, S. Y. (2024). Age-related digital disparities, functional limitations, and social isolation: Unraveling the grey digital divide between baby boomers and the silent generation in senior living facilities. *Aging & Mental Health*, *28*(4), 621–632. DOI: 10.1080/13607863.2023.2233454 PMID: 37424361

Chemnad, K., & Othman, A. (2024). Digital accessibility in the era of artificial intelligence—Bibliometric analysis and systematic review. *Frontiers in Artificial Intelligence*, *7*, 1349668. DOI: 10.3389/frai.2024.1349668 PMID: 38435800

Chen, M. L. (2022). The impact of mobile learning on the effectiveness of English teaching and learning—A meta-analysis. *IEEE Access : Practical Innovations, Open Solutions*, *10*, 38324–38334. DOI: 10.1109/ACCESS.2022.3165017

Chui, M., Manyika, J., & Miremadi, M. (2018). What AI can and can't do (yet) for your business. *McKinsey Quarterly*. https://www.mckinsey.com/business-functions/mckinsey-analytics/our-insights/what-ai-can-and-cant-do-yet-for-your-business

Clark, H., & Wu, H. (2016). The sustainable development goals: 17 goals to transform our world. *Furthering the work of the United Nations*, 36-54.

Clark, R. E. (1989). Current progress and future directions for research in instructional technology. *Educational Technology Research and Development*, *37*(1), 57–66. DOI: 10.1007/BF02299046

Connell, J. (2015, June 30). *3 Steps to Become the Empowered Entrepreneur You Want to Be*. Entrepreneur. https://www.entrepreneur.com/growing-a-business/3-steps-to-become-the-empowered-entrepreneur-you-want-to-be/246962

Costa, P., & Rodrigues, H. (2024). The ever-changing business of e-commerce-net benefits while designing a new platform for small companies. *Review of Managerial Science*, *18*(9), 2507–2545. DOI: 10.1007/s11846-023-00681-6

Coursera & Google. (2021). *The economic impact of Google Career Certificates*. Coursera. https://www.coursera.org/google-career-certificates

Cowie, A. L., & Cowie, B. (2018). Plastic waste and recycling: Environmental impact, societal issues, prevention, and solutions. *Annual Review of Environment and Resources*, *43*(1), 173–196. DOI: 10.1146/annurev-environ-102017-030147

Cui, H., & Yasseri, T. (2024). AI-enhanced Collective Intelligence: The State of the Art and Prospects. *arXiv preprint arXiv:2403.10433*.

Dahlström, H. (2019). Digital writing tools from the student perspective: Access, affordances, and agency. *Education and Information Technologies*, *24*(2), 1563–1581. DOI: 10.1007/s10639-018-9844-x

Daniela, L., & Visvizi, A. (2022). *Remote learning in times of pandemic*. Routledge.

Davis, K., & Li, J. (2023). Next-generation GPS tracking for women's safety. *Geospatial Innovations Journal*, *18*(2), 50–70.

Dinika, A. A.-A. T. (2024). A critical analysis of Rwanda's digital skills and entrepreneurship training toward solving youth unemployment. *Journal of Business and Enterprise Development*, *12*(1). Advance online publication. DOI: 10.47963/jobed.v12i.1526

Doe, A., & Lee, B. (2021). Blockchain for secure digital identities. *International Cybersecurity Review*, *28*(2), 55–72.

Dong, Z., Peng, J., & Liu, S. (2024). Gender Pay Gap in the Gig Economy. *China Finance and Economic Review*, *13*(1), 3–22. DOI: 10.1515/cfer-2024-0001

Du, J. T., Xie, I., & Waycott, J. (2020). Marginalized communities, emerging technologies, and social innovation in the digital age: Introduction to the special issue. *Information Processing & Management*, *57*(3), 102235. DOI: 10.1016/j.ipm.2020.102235

Eden, C. A., Chisom, O. N., & Adeniyi, I. S. (2024). Cultural competence in education: Strategies for fostering inclusivity and diversity awareness. *International Journal of Applied Research in Social Sciences*, *6*(3), 383–392. DOI: 10.51594/ijarss.v6i3.895

El-Hajj, M. (2024). Leveraging digital twins and intrusion detection systems for enhanced security in IoT-based smart city infrastructures. *Electronics (Basel)*, *13*(19), 3941. DOI: 10.3390/electronics13193941

Elmoazen, R., Saqr, M., Khalil, M., & Al-Ali, A. K. (2023). Learning analytics in virtual laboratories: A systematic literature review of empirical research. *Smart Learning Environments*, *10*(1), 23. DOI: 10.1186/s40561-023-00244-y PMID: 40477836

Esposito, G., Terlizzi, A., Guarino, M., & Crutzen, N. (2024). Interpreting digital governance at the municipal level: Evidence from smart city projects in Belgium. *International Review of Administrative Sciences*, *90*(2), 301–317. DOI: 10.1177/00208523231167538

European Commission on Safety. (2022). *Innovative approaches to women's safety in urban and rural travel.* Retrieved from www.ec.europa.eu

European Commission. (2022). *Women's safety in public transport: Policy recommendations.* Retrieved from www.ec.europa.eu

European Travel Security Agency. (2022). *Enhancing traveler safety through next-gen technologies.* Retrieved from www.etsa.eu

Fazil, A. W., Hakimi, M., Akrami, K., Akrami, M., & Akrami, F. (2024). Exploring the Role of Social Media in Bridging Gaps and Facilitating Global Communication. *Studies in Media. Journal of Communication*, *2*(1), 13–21.

Federation of International Travel Associations. (2023). *Enhancing women's safety in global travel.* Retrieved from www.fita.org

Feyen, E., Frost, J., Gambacorta, L., Natarajan, H., & Saal, M. (2021). Fintech and the digital transformation of financial services: implications for market structure and public policy. *BIS papers.*

Finley, M. I. (1965). Technical innovation and economic progress in the ancient world. *The Economic History Review*, *18*(1), 29–45. DOI: 10.2307/2591872

Fisher, T. (2006). Educational transformation: Is it, like 'beauty', in the eye of the beholder, or will we know it when we see it? *Education and Information Technologies*, *11*(3-4), 293–303. DOI: 10.1007/s10639-006-9009-1

Floridi, L. (2007). A look into the future impact of ICT on our lives. *The Information Society*, *23*(1), 59–64. DOI: 10.1080/01972240601059094

Floridi, L., Cowls, J., Beltrametti, M., Chatila, R., Chazerand, P., Dignum, V., Luetge, C., Madelin, R., Pagallo, U., Rossi, F., Schafer, B., Valcke, P., & Vayena, E. (2018). AI4People—An ethical framework for a good AI society: Opportunities, risks, principles, and recommendations. *Minds and Machines*, *28*(4), 689–707. DOI: 10.1007/s11023-018-9482-5 PMID: 30930541

Fornander, L., Laukkanen, K., Molin, I., Nilsson, L., & Berggren, P. (2024). Team communication patterns during real and simulated trauma resuscitation—A social network analysis. *Ergonomics*, *67*(2), 225–239. DOI: 10.1080/00140139.2023.2221000 PMID: 37273191

Fortuna, A., Prasetya, F., Samala, A. D., Rawas, S., Criollo-C, S., Kaya, D., Raihan, M., Andriani, W., Safitri, D., & Nabawi, R. A. (2025). Artificial intelligence in personalized learning: A global systematic review of current advancements and shaping future opportunities. *Social Sciences & Humanities Open*, *12*, 102114. Advance online publication. DOI: 10.1016/j.ssaho.2025.102114

García Zaballos, A., Jorge, S., Dalio, M., Makwakwa, O., & Albornoz Basto, N. (2024). *Digital inclusion strategies: A primer for Latin American policymakers* (IDB Monograph No. 1232). Inter-American Development Bank. https://publications.iadb.org/en/digital-inclusion-strategies-primer-latin-american-policymakers

Garcia, M., & Thompson, L. (2021). The role of community-based apps in enhancing travel security. *Journal of Social Tech*, *11*(3), 120–140.

Geladi, N. (2018). Technology is affecting the quality of human face-to-face interaction. *Digital Society. Retrieved from:* https://medium. com/digital-society/technology-is-affecting-the-quality-of-human-face-to-face-interaction-146fe72a29c5

Geyer, R., Jambeck, J. R., & Law, K. L. (2017). Production, use, and fate of all plastics ever made. *Science Advances*, *3*(7), e1700782. DOI: 10.1126/sciadv.1700782 PMID: 28776036

Giacobone, G. A., Mincolelli, G., & Imbesi, S. (2024). Inclusive cultural heritage in Europe: Co-designing an accessible user experience for digital architectural conservation. *Journal of Architectural Conservation*, *30*(1), 19–34. DOI: 10.1080/13556207.2023.2296216

Giere, R. N., & Moffatt, B. (2003). Distributed cognition: Where the cognitive and the social merge. *Social Studies of Science*, *33*(2), 301–310. DOI: 10.1177/03063127030332017

Gilbert, C., & Gilbert, M. A. (2024). The Convergence of Artificial Intelligence and Privacy: Navigating Innovation with Ethical Considerations. *International Journal (Toronto, Ont.)*, *3*(9).

Gleeson, B. (2012). Critical commentary. The urban age: Paradox and prospect. *Urban Studies (Edinburgh, Scotland)*, *49*(5), 931–943. DOI: 10.1177/0042098011435846

Global Security Initiative. (2023). *Public safety and emerging technologies.* Retrieved from www.globalsecurity.org

Gomber, P., Koch, J. A., & Siering, M. (2017). Digital finance and fintech: Current research and future research directions. *Journal of Business Economics*, *87*(5), 537–580. DOI: 10.1007/s11573-017-0852-x

Gonçalves, J. F. N. (2019). Self-perceived Empathy and Empathic Performance in an Organizational Context: Relationship with Job Satisfaction. [Master's thesis unpublished]. Minho's university.

Gottschalk, F., & Weise, C. (2023). *Digital equity and inclusion in education: An overview of practice and policy in OECD countries* (OECD Education Working Papers No. 299). OECD Publishing. https://www.oecd.org/en/publications/digital-equity-and-inclusion-in-education_7cb15030-en.html

Gratchev, I., & Espinosa, H. G. Advancing Engineering Education Beyond COVID.

Grover, V., & Nandal, M. (2024). Education System Using Cloud Computing: A Proposed Model. In *Educational Perspectives on Digital Technologies in Modeling and Management* (pp. 178-194). IGI Global. DOI: 10.4018/979-8-3693-2314-4.ch009

Guo, B., Hu, P., & Lin, J. (2024). The effect of digital infrastructure development on enterprise green transformation. *International Review of Financial Analysis, 92*, 103085. DOI: 10.1016/j.irfa.2024.103085

Gupta, P., & Pandey, M. K. (2024). Role of AI for Smart Health Diagnosis and Treatment. In *Smart Medical Imaging for Diagnosis and Treatment Planning* (pp. 23–45). Chapman and Hall/CRC. DOI: 10.1201/9781003464884-4

Hajat, A., Andrea, S. B., Oddo, V. M., Winkler, M. R., & Ahonen, E. Q. (2024). Ramifications of precarious employment for health and health inequity: Emerging trends from the Americas. *Annual Review of Public Health, 45*(1), 45. DOI: 10.1146/annurev-publhealth-071321-042437 PMID: 38012123

Haleem, A., Javaid, M., Qadri, M. A., & Suman, R. (2022). Understanding the role of digital technologies in education: A review. *Sustainable operations and computers, 3*, 275-285.

Hamilton, E. R., Rosenberg, J. M., & Akcaoglu, M. (2016). The substitution augmentation modification redefinition (SAMR) model: A critical review and suggestions for its use. *TechTrends, 60*(5), 433–441. DOI: 10.1007/s11528-016-0091-y

Hanna, K. T. (2022). What Is The Digital Divide and How Is It Being Bridged. *TechTarget. Retrieved March, 15*, 2023.

Harlos, K., Gulseren, D., O'Farrell, G., Josephson, W., Axelrod, L., Hinds, A., & Montanino, C. (2023). Gender and perceived organizational support as moderators in the relationship between role stressors and workplace bullying of targets. *Frontiers in Communication, 8*, 1176846. Advance online publication. DOI: 10.3389/fcomm.2023.1176846

Harvard Business School. (2021). *Annual report 2021*. https://www.hbs.edu/about/annualreport/2021/annual.pdf

Hassan, M., & Zhao, L. (2022). AI-based threat detection for solo female travelers. *Machine Learning in Security*, *13*(4), 120–138.

Healy, T. (2012). The unanticipated consequences of technology. *Nanotechnology: ethical and social Implications*, 155-173.

Hemathilake, D. M. K. S., & Gunathilake, D. M. C. C. (2022). Agricultural productivity and food supply to meet increased demands. In *Future foods* (pp. 539–553). Academic Press. DOI: 10.1016/B978-0-323-91001-9.00016-5

Henderson, M., Selwyn, N., & Aston, R. (2017). What works and why? Student perceptions of useful digital technology in university teaching and learning. *Studies in Higher Education*, *42*(8), 1567–1579. DOI: 10.1080/03075079.2015.1007946

Herrada-Lores, S., Estrella-Ramón, A., Gálvez-Rodríguez, M. M., & Iniesta-Bonillo, M. A. (2024). The role of hashtags for non-profit causes: The# fridaysforfuture movement. *International Review on Public and Nonprofit Marketing*, •••, 1–22. DOI: 10.1007/s12208-024-00401-0

Herring, M. C., Koehler, M. J., Mishra, P., Rosenberg, J. M., & Teske, J. (2016). Introduction to the second edition of the TPACK handbook. In *Handbook of technological pedagogical content knowledge (TPACK) for educators* (pp. 1-8). Routledge.

Hidayat, A. S., Sutanto, M. H., & Wirawan, A. (2020). The impact of AI-based technologies on recycling efficiency: A study on plastic waste management. *Journal of Environmental Management*, *254*, 109798. DOI: 10.1016/j.jenvman.2019.109798

Hilbert, M. (2020). Digital technology and social change: The digital transformation of society from a historical perspective. *Dialogues in Clinical Neuroscience*, *22*(2), 189–194. DOI: 10.31887/DCNS.2020.22.2/mhilbert PMID: 32699519

Hirsch-Kreinsen, H. (2024). Artificial intelligence: A "promising technology". *AI & Society*, *39*(4), 1641–1652. DOI: 10.1007/s00146-023-01629-w

Hodges, H. (1992). *Technology in the ancient world*. Barnes & Noble Publishing.

Hofstede, G., Hofstede, G. J., & Minkov, M. (2010). *Cultures and organizations: Software of the mind* (3rd ed.). McGraw-Hill.

Hopewell, J., Dvorak, R., & Kosior, E. (2009). Plastics recycling: Challenges and opportunities. *Philosophical Transactions of the Royal Society of London. Series B, Biological Sciences*, *364*(1526), 2115–2126. DOI: 10.1098/rstb.2008.0311 PMID: 19528059

Huang, C., Wu, J., & Zhao, W. (2019). Optimization of mechanical recycling processes for post-consumer plastics: A case study. *Journal of Cleaner Production*, *228*, 1176–1187. DOI: 10.1016/j.jclepro.2019.04.314

Hussain, S., Rasheed, A., & Rehman, S. U. (2024). Driving sustainable growth: exploring the link between financial innovation, green finance and sustainability performance: banking evidence. *Kybernetes*, *53*(11), 4678–4696. DOI: 10.1108/K-05-2023-0918

Hutson, J., Lively, J., Robertson, B., Cotroneo, P., & Lang, M. (2023). Conclusion: Future Perspectives—Embracing the AI Renaissance. In *Creative Convergence: The AI Renaissance in Art and Design* (pp. 225–237). Springer Nature Switzerland.

Hwang, G. J., Lai, C. L., & Wang, S. Y. (2015). Seamless flipped learning: A mobile technology-enhanced flipped classroom with effective learning strategies. *Journal of Computers in Education*, *2*(4), 449–473. DOI: 10.1007/s40692-015-0043-0

IBM. (2021). *IBM SkillsBuild: Empowering future-ready talent*. IBM. https://www.ibm.com

Iida, T., Song, J., Estrada, J. L., & Takahashi, Y. (2024). Fake news and its electoral consequences: A survey experiment on Mexico. *AI & Society*, *39*(3), 1065–1078. DOI: 10.1007/s00146-022-01541-9

Imtiaz, H., & Mohd Suki, N. (2022). Mobile travel apps engagement: Measuring tourists' perception. [iJIM]. *International Journal of Interactive Mobile Technologies*, *16*(14), 171–181. DOI: 10.3991/ijim.v16i14.31445

INSEAD. (2022). *Executive education and digital learning innovation*. INSEAD. https://www.insead.edu

International Air Transport Association (IATA). (2023). Improving airline safety for women passengers. *Aviation Security Review*, *21*(2), 88–105.

International Labour Organization. (2022). *Digital skills and the future of work*. International Labour Organization. https://www.ilo.org

International Transport Forum. (2022). *Improving public transport for women's safety and security*. Retrieved from www.itf-oecd.org

Istrate, O., & Velea, S. (2024). *Guidelines for online and blended learning: Design, delivery, assessment, evaluation of study programmes. Premises of academic curriculum digitalisation* (6th ed.). Institute for Education., DOI: 10.61071/JDP.2400

Iyer, S., Kabanda, S., & Al-Haidari, N. N. (2021). The Use of Social Media by SMEs. In *AMCIS*.

Jafarpanah, I., & Karshenas, A. (2023). Technological Trends in Smart Agriculture. *Journal of Entrepreneurship and Agriculture, 10*(2), 100–115.

Jaman, S. F. I. H., Damit, N. J. H., Ishak, N. A., Ason, M. L. A., Tamin, M. R., Tangphadungrutch, K., & Almunawar, M. N. (2020). The adoption of social media as marketing tools: Case small and medium enterprises in Brunei Darussalam. *International Journal of Asian Business and Information Management, 11*(2), 28–50. DOI: 10.4018/IJABIM.2020040103

Jambeck, J. R., Geyer, R., Wilcox, C., Siegler, T. R., Perryman, M., Andrady, A., Narayan, R., & Law, K. L. (2015). Plastic waste inputs from land into the ocean. *Science, 347*(6223), 768–771. DOI: 10.1126/science.1260352 PMID: 25678662

Jelani, F., & Nordini, N. S. (2019). Barriers to Effective Communication at the Workplace. *International Journal of Modern Languages and Applied Linguistics, 3*(2), 7–18. DOI: 10.24191/ijmal.v3i2.7642

Jemala, M. (2021). Long-term research on technology innovation in the form of new technology patents. *International Journal of Innovation Studies, 5*(4), 148–160. DOI: 10.1016/j.ijis.2021.09.002

Jiali, S., Dayo, F., Jun, G., Shuangyao, L., & Najam, S. The Impact of Artificial Intelligence on Personalized Learning in Education: A Systematic Review.

Jiang, J., Li, M., & Chen, C. (2021). Automated plastic waste sorting using deep learning and computer vision. *Journal of Cleaner Production, 278*, 123982. DOI: 10.1016/j.jclepro.2020.123982

Jianing, P., Bai, K., Solangi, Y. A., Magazzino, C., & Ayaz, K. (2024). Examining the role of digitalization and technological innovation in promoting sustainable natural resource exploitation. *Resources Policy, 92*, 105036. DOI: 10.1016/j.resourpol.2024.105036

Jiménez-Zarco, A. I., Clemente-Almendros, J. A., González-González, I., & Aracil-Jordà, J. (2021). Female micro-entrepreneurs and social networks: Diagnostic analysis of the influence of social-media marketing strategies on brand financial performance. *Frontiers in Psychology, 12*, 630058. DOI: 10.3389/fpsyg.2021.630058 PMID: 33912108

Johnson, R. (2023). Smart wearables and travel safety: A market analysis. *Technology in Society, 40*(1), 88–101.

Kaledio, E., Russell, E., Oloyede, J., & Olaoye, F. (2023). Cultivating Innovation: A Comprehensive Exploration of Agtech's Impact on Agriculture and Sustainable Food Systems.

Kang, H. S., & Exworthy, M. (2022). Wearing the future—wearables to empower users to take greater responsibility for their health and care: Scoping review. *JMIR mHealth and uHealth*, *10*(7), e35684. DOI: 10.2196/35684 PMID: 35830222

Kasula, B. Y. (2024). Advancements in AI-driven Healthcare: A Comprehensive Review of Diagnostics, Treatment, and Patient Care Integration. *International Journal of Machine Learning for Sustainable Development*, *6*(1), 1–5.

Kavanagh, C. (2022). *New tech, new threats, and new governance challenges: an opportunity to craft smarter responses?* Carnegie Endowment for International Peace.

Kellner, D. (2004). Technological transformation, multiple literacies, and the re-visioning of education. *E-Learning and Digital Media*, *1*(1), 9–37. DOI: 10.2304/elea.2004.1.1.8

Kelly, G., & McAdam, M. (2023). Women entrepreneurs negotiating identities in liminal digital spaces. *Entrepreneurship Theory and Practice*, *47*(5), 1942–1970. DOI: 10.1177/10422587221115363

Khalil, S., Kallmuenzer, A., & Kraus, S. (2024). Visiting museums via augmented reality: An experience fast-tracking the digital transformation of the tourism industry. *European Journal of Innovation Management*, *27*(6), 2084–2100. DOI: 10.1108/EJIM-09-2022-0479

Khawaja, M. K., Alkayyali, K., Almanasreh, M., & Alkhalidi, A. (2024). Waste-to-energy barriers and solutions for developing countries with limited water and energy resources. *The Science of the Total Environment*, *926*, 172096. DOI: 10.1016/j.scitotenv.2024.172096 PMID: 38556009

Khogali, H. O., & Mekid, S. (2023). The blended future of automation and AI: Examining some long-term societal and ethical impact features. *Technology in Society*, *73*, 102232. DOI: 10.1016/j.techsoc.2023.102232

Kim, H., & Patel, R. (2023). Smartphone-based travel safety tools for women. *International Journal of Mobile Security*, *14*(3), 75–92.

Kim, S., Chen, Z. W., Tan, J. Q. G., & Mussagulova, A. (2021). A case study of the Singapore SkillsFuture Credit scheme: Preliminary insights for making lifelong learning policy more effective. *Asian Journal of Political Science*, *29*(2), 192–214. DOI: 10.1080/02185377.2021.1917431

Kitchenham, A. (2008). The evolution of John Mezirow's transformative learning theory. *Journal of Transformative Education*, *6*(2), 104–123. DOI: 10.1177/1541344608322678

Kizilcec, R. F. (2024). To advance AI use in education, focus on understanding educators. *International Journal of Artificial Intelligence in Education, 34*(1), 12–19. DOI: 10.1007/s40593-023-00351-4 PMID: 37359103

Koessmeier, C., & Büttner, O. B. (2021). Why are we distracted by social media? Distraction situations and strategies, reasons for distraction, and individual differences. *Frontiers in Psychology, 12*, 711416. DOI: 10.3389/fpsyg.2021.711416 PMID: 34925123

Komolafe, M. O., Agu, E. E., Ejike, O. G., Ewim, C. P. M., & Okeke, I. C. (2024). A digital service standardization model for Nigeria: The role of NITDA in regulatory compliance. *International Journal of Frontier Research in Science, 2*(2), 069-079.

Kondraganti, A. (2021). Big Data Analytics in Humanitarian and Disaster Operations: A Systematic Review. *arXiv preprint arXiv:2108.09800.*

Kraus, S., Durst, S., Ferreira, J. J., Veiga, P., Kailer, N., & Weinmann, A. (2022). Digital transformation in business and management research: An overview of the current status quo. *International Journal of Information Management, 63*, 102466. DOI: 10.1016/j.ijinfomgt.2021.102466

Kreiss, D., & McGregor, S. C. (2024). A review and provocation: On polarization and platforms. *New Media & Society, 26*(1), 556–579. DOI: 10.1177/14614448231161880

Kultawanich, K., Koraneekij, P., & Na-Songkhla, J. (2015). A proposed model of connectivism learning using cloud-based virtual classroom to enhance information literacy and information literacy self-efficacy for undergraduate students. *Procedia: Social and Behavioral Sciences, 191*, 87–92. DOI: 10.1016/j.sbspro.2015.04.394

Kurniadi, W., & Mahaputra, M. R. (2021). Determination of Communication in the Organization: Non Verbal, Oral and Written. Journal of law politics and humanities, 1(4), 164-172.

Kuteesa, K. N., Akpuokwe, C. U., & Udeh, C. A. (2024). Gender equity in education: Addressing challenges and promoting opportunities for social empowerment. *International Journal of Applied Research in Social Sciences, 6*(4), 631–641. DOI: 10.51594/ijarss.v6i4.1034

Lajoie, S. P., & Poitras, E. (2023). Technology-Rich Learning Environments: Theories and Methodologies for Understanding Solo and Group Learning. In *Handbook of educational psychology* (pp. 630-653). Routledge.

Lambertini, M. (2018, August). Technology can help us save the planet. But more than anything, we must learn to value nature. In *World Economic Forum* (Vol. 23).

Lee, K. R. (2002). Impacts of Information Technology on Society in the New Century. *Business and management, 5*(6), 46-55.

Lee, M. F. R. (2023). A Review on intelligent control theory and applications in process optimization and smart manufacturing. *Processes (Basel, Switzerland), 11*(11), 3171. DOI: 10.3390/pr11113171

Liu, G., & Darvin, R. (2024). From Rural China to the Digital Wilds: Negotiating digital repertoires to claim the right to speak. *TESOL Quarterly, 58*(1), 334–362. DOI: 10.1002/tesq.3233

Lowenthal, P. R., Persichini, G., Conley, Q., Humphrey, M., & Scheufler, J. (2022). Digital literacy in special education: Preparing students for college and the workplace. In *Research anthology on inclusive practices for educators and administrators in special education* (pp. 524–537). IGI Global. DOI: 10.4018/978-1-6684-3670-7.ch029

Lo, Y. F., & Kun-Lin, H. (2024). The study of working patterns in the Gig Economy. *Management Analytics and Social Insights, 1*(1), 70–87.

Luckin, R., & Holmes, W. (2016). Intelligence unleashed: An argument for AI in education.

Machado, M. E. A. (2021). The influence of the project manager's communication style on team motivation. Masters dissertation. Higher School of Technology and Management. Polytechnic of Porto.

Macht, S. A., & Weatherston, J. (2014). The benefits of online crowdfunding for fund-seeking business ventures. *Strategic Change, 23*(1-2), 1–14. DOI: 10.1002/jsc.1955

Mager, W. (1993). Proto-industrialization and proto-industry: The uses and drawbacks of two concepts. *Continuity and Change, 8*(2), 181–215. DOI: 10.1017/S026841600000206X

Malhotra, C. (2024). Digital India: Past, Present and Future. In *Indien im 21. Jahrhundert– Auf dem Weg zur postindustriellen Ökonomie: India in the 21st Century–On its way to a post-industrial economy* (pp. 325–345). Springer Fachmedien Wiesbaden.

Manoharan, G., Razak, A., Rajchandar, K., Nithya, G., Durai, S., & Ashtikar, S. P. (2024). Digital Learning for Professional Development in Varied Fields of Service Sectors: Embracing Technological Advancements. In *Embracing Technological Advancements for Lifelong Learning* (pp. 111-137). IGI Global.

Manoharan, G., Ashtikar, S. P., Rao, C. G., & Nivedha, M. (2024). A Pedagogical Landscape: Narrative Study on Emerging Artificial Intelligence Trends in Education. In *Inclusive Educational Practices and Technologies for Promoting Sustainability* (pp. 22–41). IGI Global. DOI: 10.4018/979-8-3693-6955-5.ch002

Marais, N. (2011). Connectivism as learning theory: The force behind changed teaching practice in higher education. *Education, Knowledge & Economy*, *4*(3), 173–182.

Marquardt, M. J., & Kearsley, G. (2024). *Technology-based learning: Maximizing human performance and corporate success*. CRC Press. DOI: 10.4324/9781003579175

Marsh, J. A., & Farrell, C. C. (2015). How leaders can support teachers with data-driven decision making: A framework for understanding capacity building. *Educational Management Administration & Leadership*, *43*(2), 269–289. DOI: 10.1177/1741143214537229

Martindale, N., Wood, A. J., & Burchell, B. J. (2024). What do platform workers in the UK gig economy want? *British Journal of Industrial Relations*, *62*(3), 542–567. DOI: 10.1111/bjir.12797

Martinez, P., & Kim, L. (2021). Wearable tech for women's safety: Trends and challenges. *International Journal of Wearable Innovation*, *12*(2), 45–60.

Martins, M. I. S., Oliveira, F. A., Alcântara, D. G., Dias, P. R. G., Vieria, E. M., Sousa, F. S., Almeida, A. N. S., & Silva, J. P. F. (2023). Generalizability and transferability: The possibilities of qualitative research. *Revista Foco*, *16*(2), 1–10.

Mason, A. P. U., Santos, M., Spanhol, F., Bichet, K., & Giuriatti, T. (2021). New Information and Communication Technologies Associated with Active Methodologies in the Current Educational Scenario. Proceedings of the International Congress on Knowledge and Innovation – Ciki, 1(1). DOI: 10.48090/ciki.v1i1.1158

Mayo, M. (2004). Exclusion, inclusion and empowerment: community empowerment? Reflecting on the lessons of strategies to promote empowerment. In *The politics of inclusion and empowerment: Gender, class and citizenship* (pp. 139–158). Palgrave Macmillan UK. DOI: 10.1057/9781403990013_9

McKendrick, J. (2023, January). The Coming Democratization Of Financial Services, Thanks To Artificial Intelligence. Forbes. https://www.forbes.com/sites/joemckendrick/2023/01/14/the-coming-democratization-of-financial-services-thanks-to-ai/

Meeks, L., & Howe, W. (2020). Manager–Employee Communication in the #MeToo Era: The Role of Gender Similarity and Context Ambiguity in Ethical Leadership. *International Journal of Communication, 14*, 19. https://ijoc.org/index.php/ijoc/article/view/13416

Meka, J. S., & Venkateswarlu, P. (2024). Progress, Challenges, and Strategies towards attaining Sustainable Development Goals. *Educational Administration: Theory and Practice, 30*(4), 2145–2161.

Melissa, E., Hamidati, A., Saraswati, M. S., & Flor, A. G. (2013). Investigating the potentials of social media to support women entrepreneurship in Indonesian urban areas. *Proceedings of the Sixth International Conference on Information and Communications Technologies and Development: Notes* - Volume 2. DOI: 10.1145/2517899.2517921

Mezirow, J. (1991). Transformative dimensions of adult learning.

Mirzabaev, A., Kerr, R. B., Hasegawa, T., Pradhan, P., Wreford, A., von der Pahlen, M. C. T., & Gurney-Smith, H. (2023). Severe climate change risks to food security and nutrition. *Climate Risk Management, 39*, 100473. DOI: 10.1016/j.crm.2022.100473

Mishra, P., & Koehler, M. J. (2006). Technological pedagogical content knowledge: A framework for teacher knowledge. *Teachers College Record, 108*(6), 1017–1054. DOI: 10.1111/j.1467-9620.2006.00684.x

Molloy, C., Bankins, S., Kriz, A., & Barnes, L. (2024). Innovating for the greater good: Examining innovation champions and what motivates them. *Australian Journal of Public Administration, 83*(1), 24–49. DOI: 10.1111/1467-8500.12577

Monica, J. A., Malar, J. H., Arun, C., Sharmila, L., & Arif, M. (2025). Leveraging Technology and Universal Design for Inclusive and Engaging Learning in Indian Higher Education. In *Educational Philosophy and Sociological Foundation of Education* (pp. 177–212). IGI Global.

Moosavian, S. F., Noorollahi, Y., & Shoaei, M. (2024). Renewable energy resources utilization planning for sustainable energy system development on a stand-alone island. *Journal of Cleaner Production, 439*, 140892. DOI: 10.1016/j.jclepro.2024.140892

Mwangi, E. (2023). Technology and fake news: shaping social, political, and economic perspectives. *Authorea Preprints.*

Nash, J., & Boswell, J. (2019). Predicting the environmental fate of plastic waste using machine learning models. *Environmental Science & Technology, 53*(9), 5495–5504. DOI: 10.1021/acs.est.9b00094

National Research Council. (2000). *How people learn: Brain, mind, experience, and school: Expanded edition*. National Academies Press., DOI: 10.17226/9853

National Skill Development Corporation. (2025). *Skill India Digital Hub: Digital skill courses and upskilling*. https://skillindiadigital.gov.in/

National Transportation Safety Board. (2022). *Enhancing public transit safety through AI.* Retrieved from www.ntsb.gov

Neethirajan, S. (2024). Artificial intelligence and sensor innovations: Enhancing livestock welfare with a human-centric approach. *Human-Centric Intelligent Systems*, *4*(1), 77–92. DOI: 10.1007/s44230-023-00050-2

Ng, D. (2023, September). How Technology is Democratizing Access to Quality Education in the Digital Era. Medium. https://medium.com/@nclairline/how-technology-is-democratizing-access-to-quality-education-in-the-digital-era-29f16d9897ea

Nguyen, A., Kremantzis, M., Essien, A., Petrounias, I., & Hosseini, S. (2024). Enhancing student engagement through artificial intelligence (AI): Understanding the basics, opportunities, and challenges. *Journal of University Teaching & Learning Practice*, *21*(06). Advance online publication. DOI: 10.53761/caraaq92

Njema, G. G., Ouma, R. B. O., & Kibet, J. K. (2024). A review on the recent advances in battery development and energy storage technologies. *Journal of Renewable Energy*, *2024*(1), 2329261. DOI: 10.1155/2024/2329261

Nkrumah, T., & Scott, K. A. (2022). Mentoring in STEM higher education: A synthesis of the literature to (re)present the excluded women of color. *International Journal of STEM Education*, *9*(1), 50. DOI: 10.1186/s40594-022-00367-7 PMID: 35919282

Noble, S. U. (2018). *Algorithms of oppression: How search engines reinforce racism*. NYU Press. DOI: 10.18574/nyu/9781479833641.001.0001

Nohria, N., & Taneja, H. (2021). Managing the unintended consequences of your innovations. *Harvard Business Review*, •••, 19.

O'Neil, C. (2017). *Weapons of math destruction: How big data increases inequality and threatens democracy*. Crown.

O'Reilly, T. (1999). Lessons from open-source software development. *Communications of the ACM*, *42*(4), 32–37. DOI: 10.1145/299157.299164

Odoom, D., Mensah, E. O., Dick-Sagoe, C., Lee, K. Y., Opoku, E., & Obeng-Baah, J. (2024). Examining the level of public awareness on the Sustainable Development Goals in Africa: An empirical evidence from Ghana. *Environment, Development and Sustainability*, *26*(3), 6221–6238. DOI: 10.1007/s10668-023-02959-x PMID: 36721466

OECD. (2020). *Building digital workforce capacity and skills for data-intensive science* (OECD Science, Technology and Industry Policy Papers No. 90). OECD Publishing. https://www.oecd.org/en/publications/building-digital-workforce-capacity-and-skills-for-data-intensive-science_e08aa3bb-en.html

Okoro, Y. O., Ayo-Farai, O., Maduka, C. P., Okongwu, C. C., & Sodamade, O. T. (2024). The Role of technology in enhancing mental health advocacy: A systematic review. *International Journal of Applied Research in Social Sciences*, *6*(1), 37–50. DOI: 10.51594/ijarss.v6i1.690

Oladokun, B. D., Ajani, Y. A., Ukaegbu, B. C., & Oloniruha, E. A. (2024). Cultural Preservation Through Immersive Technology: The Metaverse as a Pathway to the Past. *Preservation. Digital Technology & Culture*, *53*(3), 157–164. DOI: 10.1515/pdtc-2024-0015

Olaniran, B., & Williams, I. (2020). Social media effects: Hijacking democracy and civility in civic engagement. *Platforms, Protests, and the Challenge of Networked Democracy*, 77-94.

Olorunfemi, O. L., Amoo, O. O., Atadoga, A., Fayayola, O. A., Abrahams, T. O., & Shoetan, P. O. (2024). Towards a conceptual framework for ethical AI development in IT systems. *Computer Science & IT Research Journal*, *5*(3), 616–627. DOI: 10.51594/csitrj.v5i3.910

Olorunsogo, T., Jacks, B. S., & Ajala, O. A. (2024). Leveraging quantum computing for inclusive and responsible AI development: A conceptual and review framework. *Computer Science & IT Research Journal*, *5*(3), 671–680. DOI: 10.51594/csitrj.v5i3.927

Osman, A. I., Chen, L., Yang, M., Msigwa, G., Farghali, M., Fawzy, S., Rooney, D. W., & Yap, P. S. (2023). Cost, environmental impact, and resilience of renewable energy under a changing climate: A review. *Environmental Chemistry Letters*, *21*(2), 741–764. DOI: 10.1007/s10311-022-01532-8

Owston, R. O. N. (2018, January). Empowering learners through blended learning. [). Association for the Advancement of Computing in Education] [AACE]. *International Journal on E-Learning*, *17*(1), 65–83.

Parjanen, S., & Rantala, T. (2021). Building an open innovation platform as a part of city renewal initiatives. *European Planning Studies*, *29*(12), 2165–2183. DOI: 10.1080/09654313.2021.1903397

Parker, E., & Johnson, T. (2023). Cybersecurity for female travelers: Best practices and emerging technologies. *Cybersecurity & Privacy Journal*, *22*(3), 90–115.

Parodi, J. B., Burgos, L. M., Garcia-Zamora, S., Liblik, K., Pulido, L., Gupta, S., Saldarriaga, C., Puente-Barragan, A. C., Morejón-Barragán, P., Alexanderson-Rosas, E., Sosa-Liprandi, A., Botto, F., Sosa-Liprandi, M. I., Lopez-Santi, R., Vazquez, G., Gulati, M., & Baranchuk, A. (2023). Gender differences in workplace violence against physicians and nurses in Latin America: A survey from the Interamerican Society of Cardiology. *Public Health*, *225*, 127–132. DOI: 10.1016/j.puhe.2023.09.030 PMID: 37924636

Patel, S. (2021). Blockchain and travel security: Addressing digital identity theft. *Journal of Digital Security*, *29*(3), 67–84.

Pereira, M. R. (2022). Communication management in community pharmacy. Dissertation to obtain a Master's Degree in Pharmaceutical Sciences. Faculty of Science and Technology.

Peruzzo, F., & Allan, J. (2024). Rethinking inclusive (digital) education: Lessons from the pandemic to reconceptualise inclusion through convivial technologies. *Learning, Media and Technology*, *49*(2), 244–258. DOI: 10.1080/17439884.2022.2131817

Phuyal, S., Bista, D., & Bista, R. (2020). Challenges, opportunities and future directions of smart manufacturing: A state of art review. *Sustainable Futures : An Applied Journal of Technology, Environment and Society*, *2*, 100023. DOI: 10.1016/j.sftr.2020.100023

Pires, S. F. S. (2023). Understanding non-verbal communication: Applications in healthcare. Retrieved on February 10, 2024, fromhttps://homepublishing.com.br/index.php/cadernodeanais/article/view/991/1102

Porter, S. M. (2024). Making big bets and leaning into operational excellence: Building the future of cultural heritage institutions. *Journal of Library Administration*, *64*(2), 168–193. DOI: 10.1080/01930826.2024.2305071

Prestoza, M. J. (2024). Assessing remote learning's feasibility: A comprehensive analysis of Philippine public-school teachers' use of learning management systems and blended learning approaches. *Journal of Research. Policy & Practice of Teachers and Teacher Education*, *14*(1), 21–27. DOI: 10.37134/jrpptte.vol14.1.3.2024

Puentedura, R. (2006). Transformation, technology, and education.[Blog post]. hippasus. Com/resources/tte. *Abfrage*, *14*, 2023.

Purushottamashtikar, S., & Manoharan, G. (2024, June). Emotional intelligence on higher education educators: A systematic literature review. In *AIP Conference Proceedings* (Vol. 2971, No. 1). AIP Publishing. DOI: 10.1063/5.0195788

Quinlan, C. L. (2024). Framing and determining science content and standards for cultural representation of African American heritage in science content knowledge. *Cultural Studies of Science Education*, *19*(1), 47–75. DOI: 10.1007/s11422-023-10195-y

Qureshi, S. (2023). Digital transformation for development: A human capital key or system of oppression? *Information Technology for Development*, *29*(4), 423–434. DOI: 10.1080/02681102.2023.2282269

Rafferty, J. P. (2017). The rise of the machines: Pros and cons of the industrial revolution.

Rafiq, S., Iqbal, S., & Afzal, A. (2024). The Impact of Digital Tools and Online Learning Platforms on Higher Education Learning Outcomes. [MRJ]. *Al-Mahdi Research Journal*, *5*(4), 359–369.

Ragaert, K., Delva, L., & Van Geem, K. (2017). Mechanical and chemical recycling of solid plastic waste. *Waste Management (New York, N.Y.)*, *69*, 24–58. DOI: 10.1016/j.wasman.2017.07.044 PMID: 28823699

Ragland, M., Harrell, J., Ripper, M., Pearson, S., Granberg, R., & Verble, R. (2023). Gender, sexual orientation, ethnicity and socioeconomic factors influence how wildland firefighters communicate their work experiences. *Frontiers in Communication*, *8*, 1021914. Advance online publication. DOI: 10.3389/fcomm.2023.1021914

Rahiem, M. D. (2024). Early childhood education contingencies for sustaining learning during school closures: Lessons from preschool remote education home visits in Indonesia during the COVID-19 pandemic. *Children and Youth Services Review*, *166*, 107955. DOI: 10.1016/j.childyouth.2024.107955

Raihan, M. M., Subroto, S., Chowdhury, N., Koch, K., Ruttan, E., & Turin, T. C. (2024). *Dimensions and barriers for digital (in) equity and digital divide: A systematic integrative review*. Digital Transformation and Society.

Raja, R., & Nagasubramani, P. C. (2018). Impact of modern technology in education. *Journal of Applied and Advanced Research*, *3*(1), 33–35. DOI: 10.21839/jaar.2018.v3iS1.165

Ramolobe, K. S., & Khandanisa, U. (2024). The role of public–private partnership in achieving local government sustainable development. *Africa's Public Service Delivery & Performance Review*, *12*(1), 6. DOI: 10.4102/apsdpr.v12i1.816

Ramtohul, A., & Khedo, K. K. (2024). Augmented reality systems in the cultural heritage domains: A systematic review. *Digital Applications in Archaeology and Cultural Heritage*, *32*, 00317. DOI: 10.1016/j.daach.2024.e00317

Ransbotham, S., Kiron, D., Gerbert, P., & Reeves, M. (2017). *Reshaping business with artificial intelligence: Closing the gap between ambition and action*. MIT Sloan Management Review in collaboration with The Boston Consulting Group. https://sloanreview.mit.edu/projects/reshaping-business-with-artificial-intelligence/

Reich, Y. (2010). My method is better! *Research in Engineering Design*, *21*(3), 137–142. DOI: 10.1007/s00163-010-0092-3

Reis, F. (2024). [Lusófona University]. *Organizational Communication*, *2023*, 2024.

Ribeiro, N., & Subrahmanyam, S. (2021). Emotional challenges of teaching online during the pandemic. In Uddin, M., Sony, K. K., & Verma, N. (Eds.), *Psychosocial issues in COVID-19 pandemic* (pp. 244–255). SHINE Publication. RED.

Rincon-Flores, E. G., Castaño, L., Guerrero Solis, S. L., Olmos Lopez, O., Rodríguez Hernández, C. F., Castillo Lara, L. A., & Aldape Valdés, L. P. (2024). Improving the learning-teaching process through adaptive learning strategy. *Smart Learning Environments*, *11*(27), 27. Advance online publication. DOI: 10.1186/s40561-024-00314-9

Roberts-Mahoney, H., Means, A. J., & Garrison, M. J. (2016). Netflixing human capital development: Personalized learning technology and the corporatization of K-12 education. *Journal of Education Policy*, *31*(4), 405–420. DOI: 10.1080/02680939.2015.1132774

Robinson, L., Cotten, S. R., Ono, H., Quan-Haase, A., Mesch, G., Chen, W., Schulz, J., Hale, T. M., & Stern, M. J. (2015). Digital inequalities and why they matter. *Information Communication and Society*, *18*(5), 569–582. DOI: 10.1080/1369118X.2015.1012532

Robotics, A. M. P. (2020),"AMP Cortex: The intelligent robotics system for the recycling industry". [Online] Available at: https://www.amprobotics.com/

Rodríguez-Segura, D. (2022). *EdTech in developing countries: A review of the evidence*. World Bank Research Observer. World Bank. https://openknowledge.worldbank.org/bitstreams/6ac08b1a-d072-4727-8678-d42bbee86a8a/download

Rohatgi, S., Gera, N., & Nayak, K. (2024). Has digital banking usage reshaped economic empowerment of urban women? *The Journal of Management and Governance, 28*(2), 543–563. DOI: 10.1007/s10997-023-09676-7

Romano, V., Lozano, S., & Fernández-López de Pablo, J. (2020). A multilevel analytical framework for studying cultural evolution in prehistoric hunter–gatherer societies. *Biological Reviews of the Cambridge Philosophical Society, 95*(4), 1020–1035. DOI: 10.1111/brv.12599 PMID: 32237025

Rosário, A. T., & Raimundo, R. (2024). Enhancing business higher education through simulation-based learning, problem-based learning, and challenge-based learning (Preprint). *Preprints.org*. https://doi.org/DOI: 10.20944/preprints202407.0747.v1

Roschelle, J. (1995). *The construction of shared knowledge in collaborative problem solving*. Computer Supported Collaborative Learning/Springer-Verlag. DOI: 10.1007/978-3-642-85098-1_5

Rubeis, G., Dubbala, K., & Metzler, I. (2022). "Democratizing" artificial intelligence in medicine and healthcare: Mapping the uses of an elusive term. *Frontiers in Genetics, 13*, 902542. DOI: 10.3389/fgene.2022.902542 PMID: 36046243

Rúbio, I. (2022). Human resource management practices for gender equality and organizational quality. *University of Évora - School of Social Sciences*. http://hdl.handle.net/10174/33540

Sa'idah, S., & Juhana, A. (2024). The Effectiveness of Virtual Reality in Increasing Visitor Satisfaction of Cultural Heritage Sites: A Systematic Literature Review:-. [JOINT]. *Journal of Information System and Technology, 5*(3), 7–14. DOI: 10.37253/joint.v5i3.9981

Sabarirajan, A., Reddi, L. T., Rangineni, S., Regin, R., Rajest, S. S., & Paramasivan, P. (2024). Leveraging MIS Technologies for Preserving India's Cultural Heritage on Digitization, Accessibility, and Sustainability. In *Data-Driven Intelligent Business Sustainability* (pp. 122–135). IGI Global.

Sá, C. (2018). *Oral and Written Communication Techniques* (1st ed.). UA Publishing., https://ria.ua.pt/bitstream/10773/24945/1/20181212_CEF_CD_Tec nicas%20Comunicacao%20Oral%20e%20Escrita.pdf

Salmah, E., Astuti, E., & Harsono, I. (2024). Employee Engagement in the Gig Economy. [PRODUCTIVITY]. *Management Studies and Business Journal, 1*(1), 116–122.

Salykov, A., Aimbetov, A., Yesmagulova, N., & Jussibaliyeva, A. (2024). Factors and trends in the development of the space industry in the context of the digitalization of the economy of the Republic of Kazakhstan. *Environment, Development and Sustainability*, *26*(3), 6703–6718. DOI: 10.1007/s10668-023-02983-x PMID: 36747988

Samuel-Okon, A. D., & Abejide, O. O. (2024). Bridging the digital divide: Exploring the role of artificial intelligence and automation in enhancing connectivity in developing nations. *Journal of Engineering Research and Reports*, *26*(6), 165–177. DOI: 10.9734/jerr/2024/v26i61170

Sanders, M., & George, A. (2017). Viewing the changing world of educational technology from a different perspective: Present realities, past lessons, and future possibilities. *Education and Information Technologies*, *22*(6), 2915–2933. DOI: 10.1007/s10639-017-9604-3

Santos, O., & Radanliev, P. (2024). *Beyond the Algorithm: AI, Security, Privacy, and Ethics*. Addison-Wesley Professional.

Saptasagar, K. A. (2022). Effects of Digital Technology on Adolescents: Pros and Cons. In *Impact and Role of Digital Technologies in Adolescent Lives* (pp. 19–25). IGI Global. DOI: 10.4018/978-1-7998-8318-0.ch002

Sarkar, S. (2012). The role of information and communication technology (ICT) in higher education for the 21st century. *Science*, *1*(1), 30–41.

Sarker, I. H. (2024). LLM potentiality and awareness: A position paper from the perspective of trustworthy and responsible AI modeling. *Discover Artificial Intelligence*, *4*(1), 40. DOI: 10.1007/s44163-024-00129-0

Saxena, A., Prakash Gupta, J., Tiwary, J. K., Kumar, A., Sharma, S., Pandey, G., Biswas, S., & Raghav Chaturvedi, K. (2024). Innovative Pathways in Carbon Capture: Advancements and Strategic Approaches for Effective Carbon Capture, Utilization, and Storage. *Sustainability (Basel)*, *16*(22), 10132. DOI: 10.3390/su162210132

Schuett, J., Reuel, A. K., & Carlier, A. (2024). How to design an AI ethics board. *AI and Ethics*, •••, 1–19.

Selwyn, N. (2022). *Education and technology: Key issues and debates* (3rd ed.). Bloomsbury Academic. DOI: 10.5040/9781350145573

Shaamala, A., Yigitcanlar, T., Nili, A., & Nyandega, D. (2024). Algorithmic green infrastructure optimisation: Review of artificial intelligence driven approaches for tackling climate change. *Sustainable Cities and Society*, *101*, 105182. DOI: 10.1016/j.scs.2024.105182

Shahbazi, M., & Bunker, D. (2024). Social media trust: Fighting misinformation in the time of crisis. *International Journal of Information Management*, *77*, 102780. DOI: 10.1016/j.ijinfomgt.2024.102780

Sharma, A., Arya, S. K., Singh, J., Kapoor, B., Bhatti, J. S., Suttee, A., & Singh, G. (2024). Prospects of chitinase in sustainable farming and modern biotechnology: An update on recent progress and challenges. *Biotechnology & Genetic Engineering Reviews*, *40*(1), 310–340. PMID: 36856523

Sharma, A., & Singh, B. J. (2020). Evolution of industrial revolutions: A review. *International Journal of Innovative Technology and Exploring Engineering*, *9*(11), 66–73. DOI: 10.35940/ijitee.I7144.0991120

Shehzadi, S. (2024). Privacy by Design: Integrating Information Theoretical Privacy in AI Development. *Integrated Journal of Science and Technology, 1*(2).

Sia, P. Y., Saidin, S. S., & Iskandar, Y. H. P. (2023). Systematic review of mobile travel apps and their smart features and challenges. *Journal of Hospitality and Tourism Insights*, *6*(5), 2115–2138. DOI: 10.1108/JHTI-02-2022-0087

Singh, A., & Rao, P. (2022). Machine learning applications for women's travel safety. *Journal of AI in Transportation*, *9*(1), 30–50.

Singh, N., Hui, D., Singh, R., Ahuja, I. P., Feo, L., & Fraternali, F. (2017). Recycling of plastic solid waste: A state of art review and future applications. *Composites. Part B, Engineering*, *115*, 409–422. DOI: 10.1016/j.compositesb.2016.09.013

Sinha, A. K., Rakesh, S., Mitra, B., Roy, N., Sahoo, S., Saha, B. N., ... & Bhattacharya, P. M. (2021). Agricultural waste management policies and programme for environment and nutritional security. *Input use efficiency for food and environmental security*, 627-664.

Smith, J. (2022). The role of AI in personal security. *Journal of Advanced Technology*, *35*(4), 112–130.

Sparkling, A. E., & Sengupta, R. (2023). Mapping Student's Perspective of a Redesigned Curriculum in Construction Management Using Self-Determination Theory. *International Journal of Construction Education and Research*, *19*(4), 443–459. DOI: 10.1080/15578771.2022.2148025

Spinellis, D., & Szyperski, C. (2004). How is open source affecting software development? *IEEE Software*, *21*(1), 28–33. DOI: 10.1109/MS.2004.1259204

Stachel, C., & Cantoni, L. (2024, June). Creating an Online Exhibition About Shoe Heritage: A Story on Swiss Footwear on Google Arts & Culture. In *International Conference on Human-Computer Interaction* (pp. 369-385). Cham: Springer Nature Switzerland. DOI: 10.1007/978-3-031-61353-1_25

Stahl, B. C., & Eke, D. (2024). The ethics of ChatGPT–Exploring the ethical issues of an emerging technology. *International Journal of Information Management*, *74*, 102700. DOI: 10.1016/j.ijinfomgt.2023.102700

Statista (n.d.). Estimated transaction value of crowdfunding worldwide from 2017 to 2023, with forecasts from 2024 to 2028. https://www.statista.com/statistics/1078273/global-crowdfunding-market-size/

Stjernborg, V., & Svensson, G. L. (2024). Rural mobility in later life; counteracting accessibility poverty with digital service solutions. *Transportation Research Part D, Transport and Environment*, *126*, 104030. DOI: 10.1016/j.trd.2023.104030

Strubell, E., Ganesh, A., & McCallum, A. (2019)," Energy and Policy Considerations for Deep Learning in NLP", *Proceedings of the 57th Annual Meeting of the Association for Computational Linguistics*, 3645-3650. DOI: 10.18653/v1/P19-1355

Subrahmanyam, S. (2025). Business, Digital Transformation, and Entrepreneurship. In Ordóñez de Pablos, P. (Ed.), *Shaping Green and Inclusive Economies Through Innovative Entrepreneurship* (pp. 1–34). IGI Global Scientific Publishing., DOI: 10.4018/979-8-3373-1097-8.ch001

Su, Z., Li, C., Fu, H., Wang, L., Wu, M., & Feng, X. (2024). Development and prospect of telemedicine. *Intelligent Medicine*, *4*(1), 1–9. DOI: 10.1016/j.imed.2022.10.004

Tang, C. S. (2022). Innovative technology and operations for alleviating poverty through women's economic empowerment. *Production and Operations Management*, *31*(1), 32–45. DOI: 10.1111/poms.13349

Thomason, J. (2021). Big tech, big data and the new world of digital health. *Global Health Journal (Amsterdam, Netherlands)*, *5*(4), 165–168. DOI: 10.1016/j.glohj.2021.11.003

TOMRA. (2019). TOMRA Sorting Solutions: AI-powered plastic sorting for a sustainable future", [Online] Available at: https://www.tomra.com/sorting/recycling

Top, C., & Ali, B. J. (2021). Customer satisfaction in online meeting platforms: Impact of efficiency, fulfillment, system availability, and privacy. *Amazonia Investiga*, *10*(38), 70–81. DOI: 10.34069/AI/2021.38.02.7

Topol, E. (2019). *Deep medicine: how artificial intelligence can make healthcare human again.*

Tortora, L. (2024). Beyond Discrimination: Generative AI Applications and Ethical Challenges in Forensic Psychiatry. *Frontiers in Psychiatry, 15*, 1346059. DOI: 10.3389/fpsyt.2024.1346059 PMID: 38525252

Tran, J. (2022). AI-powered crime prediction and prevention. *Cybersecurity Advances, 18*(4), 123–140.

Treiblmaier, H. (2019). Toward more rigorous blockchain research: Recommendations for writing blockchain case studies. *Frontiers in Blockchain, 2*, 3. Advance online publication. DOI: 10.3389/fbloc.2019.00003

Trindade, J. (2023). Health and gender: a study based on the National Health Survey. *Higher Institute of Social and Political Sciences.* https://www.repository.utl.pt/bitstream/10400.5/27562/1/Dissertac%cc%a7a%cc %83o%20-%20Jos%c3%a9lia%20Trindade.pdf

Troxler, P. (2013). *Making the 3rd industrial revolution. Fab Labs: Of Machines, Makers and Inventors*. Transcript Publishers.

Troyer, M., Benjamin, E. V., & Gevorkian, A. (2024). Quantum for good and the societal impact of quantum computing. *arXiv preprint arXiv:2403.02921.*

Turaga, U., Gupta, S., & Soni, N. (2020). AI-powered waste management: A review on computer vision techniques for plastic waste sorting and recycling. *Environmental Technology & Innovation, 20*, 101067. DOI: 10.1016/j.eti.2020.101067

UNCTAD. (2021). *Digital economy report 2021: Cross-border data flows and development: For whom the data flow* (UNCTAD/DER/2021). United Nations Conference on Trade and Development. https://unctad.org/publication/digital-economy-report-2021

UNESCO. (2017). *Cracking the code: Girls' and women's education in science, technology, engineering and mathematics (STEM)* (ISBN 978-92-3-100233-5). UNESCO. https://unesdoc.unesco.org/ark:/48223/pf0000253479

UNESCO. (2023). *Global education monitoring report 2023: Technology in education – A tool on whose terms?* UNESCO. https://unesdoc.unesco.org/ark:/48223/pf0000385723

United Nations Department of Economic and Social Affairs. (2021). *Leveraging digital technologies for social inclusion: Policy brief no. 92*. UN DESA. https://desapublications.un.org/policy-briefs/undesa-policy-brief-92-leveraging-digital-technologies-social-inclusion

United Nations Office on Drugs and Crime. (2022). *Women's safety and crime prevention strategies*. Retrieved from www.unodc.org

United Nations Women. (2022). *Technology solutions for women's safety in public spaces*. Retrieved from www.unwomen.org

United States Department of State. (2023). *Travel advisory and safety measures for women abroad*. Retrieved from www.travel.state.gov

University of Wollongong in Dubai. (2025). *Blended learning*. University of Wollongong in Dubai. Retrieved December 19, 2025, from https://www.uowdubai.ac.ae/students/blended-learning

Upreti, G. (1994). Environmental conservation and sustainable development require a new development approach. *Environmental Conservation*, *21*(1), 18–29. DOI: 10.1017/S0376892900024036

Usera, D. (2024). Communicating to Connect - Interpersonal Communication for Today. Social Sci LibreTexts. https://socialsci.libretexts.org/Bookshelves/Communication/Introd uction_to_Communication/Communicating_to_Connect_-_Interpersonal_Communication_for_Today_(Usera)

Val, S., & López-Bueno, H. (2024). Analysis of Digital Teacher Education: Key Aspects for Bridging the Digital Divide and Improving the Teaching–Learning Process. *Education Sciences*, *14*(3), 321. DOI: 10.3390/educsci14030321

van Dijk, J. (2020). *The digital divide*. Polity Press.

van Grunsven, J., Stone, T., & Marin, L. (2024). Fostering responsible anticipation in engineering ethics education: How a multi-disciplinary enrichment of the responsible innovation framework can help. *European Journal of Engineering Education*, *49*(2), 283–298. DOI: 10.1080/03043797.2023.2218275

van Laar, E., van Deursen, A. J. A. M., van Dijk, J. A. G. M., & de Haan, J. (2019). Determinants of 21st-century digital skills: A large-scale survey among working professionals. *Computers in Human Behavior*, *100*, 93–104. DOI: 10.1016/j.chb.2019.06.017

Vann Yaroson, E., Chowdhury, S., Mangla, S. K., Dey, P., Chan, F. T., & Roux, M. (2024). A systematic literature review exploring and linking circular economy and sustainable development goals in the past three decades (1991–2022). *International Journal of Production Research*, *62*(4), 1399–1433. DOI: 10.1080/00207543.2023.2270586

Vannoy, S. A., & Palvia, P. (2010). The social influence model of technology adoption. *Communications of the ACM*, *53*(6), 149–153. DOI: 10.1145/1743546.1743585

Vasist, P. N., Chatterjee, D., & Krishnan, S. (2024). The polarizing impact of political disinformation and hate speech: A cross-country configural narrative. *Information Systems Frontiers*, *26*(2), 663–688. DOI: 10.1007/s10796-023-10390-w PMID: 37361884

Veluvali, P., & Surisetti, J. (2022). Learning management system for greater learner engagement in higher education—A review. *Higher Education for the Future*, *9*(1), 107–121. DOI: 10.1177/23476311211049855

Venkadesh, P., Divya, S. V., Marymariyal, P., & Keerthana, S. (2024). Predicting Natural Disasters With AI and Machine Learning. In *Utilizing AI and Machine Learning for Natural Disaster Management* (pp. 39–64). IGI Global. DOI: 10.4018/979-8-3693-3362-4.ch003

Veolia (2021)," Veolia's AI-enhanced plastic recycling: Improving quality and efficiency", [Online] Available at: https://www.veolia.com/en/our-services/plastic-recycling

Vial, G. (2019). Understanding digital transformation: A review and a research agenda. *The Journal of Strategic Information Systems*, *28*(2), 118–144. DOI: 10.1016/j.jsis.2019.01.003

Vieriu, A. M., & Petrea, G. (2025). The impact of artificial intelligence (AI) on students' academic development. *Education Sciences*, *15*(3), 343. DOI: 10.3390/educsci15030343

Vinuesa, R., Azizpour, H., Leite, I., Balaam, M., Dignum, V., Domisch, S., Felländer, A., Langhans, S. D., Tegmark, M., & Fuso Nerini, F. (2020). The role of artificial intelligence in achieving the Sustainable Development Goals. *Nature Communications*, *11*(1), 233. DOI: 10.1038/s41467-019-14108-y PMID: 31932590

Vygotsky, L. S. (1978). *Mind in society: The development of higher psychological processes* (Vol. 86). Harvard university press.

Wang, L., & Gupta, N. (2023). Smart cities and AI-based security: Implications for female travelers. *International Journal of Smart Infrastructure*, *10*(1), 22–38.

Wang, X., Wu, Y. C., Zhou, M., & Fu, H. (2024). Beyond surveillance: Privacy, ethics, and regulations in face recognition technology. *Frontiers in Big Data*, *7*, 1337465. DOI: 10.3389/fdata.2024.1337465 PMID: 39027377

WHO. (2022). *Violence against women prevalence estimates*. Retrieved from www.who.int

Wilson, H. (2020). The evolution of hotel security systems. *Hospitality & Technology Review*, *33*(1), 99–115.

Women, U. N. (2021). *Safe cities and safe public spaces for women and girls.* Retrieved from www.unwomen.org

Wood, J., & Khan, G. F. (2016). Social business adoption: An empirical analysis. *Business Information Review*, *33*(1), 28–39. DOI: 10.1177/0266382116631851

World Bank. (2022). COVID-19 drives a global surge in use of digital payments. https://www.worldbank.org/en/news/press-release/2022/06/29/covid-19-drives-global-surge-in-use-of-digital-payments

World Bank. (2023). *Gender equality and transport: Improving safety for women.* Retrieved from www.worldbank.org

World Economic Forum. (2023). *Future of travel security: Innovations and challenges.* Retrieved from www.weforum.org

World Economic Forum. (2023). *The future of jobs report 2023*. World Economic Forum. https://www.weforum.org/publications/the-future-of-jobs-report-2023/

World Economic Forum. (2025). *This is how we upskill future leaders to drive the digital transformation of manufacturing*. World Economic Forum. https://www.weforum.org/stories/2025/04/this-is-how-we-upskill-future-leaders-to-drive-the-digital-transformation-of-manufacturing

Wu, W. H., Wu, Y. C. J., Wu, C. Y., Kao, H. Y., Lin, C. H., & Huang, S. H. (2012). Review of trends from mobile learning studies: A meta-analysis. *Computers & Education*, *59*(2), 817–827. DOI: 10.1016/j.compedu.2012.03.016

Wu, X., Duan, R., & Ni, J. (2024). Unveiling security, privacy, and ethical concerns of ChatGPT. *Journal of Information and Intelligence*, *2*(2), 102–115. DOI: 10.1016/j.jiixd.2023.10.007

Xinzhou, H. (2015, April). The development trend of mobile Internet and its impact on the global economy. In *2015 International Conference on Social Science and Technology Education* (pp. 598-600). Atlantis Press. DOI: 10.2991/icsste-15.2015.159

Xue, C., & Wang, J. (2024). Proactive boundary-spanning search, organizational resilience, and radical green innovation. *Business Strategy and the Environment, 33*(3), 1834–1852. DOI: 10.1002/bse.3576

Yáñez-Valdés, C., & Guerrero, M. (2024). Determinants and impacts of digital entrepreneurship: A pre-and post-COVID-19 perspective. *Technovation*, 132, 102983.

Yáñez-Valdés, C., & Guerrero, M. (2024). Equity crowdfunding platforms and sustainable impacts: Encountering investors and technological initiatives for tackling social and environmental challenges. *European Journal of Innovation Management, 27*(7), 2326–2350. DOI: 10.1108/EJIM-03-2022-0127

Yang, Y., & Su, Y. (2020). Public voice via social media: Role in cooperative governance during public health emergencies. *International Journal of Environmental Research and Public Health, 17*(18), 6840. DOI: 10.3390/ijerph17186840 PMID: 32962172

Yap, J. M., Barat, A. H., & Kiszl, P. (2024). Civic roles of libraries in combating information disorders in social media: A scoping review. *Education for Information*, (Preprint), 1-24.

Yelne, S., Chaudhary, M., Dod, K., Sayyad, A., & Sharma, R. (2023). Harnessing the power of AI: A comprehensive review of its impact and challenges in nursing science and healthcare. *Cureus, 15*(11). Advance online publication. DOI: 10.7759/cureus.49252 PMID: 38143615

Yin, Y., Stecke, K. E., & Li, D. (2018). The evolution of production systems from Industry 2.0 through Industry 4.0. *International Journal of Production Research, 56*(1-2), 848–861. DOI: 10.1080/00207543.2017.1403664

Yusniza, K. (2011). E-Consumer Behaviour: Exploring the Drivers of E-Shopping. *European Journal of Social Sciences, 23.*

ZenRobotics. (2018). ZenRobotics Recycler,"The world's first AI-powered robotic waste sorting system", [Online] Available at: https://zenrobotics.com/recycler/

Zhao, Y., Lei, J., & Conway, P. F. (2006). Global perspective on political definitions of e-learning: Commonalities and differences in national educational technology strategy discourses. In *The international handbook of virtual learning environments* (pp. 673–697). Springer Netherlands. DOI: 10.1007/978-1-4020-3803-7_26

Zhou, H., & Yuan, W. (2017). A novel deep learning model for efficient plastic waste sorting. *Waste Management (New York, N.Y.), 68*, 561–569. DOI: 10.1016/j.wasman.2017.07.023

Zhu, G., Huang, J., Lu, J., Luo, Y., & Zhu, T. (2024). Gig to the left, algorithms to the right: A case study of the dark sides in the gig economy. *Technological Forecasting and Social Change*, *199*, 123018. DOI: 10.1016/j.techfore.2023.123018

Zhuk, A. (2024). Crypto-anarchy: a paradigm shift for society and the legal system. *Journal of Computer Virology and Hacking Techniques*, 1-27.

Zhu, Y. (2024). Research on the Branding of Intangible Cultural Heritage Enabled by Digital Technology. *International Journal of Education and Humanities*, *13*(2), 104–107. DOI: 10.54097/ks839493

About the Contributors

Miftachul Huda is a senior lecturer at the Faculty of Human Sciences, Universiti Pendidikan Sultan Idris Malaysia. His research interests include education studies, learning technology and digital ethics. He has over fifteen years of research experience. Having contributed several works, he currently serves on the advisory editorial board for several international journals. Traveling to several countries for scholarly purposes gives him extensive experience regarding international trends and issues in his research expertise. Thus, he commits to contributing his knowledge to benefit society through professional and social activities.

***

A.V. Senthil Kumar is working as a Professor and Principal, Nehru Institute of Information Technology and Management, Coimbatore, India. He has worked as Professor and Director, PG and Research Department of Computer Applications, Hindusthan College of Arts & Science, Coimbatore, Tamilnadu for 15 years and as Senior Grade Lecturer in CMS College of Science and Commerce for 14 years. To his credit he has industrial experience for five years and teaching experience of 29 years. He has also received his Doctor of Science (D.Sc in Computer Science). He has to his credit 86 Book Chapters, 234 papers in International and National Journals, 85 papers in International Conferences in International and National Conferences, and edited 17 books and 3 Text books. He is as Associate Editor of IEEE Access. He is an Editor-in-Chief for many journals and Key Member for India, Machine Intelligence Research Lab (MIR Labs). He is an Editorial Board Member and Reviewer for various International Journals. He is also a Committee member for various International Conferences. He has guided 16 Ph.D scholars and guiding 3 Ph. D scholars now.

Diogo Belejo received her Graduate Studies in Management from Universidade Lusófona, with a degree in Management from Lusofona University (Portugal).

Ankita Chaturvedi is currently working as an Associate Professor at IIS (deemed to be University), Jaipur and has over 16+ years of teaching experience. She received her Ph.d degree (2011), Master's in Accounting and Business Statistics(2006), and Master's in Economics and Financial Management (2018) from University of Rajasthan, India. She has qualified NET in Commerce in 2015. She is an author or Co-author of more than 46 research papers published in national or international refereed journals, 11 chapters in edited books, 3 books with ISBN number and more than 50 conference contributions. She has received several (22) awards in the field of academics and research. She has supervised around 18 PG dissertations. She is supervising 6 Ph.d Thesis and 6 Ph.d degrees has been awarded under her guidance. She has been convener of various academic events like international conference, training programmes, Research workshop, Board of Studies etc. She has attended various more than 22 FDP's and training programmes.

Shanmugasundaram Hariharan received his B.E degree specialized in Computer Science and Engineering from Madurai Kammaraj University, Madurai, India in 2002, M.E degree specialized in the field of Computer Science and Engineering from Anna University, Chennai, India in 2004. He holds his Ph.D degree in the area of Information Retrieval from Anna University, Chennai, India. He is a member of IAENG, IACSIT, ISTE, CSTA and has 22 years of experience in teaching. Currently he is working as Professor in Department of Computer Science and Engineering, Vel Tech Rangarajan Dr. Sagunthala R&D Institute of Science and Technology, Chennai,India. His research interests include Information Retrieval, Data mining, Opinion Mining, Web mining. He has to his credit several papers in referred journals and conferences. He also serves as editorial board member and as program committee member for several international journals and conferences.

S. Ida Evangeline is an Assistant Professor in the Department of Electrical and Electronics Engineering at Government College of Engineering, Tirunelveli, Tamil Nadu, India. She holds a Bachelor's degree in Electrical and Electronics Engineering from Manonmaniam Sundaranar University (2003) and a Master's degree in Power Systems Engineering from Anna University, Chennai (2005). She earned her Ph.D. from Anna University, Chennai, in 2023. She has published six research papers in international journals. Her areas of interest include optimal power flow, renewable energy, soft computing, artificial intelligence, machine learning, and deep learning.

Jipson Joseph has a PhD in Ethics from DVK Bangalore. Currently, he is a Research Scholar in the School of Law at Christ University, Bangalore. His research interests are in the fields of ethics, gender studies, constitutional law, human rights, human security, food security, environmental justice, developmental policies and global poverty.

Shaji Joseph did his graduation and postgraduation in Sociology from Pune University (SPPU) and PhD in Management from Symbiosis International University in 2020. Currently, he is an associate professor at Symbiosis International Deemed University Pune. His area of expertise is in sustainability standards and reporting, Human resources management, and corporate governance and ethics. His research interests include sustainable development, ethical leadership, leadership assessment, and human resources management. Dr Shaji Joseph can be reached at shaji@scit.edu

Gaganpreet Kaur is currently working as an Professor at Department of Computer Science & Engineering, Chitkara University, Punjab, India. She has obtained Ph.D (CSE),from I.K. Gujral Punjab Technical University, Jalandhar, M.Tech (CSE), from I.K. Gujral Punjab Technical University, Jalandhar and B.Tech (CSE), from Kurukshetra University. She has rich teaching experience of 18+ years. She has published more than 100+ research articles in various peer reviewed, SCI, Scopus Journals, International and National Conferences in the field of computer science. She has published more than 17 Indian patents. She has authored a book on biometrics. She has guided a Ph.D scholar and 38 students have M. Tech students. She has acted as a guest editor for special issue in various Special Issues.

Benu Kesar did her Masters in Business Administration (MBA) from NMIMS Mumbai and is pursuing her PhD from Symbiosis International Deemed University Pune. Dr. Kesar's research interests lie at the intersection of technology, communication, and societal impact, focusing on how digital platforms are reshaping human interaction and influencing organisational strategies. She can be reached at drbenukesar@gmail.com.

Dev Kesar is an Analyst at a Finance firm, where he contributes to data-driven financial strategies and technology solutions. He holds a B.Tech in Computer Science and Engineering from VIT Chennai. His interests lie at the intersection of finance, analytics, and emerging technologies.Dev Kesar can be reached at devkesar4210@ gmail.com.

Saifullah Khalid is a beacon of innovation and excellence in Electrical Engineering and Aviation Technology. With a distinguished career that spans over two decades, his contributions have been instrumental in shaping the future of air traffic management and engineering research. His impressive credentials include serving as a Visiting Researcher at Nanyang Technological University, Singapore, and holding a pivotal role as an Assistant General Manager (ATM) at SGRDJI Airport Amritsar, in addition to his association with the Civil Aviation Research Organization (CARO) in Indi. Dr. Khalid's academic prowess is underlined by a Doctorate of Philosophy in Electrical Engineering from Dr. APJ Abdul Kalam Technical University, India. His commitment to education and research is further evidenced by his role in nurturing the next generation of engineers and researchers and his mentorship of PhD students focusing on cutting-edge technologies in aviation. A testament to his inventive genius, Dr. Khalid has secured 58 patents, showcasing groundbreaking technologies that range from AI-enhanced fault detection systems to innovative solutions in UAV technologies.

Geetha Manoharan is currently working in Telangana as an assistant professor at SR University. She is the university-level PhD program coordinator and has also been given the additional responsibility of In Charge Director of Publications and Patents under the Research Division at SR University.

Ananya Pandey is a Research Scholar in School of Law at Christ University, Bangalore. She has her research interests in the field of Constitutional Law, Environment Law, Human Rights, Food Security, Intellectual Property Law and Jurisprudence.

S. Vinod Kumar is an Associate Professor in the Department of Chemical Engineering at St. Joseph's College of Engineering, OMR, Chennai, India. He earned his B.Tech degree in Chemical Engineering from Anna University, India, in 2005, followed by an M.Tech degree in Chemical Engineering from AC Tech, Anna University, Chennai, India, in 2010. He successfully obtained his PhD from Sathyabama University in 2021. With over 13 years of dedicated teaching experience, his focus lies in the realm of Water Treatment, Wastewater Treatment, Membrane Desalination, as well as Machine Learning and Artificial Intelligence.

Henrique Ribeiro Sá received her Graduate Studies in Management from Universidade Lusófona, with a degree in Management from Lusofona University (Portugal).

Ana Simões received her Graduate Studies in Management from Universidade Lusófona, with a degree in Management from Lusofona University (Portugal).

Maria Trigo received her Graduate Studies in Management from Universidade Lusófona, with a degree in Aeronautical Management from Lusofona University (Portugal).

Index

W

www.ingramcontent.com/pod-product-compliance
Lightning Source LLC
LaVergne TN
LVHW062223200926
848484LV00006B/1464